THE TRADING STATES OF
THE OIL RIVERS

*A Study of Political Development
in Eastern Nigeria*

The Trading States of the Oil Rivers

A STUDY OF POLITICAL DEVELOPMENT IN EASTERN NIGERIA

G. I. JONES

Published for the
INTERNATIONAL AFRICAN INSTITUTE
by the
OXFORD UNIVERSITY PRESS
LONDON   IBADAN   ACCRA

Oxford University Press, Ely House, London W.1

GLASGOW NEW YORK TORONTO MELBOURNE WELLINGTON
CAPE TOWN SALISBURY IBADAN NAIROBI DAR ES SALAAM LUSAKA ADDIS ABABA
BOMBAY CALCUTTA MADRAS KARACHI LAHORE DACCA
KUALA LUMPUR SINGAPORE HONG KONG TOKYO

SBN 19 724151 4

© *International African Institute* 1963

*The International African Institute and the author gratefully
acknowledge a grant of £250 by the Smuts Memorial Fund
towards the cost of publication of this volume.*

First edition 1963
Reprinted 1964 *and* 1970

Printed in Great Britain by
Latimer Trend & Co. Ltd., Whitstable

PREFACE

THIS book was inspired by Dr. Dike's *Trade and Politics in the Niger Delta* and is an attempt to extend the trail blazed by that work. But in its approach it has moved from the general expanse of the Niger Delta to its Eastern margin, and from the Foreign Office and other British records to the oral traditions and social anthropology of the people living there. *Trade and Politics* is a study of the external relations of these Oil River states and of British foreign policy towards them. The present study deals with their local political development and is concerned with European documentary sources only in so far as they refer to this aspect of their total history. It has two main aims, the first historical, to trace the history of these Eastern Delta states, the second anthropological, to analyse their systems of government.

I have concentrated on the two principal Oil River states which nineteenth-century writers called New Calabar and Grand Bonny, and which today are known as Kalabari and Bonny, and I have used the latter names except when quoting from or using European documents. I have also for purposes of comparison considered the adjacent states of Brass (Nembe) and Okrika, the Andoni tribe, and the Efik state known to Europeans as Old Calabar, while in the more general chapters I have also referred to other Ibo tribes and to the Arochuku. The area occupied by the Ijo states of Kalabari, Bonny, Nembe, and Okrika I have called the Eastern Delta. In their relations with the European world this formed part of a wider area which included Old Calabar and some villages on the Cameroons River. During the nineteenth century it became known as the Oil Rivers and I have used the term Oil River states when Old Calabar was included and Eastern Delta states when referring only to the four Ijo states.

I have not extended this study beyond the year 1884. This forms a very convenient terminal point. It marks the beginning of the British Protectorate government and with it the end of the indigenous systems of government which characterized these Oil River states during the nineteenth century. The monarchies established in the eighteenth century by King Pepple of Bonny and King Amakiri of Kalabari and the political and economic organizations developed under their rule were coming or had come to an end, and the oligarchies which developed in their place under the Niger Coast Protectorate rule merit a separate study. This I hope is the present concern of Robin Horton, to whom I am deeply indebted for criticism of this work, and for placing at my disposal certain additional oral traditions and other data which I have acknowledged in the text.

My own field material was obtained during a period of six weeks in the Eastern Delta in 1956, and I should like to thank the many Bonny, Kalabari, Efik, Okrika, and Adoni kings, chiefs, and gentlemen for the wealth of traditional material which they contributed to my enquiry. To name them personally would be invidious.

I am very grateful to the International African Institute for undertaking the publication of this study and to Professor Daryll Forde, its Director, for his criticisms and suggestions for the revision of the text. My thanks are also due to Mr. R. E. Thompson, for compiling the index, and to Miss Barbara Pym, for her tireless work in seeing the volume through the press.

I have also to thank Dr. Namdi Azikiwe and the Government of the Eastern Region of Nigeria for the transport and other facilities which they placed at my disposal.

CONTENTS

I

Introduction

THE study of the earlier indigenous systems of government in Africa presents many problems to the contemporary historian and social anthropologist. In the first place, most of these systems have been replaced or drastically modified by their respective colonial or protectorate governments in the interest of more efficient local government. The anthropologist who studies them has therefore to describe something which he has never seen in action, and his reconstruction tends to be either an ideal system—the system as it is believed by his informants to have functioned before the colonial government intervened—or a hypothetical model—the system as he assumes it would function were the controls of this government removed.

In the second place, the time at his disposal and the nature of his field work tends to make his study a synchronic one, although what is really needed, unless the system is exceptionally stable, is a diachronic one. Unless documentary material is available, and in most of the Nigerian hinterland it is not, any attempt to analyse change in political systems has to be based on oral tradition and on comparisons with other related communities. At best, then, such a study can be only a hypothetical reconstruction. But in some of the coastal communities there has been contact with Europeans for several centuries and this has provided sufficient historical data to justify, it is hoped, the present study of the political systems of Kalabari, Bonny, and their neighbours before they came under British colonial rule.

In order to do this, however, one must first write the political history of the Eastern Delta and, before one can attempt to write it, make a critical evaluation of the material that has to serve for West African history. In the Eastern Delta it falls into two categories—European documentary records and local oral tradition. Historians know how to handle the former; but they have still a lot to learn about oral tradition and in this anthropologists have hindered rather than helped them. Ethnologists have sought to use it in the construction of hypothetical culture sequences or strata, social anthropologists have treated it as myth, whose main function is to validate existing institutions. Before therefore one can legitimately use oral tradition as historical data one has first to make a very thorough analysis of the myths and legends which constitute the oral history of this region.

The results which will be published elsewhere suggest that in most of these communities oral tradition is more limited in content and in historical depth than would appear at first sight; it tends to have a beginning and an end but no middle. The beginning, which one can call the remote past, is a dawn period associated with the origin of the community; the end, which can be called the recent past, is associated with episodes which still exist in living memory. Any intervening events which are still preserved in the traditions find themselves, by a process which can be termed legendary elision, pushed to one or other of these extremes. By a similar process of compression, termed legendary stereotyping, the names of actors and of places become so reduced that in extreme cases a single name has to do duty for a tribal ancestor and for a tribal home.

In dealing with these traditions one has also to distinguish between, on the one hand, a mass of unco-ordinated and often contradictory material, most of which is known only to particular individuals and small groups, and on the other a co-ordinated narrative prepared for external consumption which is known to most people and which might be called the 'Authorized version'. Political and cultural changes can and do alter this narrative and produce 'Revised versions', but once members of the community know that it has been codified, recorded for example in an ethnographic monograph or Government report, and have access to such documents, it tends to become a 'gospel' and no further changes occur.

The available documentary material for this area consists almost entirely of written records. Archaeology is no help and the few artifacts that survive, apart from some undateable bronzes,[1] belong to the nineteenth century and are valuable, for our purposes, primarily for what is written on them. For example, the great bell of King Opobo, King Okiya of Nembe's larger than life portrait in enamel, King Warri of Nembe's cast-iron memorial tablet, the brass pilot badges, and the ivory traders' bracelets. These last were given by masters or supercargoes of trading vessels to the heads of some of the houses who traded with them. They were produced by any

---

[1] E.g. bronze leopard skulls in a generalized and naturalistic Benin style, or bronze iguanas in a naturalistic European style.

trading member of the house to the supercargo to show under which house they were trading, and they probably date from the beginning of the palm oil trade. They were inscribed with the name of the house head, and usually with the name of the European trader and the date. For instance, the Oko Jumbo house of Bonny has a bracelet inscribed on one side 'Jumbo Manilla, gentleman of Grand Bonny, a good and honest trader. May be trusted to any amount', and on the other side, 'Presented by Captain Frederic Grant. Ship Hero 1841'. Or again, the Epemu house of Nembe has a bracelet with 'John Jacket, a gentleman of Nimby. A.D. 1849'.

The written records fall into two categories—the early description of the coast and the later, nineteenth century, records. The first group are three in number the *Esmeraldo de Situ Orbis* of Pachecho Pereira ,the *Description de l'Afrique* of Olfert Dapper, and the *Description of the coasts of North and South Guinea* by John Barbot, together with an abstract of his brother James Barbot's voyage to New Calabar. In so far as they relate to the Eastern Delta all the descriptions apart from this abstract are secondary sources. But apart from a few minor documents[2] they are the only relevant sources now available in this country.

The nineteenth-century records can be divided into two classes, namely the private or personal and the official records. The former are made up of the journals, trading handbooks, and memoirs of consular officials and other persons who had occasion to visit the Eastern Delta. These personal records are only historically reliable when their writers confine themselves to recording what they actually saw or did. When they leave the 'present' and describe what happened in the past they become even more unreliable than the local oral traditions and suffer from just the same defects of legendary elision and stereotyping.

The official records consist of Treaties and of Colonial, Foreign Office and Admiralty papers which, although they started in 1825, do not begin to give any continuous information until after the establishment of a British consul at Fernando Po in 1849.

POLITICAL SYSTEMS

As a definition of the term 'political system' for the purposes of this study we may begin with the broad generalization given by Radcliffe-Brown as being 'that aspect of the total organization [of a society] which is concerned with the control and regulation of the use

[2] e.g. Blake, Vol. I, Nos. 13, 26, 62, 65.

of physical force'.[3] To this we can add Schapera's modification that 'in studying political organization we have to study more than merely the maintenance or establishment or social order within a territorial framework by the organized exercise of coercive authority through the use, or the possibility of use, of physical force. We have to study in fact the system of communal leadership and all the functions (as well as the powers) of the leaders'.[4] Fortes and Evans-Pritchard have divided African political systems into two main types, A and B. Group A consists of those societies which have centralized authority, administrative machinery, and judicial institutions, and in which cleavages of wealth, privilege and status correspond to the distribution of power and authority. Group B consists of societies which lack centralized authority, administrative machinery, and constituted judicial institutions, and in which there are no sharp divisions of rank, status and wealth.[5] When they seek to go further in distinguishing between them and claim that in societies of group B it is the segmentary lineage system which primarily regulates political relations between territorial segments,[6] they are on more controversial ground. What really distinguishes societies of Group B from those of Group A is not merely the possession of a co-ordinated system of territorial segments (which may or may not be lineage segments) but the fact that these segments are politically equivalent and that they acknowledge no higher political authority than that which derives from their political association on the basis of this equality.

One of the main difficulties in studying such systems is that we are dealing not only with a number of variables which can be combined in different ways in different societies, but also with a limited number of terms which are applied to different combinations of these variables by different writers. A 'state' as defined by Nadel[7] is something which among African societies, only the Nupe and (possibly) the Hausa possess. To Barnes[8] the essential feature of a segmentary lineage system is that it continually segments. To Fortes[9] it would appear to be the equivalence of these segments. To Smith[10] segmentation is the essential concomitant of all political action and therefore characterises all political systems.

[3] Fortes and Evans-Pritchard, p. xxiii.
[4] Schapera, p. 218
[5] Fortes and Evans-Pritchard, p. 5.
[6] Ibid, p. 6.
[7] Nadel, p. 69.
[8] Barnes, p. 49
[9] Fortes and Evans-Pritchard, p. 13.
[10] M. G. Smith, p. 48.

In my own case, and in attempting to classify and differentiate between political systems in Eastern Nigeria, I find it convenient to regard the two main divisions of *African Political Systems* as polar or extreme types rather than as exclusive categories. At the one pole political authority is centralized and derives from the central government as 'personified' by the king, the head of the state. At the other there is no central government, authority remains with the members of the territorial segments which are held together by ties of common interest, traditions, descent, common ritual institutions, and similar bonds. The Zulu or Tswana systems could be said to represent the one type, the Dinka or Nuer the other, and most other African systems could be graded between these two extremes. In Nigeria the kingdoms of Benin and of Idah would fall closer to the A pole, the political system of the Tiv close to the B pole, while most of the societies of Eastern Nigeria would occupy a more central position. All Ibo, Ibibio, or Ijo societies that have been studied can be said to possess the requirements of a primitive state, in that they have some centralized administrative and judicial institutions and cleavages of wealth and status corresponding to the distribution of power and authority. They are also segmentary in Fortes's sense, in that power is ultimately resident in the segments not in the central government, which consists essentially of a federation of politically equivalent segments. In the case of Ibibio and Ijo these federations can be called villages and in that of Ibo, village groups.

It is hoped as a result of this present study to show that the political system of the Eastern Delta states developed out of the kind of segmentary political system characteristic of other communities in the Eastern Region. The hypothesis is put forward that in systems of this Eastern Delta type one is concerned with a cycle of development through which a political system, which is essentially segmentary in character, passes in moving towards a new equilibrium when it has been upset by external factors. These factors in the Eastern Delta states were, firstly, the control of the overseas trade with western Europe and, secondly, the acquisition of very considerable state revenue which was provided by European trading vessels in the form of trading dues (comey). The cycle begins with an exceptionally able and wealthy political leader who replaces a federal system of equivalent political units with a monocratic system of his own. But the political group which he has created itself divides into segments and in due course these new segments either develop into the units of a new federal system similar to the one they have replaced, or become involved in a conflict which is resolved either by political fission or by the emergence of another successful leader who develops another similar monocratic system.

Such an achievement involves leadership of a high order operating under very favourable conditions, as was found in the Eastern Delta during the eighteenth and early nineteenth century. But this pattern of an exceptional leader being able to establish himself as the supreme ruler of his community was not confined to these Delta states. It was occurring throughout the region, being least in evidence in the areas most actively involved in territorial expansion, and most common in the more populous areas, where there were greater opportunities for specialization and for the acquisition of wealth through trading and other professional occupations. The British colonial government, as it brought the region under its control, gratefully recognized such self-made rulers wherever it found them and sought to create them for communities where they were lacking. These were the 'warrant chiefs' who became their principal instruments of local government. But, at least during the recent past, such self-made chiefs were never able to alter the structure of their tribe or village group and the office in almost every case died with its creator. In the earlier stages of their development, however, such restructuring may well have taken place, to judge from the traditions of a number of these communities. But for clear examples of the processes involved in such restructuring we must refer to the Oil River states whose oral traditions can be supported by historical records.

This study has accordingly been divided into four parts. The first gives a general introduction to the ethnography of the region and then outlines the prehistory, protohistory and early history of the Eastern Delta down to the eighteenth century. The second describes the political and economic systems of the African and European communities living on these trading rivers at the beginning of the nineteenth century, by way of an introduction to the third part which gives the political history of Bonny and Kalabari down to 1884. The fourth part provides an analysis of the dynamics of these political systems.

Part One

ORAL TRADITIONS AND HISTORY

II

Ethnographic Background

BEHIND the narrow surf-beaten Nigerian coastline lie 11,000 square miles of swamps and waterways which break through to the sea in innumerable broad estuaries or converge inland up the Niger by way of its two main outlets, the Forcados and the Nun Rivers. Most of this delta is brackish tidal swamp under water at high tide and carrying mangrove forest. Wherever the land is permanently above high water, for example along the coast, it carries tropical rain forest and, as it moves inland and away from the tidal area, the banks of the waterways become higher and higher and the land behind them is only under water when the Niger and the other rivers that feed the delta are in flood. Oil and raffia palms will grow here and food crops can be cultivated on those banks that remain above the flood level. But the greater part of the delta is a barren waste of mangrove forest and most of its inhabitants live scattered over it in small widely dispersed communities of fishermen.

Although they may be isolated, these communities have never been self-sufficient; they depend on the specialized fishing of their menfolk and on the exchange of their smoke-dried fish and salt with the people of the hinterland for bulk foodstuffs, tools, clothing, and domestic gear.[1] Most of the common techniques of catching fish are used, some of African and some of European origin. Apart from fishing on the bars of estuaries, there is no fishing in the open seas, and their canoes are not designed for negotiating surf. Some of the fishing is done by women but most of it by men. The habits of the different fish vary, some are sedentary and others migrate, and men travel all over the delta in pursuit of them and in search of better fishing grounds. They take some of their women and children with them to help smoke their catch and they build themselves temporary huts at the various fishing camps along their route. Here again the delta differs from the hinterland, communication may be long and slow but except when there is an active state of war between two tribes, people can move freely, carrying with them in their larger canoes as much of their property as they might wish to, and

[1] This fishing economy of the delta has never been studied.

9

passing without interference through the territories of different political groups. All that is demanded of them by the owners of the territory is the payment of a small rent or tribute before they erect any building.[2]

European geographers divided this coast into the Bights of Benin and Biafra; more recent political boundaries have perpetuated this division and there is now a Western Delta most of which is contained in the Delta, formerly the Warri, Province of the Western Region and an Eastern Delta most of which is in the Rivers Province of the Eastern Region. This, like many other Nigerian boundaries, is an arbitrary administrative arrangement bearing little relation to the geographical and cultural realities. For this desolate, sparsely inhabited region is not a barrier between Eastern and Western Nigeria but a channel of communication between them. The real barrier between the two regions was not the Niger and its delta but the forest region on its western bank, in the heart of which was the kingdom of Benin. Geographically and ethnologically the delta is better represented as a single whole made up of a central area, the true delta of the Niger, which has become extended eastwards and westwards in a narrow belt to fuse with the coastal outlets of the other lesser rivers of Southern Nigeria. Similarly the inhabitants of the delta are culturally and linguistically homogeneous in the central area where they form the Ijo-speaking people; and, if we accept their oral traditions, it is from this central area that they have expanded westwards to mingle with Yoruba-speaking communities and eastwards to lose their cultural identity and become the Ibibio-speaking Andoni and Ibeno tribes of the Calabar Province.

Above the Ijo in the northern apex of the delta are a few other tribes and fragments of tribes, some speaking dialects of Edo and of Ibo, others with languages not yet classified and who are referred to by various names—Epie, Atissa, Engenni, Saka, Abua. Once out of the delta the Niger—Cross River hinterland is occupied by the large and numerous Ibo- and Ibibio-speaking peoples and between them and bordering Okrika and Andoni, another linguistically obscure people, the Ogoni. West of the Niger is forest sparsely populated by the Benin people and by other Edo-speaking tribes which have drifted southwards into it, or by Ibo-speaking tribes which have crossed over from the eastern side of the Niger.

[2] Opinions vary as to the extent of this mobility in the past. The data are conflicting.

Earlier ethnographers, for example Talbot,[3] have divided the Ijo into three groups, Lower, Western, and Kalabari. Later ones, for example Horton,[4] divide them into Western, Nembe, and Eastern. By Western, Horton refers to the Ijo living in the central delta and, presumably, its western extension. Under Eastern he includes those Ijo tribes which have become modified by contact with Western Europe and with the Ibo hinterland, like the Kalabari, Bonny, and Okrika (Talbot's Kalabari Ijo). The Nembe and adjacent tribes form a transitional group between them. Talbot's classification is, apparently, based on linguistic criteria, as is Horton's, and neither corresponds with the Nigerian administrative divisions or provinces.

This study refers to that part of the Bight of Biafra and its delta now included in the Eastern Region of Nigeria and for convenience I have divided it into three areas, the Eastern Delta, the Ibibio Delta, and the Cross River Delta. 'Eastern Delta' includes all the Eastern, Nembe, and Western Ijo, and is comprised of the present administrative divisions of Brass and Degema. The 'Ibibio Delta' covers the territory of the Andoni and Ibeno tribes, and the 'Cross River Delta' that of the Efik tribe. I am concerned chiefly with the Eastern Ijo and in particular the Kalabari and the Ubani (Bonny), the two communities in the Rio Real area of the Eastern Delta which emerged into history as the kingdoms or states of New Calabar and Grand Bonny and which, with the Efik state of Old Calabar, dominated the overseas trade of the Bight of Biafra.

Approximate figures for the population of these and neighbouring peoples are given below. They are taken from the 1953 census which in the case of the Rivers Province was most unreliable.[5] The population of Arochuku is much larger, since the figure does not include Aro living abroad. At least half of the population of Calabar township are Ibo and other 'strangers'. Nigerian population figures again can be very misleading unless allowance is made for uneven distribution. The three million Yoruba and four and a half million Ibo are not evenly dispersed over that portion of the map on which their name is written. The bulk of them are concentrated in one or more areas of much more limited extent and situated at some

---

[3] *Peoples of Southern Nigeria*, Vol. IV, Map 8, p. 48
[4] In a work on Ijo Art in course of publication.
[5] 'It is clear that the original figures for the Degema Division (with the exception of the Odual clan) were the result of gross over-counting. The Divisional total was more than three times the previous estimate. In order to give a relatively undistorted picture of the Province it has been necessary to adjust the figures for this division in the light of information gained in the recount'. (Note at the end of Bulletin 3. *Population Census of the Eastern Region* 1953).

distance from the coast. Similarly in the Eastern Delta the density of the Ijo population increases considerably as one moves eastwards and is highest in the Northern Kalabari and Okrika areas.

TABLE 1. POPULATION OF PRINCIPAL TRIBES AND GROUPS

1. *Ijo Groups*

Kalabari state and tribe

True Kalabari (Buguma, Abonnema, Bakana and plantations) affiliated villages (Tombia [New Town], Abalama, Ifoko, Ido)		46,363
Satellite and associated villages (Tema, Sama, Ilelema, Abissa, Angulama, Krakrama, Okpo, Udekama group, Ke, Kula, Soku, Bile, and others)		20,841
	Total	67,204

Nembe tribe

Nembe Town and plantations including coastal villages and other satellite villages	Total	24,297

Bonny tribe

Bonny Town, affiliated villages and plantations		10,226
Opobo Town, affiliated villages and plantations		7,391
	Total	17,617

Okrika tribe

Okrika village		26,575
Other villages on Okrika island and outlying villages		7,445
	Total	34,020

2. *Non-Ijo groups*

Engenni river (communities of Joinkrama and Okarki)		6,920
Abua Tribe		19,379
Ogoni Tribe		156,717
S. Ibo. Ikwerri group of tribes and village groups of Amafo, Isiokpo, Okpo-mbu-tolu		48,599
S. Ibo. Ndokki tribe		34,728
Cross River Ibo. Arochuku tribe		6,342
	Total	272,685

TABLE I—*continued*

Coastal Ibibio
Andoni Tribe 36,061
Ibeno Tribe 6,053

Total 42,114

Efik tribe
*x Calabar Township (the former Duke Town and
Old Town) 46,705
x Duke Town plantations (Akpabuyo, Odukpani
Road) 50,620
x Creek Town and plantations 9,201
Other Efik villages (Ikonetu, Ikot Offiong,
Adiabo) 10,072

Total 116,598

* Includes about 20,000 Ibo. x Includes Kwa and Efut Groups.

I. ECONOMIC SYSTEM

Neither the Eastern Delta nor its hinterland were self-sufficient in their economy. The hinterland lacked salt and protein and its nearest supply of both was the delta. Field studies in the Eastern region[6] have shown that the region possesses a highly developed system of distributive trade. This system is not recent in origin but appears to have been developed over centuries of slow and unimpeded growth. The overall pattern was the import of salt, protein, and of bulk foodstuffs by the over-populated areas of the hinterland, and in particular the Ibo hinterland, which paid for this by the export of their labour, skilled and unskilled. The skilled labour was in the form of craftsmen and artisans, for example 'medicine men', 'priests', blacksmiths, carvers, and market traders; the unskilled was mainly agricultural labourers and, particularly during the eighteenth and early nineteenth century, slaves. The unskilled labourers worked seasonally in the food-, and, when these developed, in the palm oil-producing regions, returning home for the rest of the year; the skilled travelled abroad for longer periods and any slaves who were not exported overseas became incorporated into the communities of

[6] By the Government Agricultural Department Umuahia and by myself.

their eventual masters. The bulk of the protein imported by the hinterland was in the form of smoke-dried fish from the delta, which also originally provided most of their salt. The bulk foodstuffs which fed the delta came from the food-producing areas most accessible to the delta and remote from the over-populated areas. Those closer to the over-populated areas exported food to these areas.

Goods and food were moved about the region through a complex network of markets. In the Ibo hinterland almost every local community of any size had its own market held once a week (of eight days) on a day that did not clash with neighbouring markets. In addition to women from the neighbourhood engaged in part-time petty trade, the market contained a smaller number of men who were full-time professional traders retailing rarer and more costly goods which they had bought elsewhere. Some of these markets were larger than others attracting more professional traders who came to buy or sell the special commodities for which the market was distinguished, and these more specialized products of particular areas were carried to any part of the region that demanded them along a chain of such larger markets, whence they were distributed to the smaller ones in their neighbourhood.

Travel in the hinterland was on foot along the jungle and forest paths linking one community and its market with another. These communities were in a state of armed neutrality with each other, and such travel was dangerous and could only be undertaken over long distances by those who had established a travelling relationship with particular households in the communities along the route. The householder gave the traveller food and lodging for the night, and provided him the next day with a safe conduct to the next stage along his route. Only where water transport was available was it possible to carry goods in bulk and this was confined to the delta and to the broader sections of the rivers that led out of it. Narrower rivers were always blocked to canoe traffic by the great trees which continually fell across them as the current undercut the banks on which they were growing. Apart from the Niger and the Cross River, the only rivers that led any distance into the Ibo hinterland were the Orashi (or Engenni) which was navigable to Oguta lake (which also connected with the Niger), the Imo which was blocked above the Ndokki country, and the New Calabar which led only up to Ibaa.

There were no trade guilds or analogous organizations, but skilled occupations like those of 'medicine men', diviners, blacksmiths, or traders tended to become concentrated in particular communities, and the specialists from these communities tended to have special areas at some distance from their home village, where they resided and worked. Alternatively they moved and plied their trade as they went in a particular direction from this village and then retraced their way back along the same route. In the heavily populated Ibo area, for example, the village group of Nri (Awguku) produced ritual specialists who were able to remove 'abominations' and to rehabilitate the ritually polluted and who operated particularly westwards from Nri and across the Niger. The people of Awka village group were native doctors, woodcarvers, and blacksmiths who operated over the Northern Ibo area; those of Nkwerri were blacksmiths and traders who operated southwards through the Ndokki country to the Ogoni. Among the Cross River Ibo, the people of Item were 'medicine men' who moved northwards and eastwards up the Cross River; the people of Abiriba were carvers, blacksmiths, and doctors who moved down the Enyong river to the Ibibio country; and the people of Arochuku were ritual specialists who brought people to 'consult' their tutelary deity, *chuku ibinokpabi*, the 'Long juju' of Arochuku, known in the Eastern Delta as *suka obiama*, which was famed throughout the region as a judicial oracle and as the giver of fertility and wealth. Among the Eastern Ijo the coastal villages of the Nembe tribe made salt by boiling sea water; some of the villagers of Ke were ritual specialists and peace-makers; those of Ilelema were potters; the early inhabitants of Bonny were salt-makers, the later ones and those of Kalabari were engaged in the carrying trade, taking the produce of the delta up the New Calabar and Imo rivers to sell in the up-river markets and returning to the delta markets with goods and food from the hinterland.

Not everyone in a specialist community was engaged in its particular trade or craft. Many remained simple fishermen in the delta or farmers in the hinterland, the proportion thus employed depending on the capacity of their specialist relatives to develop and extend their specialization. Practically no one farmed in Arochuku, as they could afford to buy the food they wanted from the poorer tribes around them; by way of contrast almost everyone in Ke except the priests of its tutelary deity were fishermen. Contact with Western Europe, which began with the Portuguese about the fifteenth century, did not alter this trading structure which the Portuguese records show as already functioning. It merely attracted

trade to the routes feeding and fed by the Eastern Delta by providing a strong demand for some of the products of the hinterland,
in particular ivory and slaves, and food to feed these slaves. In
return the hinterland was supplied with luxuries which in course of
time became necessities, for instance, base metals, clothes, hardware,
fire-arms, spirits, and Virginia tobacco. But the organization of this
trade with the hinterland remained unchanged, and the communities
that were able to profit most from it were those delta communities
already specialized as carrying traders and in closest contact with the
markets feeding the densely populated Ibo hinterland. These
communities were Kalabari and Bonny.[7]

2. SOCIAL STRUCTURE

This economic system is common to the whole region and the
social and political organization once again shows considerable uniformity. Whether it be the Ibo, Ibibio, or other peoples of the hinterland, or the Ijo and Andoni of the delta, one finds them dispersed
over the territory in a vast number of relatively small and virtually
independent local communities, which today average about 5,000
Ibo people, about 500 Ibibio and 250 or less among the Ijo. Each of
these units, which one can call either village groups or villages
according to their size, had its own territory and government. Some
of these villages might cherish feelings of a common cultural identity
with a number of other adjoining units in their neighbourhood, and
they might reinforce these feelings by claiming a common origin
and common religious cults, and distinguish themselves or be
distinguished by their neighbours under a common name. Some
of these villages again might also recognize stronger bonds of
political as well as cultural unity ; while others, especially among
the Northern Ibo, might recognize no common bonds except
the fact that they lived in the same neighbourhood and therefore
traded together and intermarried. Earlier Nigerian ethnologists
(for example Talbot), and following them the Nigerian government,
prefer to call all these three kinds of wider associations, 'clans',
reserving the term 'tribe' for people speaking a common language.
I prefer to use tribe to designate the groupings of the first two kinds,

---

[7] Similarly in the hinterland the Arochuku, whose organization for 'consulting'
their juju covered the whole region, came to monopolize the hinterland slave trade
to such an extent that they were able to establish trading settlements on or near
all the more important trading route intersections and terminals, notably at Oguta
and near the New Calabar and Imo rivers.

that is, communities whose members shared a common name and considered themselves a cultural and in some case also a political unity. Among the Ibibio such tribes usually had a common tutelary deity (*Idem*) and totem (*Nkpo ibet*). Ibo and Ijo tribes did not, but like the Ibibio many of them preferred to think of themselves in terms of clanship, as the descendants of a common ancestor, or as derived from a single parent village. Of the particuler groups with which this study is concerned, Nembe, Andoni, and Efik were, according to their traditions, homogeneous tribes, most of their component villages tracing their origin to a common ancestor (Efik) or a common village (Nembe, Andoni), while the rest were heterogeneous.

With a few exceptions, these tribes were incapable of coherent political action, which was confined in most Ibo tribes to the village group and in most Ibibio and Ijo to the village. A village, if the population was numerous enough, was made up of a number of residentially separate sections or wards and these, in the Ibibio communities, were autonomous in their internal government and, unless the village was a very small one, were fighting and feuding units. With the Ibo it was the village which was internally autonomous, and no fighting or feuding was permitted within it. Comparative data for the Ijo are lacking, but it would seem that most villages were too small for any further sub-division and in most political matters preferred to segment on a basis of age rather than of local residence. In the Eastern Delta, the traditions of larger communities like Kalabari, Bonny, and Okrika indicate a division into wards. An Ibo village and an Ibibio or Ijo ward considered itself a corporate group of patrilineal kin and its government consisted of a meeting of the heads of its component households, presided over by the head of the ward (or of the senior ward in the case of an Ibo village). This head was selected for his office by the members of the ward or village, the choice being governed by various criteria, of which age was the most universal. Some areas, and in particular the Eastern Ijo, attached more importance to his wealth and capacity for leadership, others again, particularly the Efik, to direct descent in the male line from the founder of the ward.[8]

Government of the Ibo village group or the Ibibio village consisted of a council of elders—the heads of its component sections and their supporters. In most Ibo and Ibibio communities segments were ranked in order of seniority and the head of the senior ranking

[8] Descent could also be traced through a female link.

segment was considered the head of the community. The traditions of Bonny, Kalabari, and Okrika make no reference to any such ranking order and imply that the headship of the community was not originally vested in any particular ward or lineage.

The nineteenth-century traders and travellers referred to these local communities and their subdivisions as 'towns'. The term had a political as well as a residential connotation, and implied a self-governing group. Thus the town of Old Calabar was said to consist of Duke Town, Creek Town, and Old Town. Duke Town again was composed of a number of lesser towns, Henshaw Town, Cobham Town, and so on, which were the units which have been referred to as wards. On the other hand the farming villages in the hinterland established by members of these wards were distinguished as plantations, since they were part of and subordinate to one of these wards. But a plantation was not represented as subordinate to a town, for, in its corporate and kinship aspect, the ward was known as a 'house', and these plantations were said to belong to particular houses.

Supporting and sanctioning this political system was a belief in local deities—nature or fertility spirits. Each village had its own special deity who watched over it and protected it, provided the people who lived there obeyed his or her laws. Similarly each ward and sub-ward had its special ancestor cult for its founder and other forebears of the ward who were associated with him.

Besides this organization based on corporate kinship and local residential groupings, there were other complementary forms of association, based on age and on occupation and interests. The men of a village were placed in three grades—elders, men, and boys and the women likewise, and even though the political organization of a village consisted of a federation of politically equivalent segments (wards) it was usually referred to in terms of this age grade organization as rule by the elders, or by a council of elders. Young men of the same relative age were also grouped into age sets and so were young women. In some communities the age sets received formal recognition and a special name as they passed from the grade of boys (or girls) into that of men (or women), in others they remained anonymous and informal.

Throughout the area those men who had distinguished themselves by killing an enemy or potential enemy of the village were given a special rank and grouped themselves into a 'man-killer' society. But perhaps the most important of these associations in the Ibibio and Ijo areas were the clubs into which the men of the village were initiated when they became adult. These so-called 'secret societies' performed a number of different functions, religious, political and recreational. They all had their special private meetings and their secret ritual known only to the initiates, but most of them also had their public pageants, when the younger members of the society mimed and danced in masked disguises and were said to be the spirits to which the society ministered. Among the Ibo and Ibibio these masked players represented ancestral spirits and the society was called after them, *mau* or *ekpo* (ghost). Among the Eastern Ijo the secret society ministered to the *owu*, the spirits of the rivers and estuaries. Among the Ekoi and other Cross River tribes the spirit was represented as a forest demon, often symbolized under the name of leopard. The masked players were usually his attendant sprites and the demon himself was heard but not seen by the uninitiated. In Old Calabar the Efiks obtained their society from their Ekoi neighbours, and called it *ekpe* (leopard). The European traders and missionaries preferred to call it Egbo.[9]

3. NOMENCLATURE

The terminology used in this study differs in some respects from that employed in a number of other recent works on African social anthropology, since the institutions and groups which it seeks to describe differ in many respects from analogous ones in other parts of the continent. Some of the more confusing terms are explained in the text, for example, 'house' and 'village'. In attempting to write a history of these Oil River states one also encounters a difficulty not often met with in African anthropology. Many of the peoples are not only bilingual in local African languages, speaking in Bonny, for example, Southern Ibo as well as their own dialect of Eastern Ijo; they are also conversant with two forms of English. The first, which can be distinguished as literate English, is English as it is usually spoken and written and is used by the wealthier members of the community who have had the advantages of a school education. The second, which can be called trade English, is known by all members of the community who travel or who trade. This coastal 'Pidgin English' uses an African syntax with a vocabulary of words which are mainly English, or derived from English or from other

[9] These Ekoi societies should not be confused with the 'leopard societies' of Sierra Leone and Liberia, whose members were believed to be able to transform themselves into leopards.

Western European languages. It is used not only between European and African traders, but serves as a common language among Africans from Southern Nigeria and the Cameroons.

Some of the literate English words used today by Bonny or Kalabari people are used in a special sense or as a translation of an Ijo expression. 'Redeem', for instance, means either buying back from European slavers a person, slave or freeborn, who ought not to have been sold away from his community, or paying the debts of a house that had gone bankrupt. In both cases the result was the same, the person redeemed, or the members of the bankrupt house, belonged to the man or to the house that had paid the money. Similarly 'adopted' son or daughter means a slave who was incorporated as a child into the household of a chief or wealthy man.

Some of the trade English words derive from other European languages, notably 'dash' (Portuguese, *doação*)—a present; 'manilla' —the local currency unit; and 'matchet'—a cutlass. Some, like 'putta-putta'—mud or clay, appear to be purely onomatopoeic inventions; some, though derived from English or from other dialects of trading English, have meanings very far removed from the normal one, for example, 'tie-tie—rope or twine; 'chop'—to eat or food; while some like 'comey'—customs dues, were peculiar to the Oil Rivers in the nineteenth century and their derivations are now forgotten.

4. PLACE NAMES

European traders thought of the Bight of Biafra as a series of rivers, some of which afforded facilities for trade while others were barren in this respect. In the time of the Portuguese empire they were designated the rivers of the Island of San Thomé, that is the rivers on the adjacent mainland in which the residents of this colony were permitted to trade. The rivers of the Bight of Benin formed a separate trading area under the Portuguese factory at Gwatto. As in the nineteenth century, the principal Biafra trading river was the Rio Real in the Eastern delta. Portuguese traders did not apparently use the Cross River and no reference is made in their published records to it and to the Efik tribe and their prawn fisheries at its mouth. When the Dutch and English traders became interested in slaves from these rivers they distinguished three principal trading states each on its own river of the same name. These were Calbaria or New Calabar (Kalabari), Bonny, and Old Calabar. The last referred to the Efik state and one can only guess how this name came to be applied to it. The Efik people have always dissociated themselves from the name, which they say they received from the Europeans, and have acknowledged no connections with the Kalabari. Kalabari traditions are complicated by the fact that Koroye, the founder of one of the Kalabari wards, is said to have come 'from Old Calabar'. This is probably a modern emendation. It was not until the end of the nineteenth century that the Efiks came into contact with the Eastern Delta states.[10] Between the Eastern Delta and the Cross River were the Andoni and Ibeno people who also according to their traditions came from the Rio del Rey 'through Efik' to their present site, and the Korome ward, as also some of the other groups in the Kalabari territory, is more likely to have been an Andoni than an Efik offshot.

Calabar was not the only name to worry nineteenth century ethnographers. There were also the Kwa (or Qua). One group of Kwa was a subtribe of the Ejagham Ekoi which, with another tribal fragment the Efut, were the original inhabitants of Old Calabar. There were also a few villages on the Cameroons river, unrelated to the Ekoi, who also called themselves Kwa, and finally there was the Western or Anang division of the Ibibio whose European name was the Kwa and later the Qua Ibo, presumably to distinguish them from the other Kwa. The Eastern division of the Ibibio, or at least those who bordered the right bank of the Cross River, were known to Europeans as Agbisherea or Egboshari. The Europeans also recognized two Ekrike (Krike). There was the Mbiabo group of Efik, whose villages were known to Europeans respectively as Old Ekrikok (Old Ikot Offiong), Tom Ekrikok (Ikot Offiong), and George Ekrikok (Ikonetu), and there was the Eastern Ijo tribe of Okrika, which they referred to variously as Cricke, Creeka, or Creek, and which should not be confused with the Creek Town (Ikot Itunko) of the Efik. Another European name that is liable to confuse is Brass. This name was given to the Nembe coastal villages because, it is said, of the brass pans and neptunes which were traded there for salt boiling. It was also extended to all the Ijo communities from Cape Formosa to the Santa Barbara river, who were known as the Brass Ijo, or restricted more specifically to the village of Twon near the anchorage for shipping on the estuary of the Brass River which led inland to the Nembe capital. Finally it

---

[10] When King Jaja of Opobo and the Henshaw ward of Duke Town were both seeking to extend their trade to the Kwa Ibo river.

was used in the treaties of 1884 and 1886 to refer to the Nembe state.

With the rise of the palm oil trade, the trading rivers of the Bight of Biafra became known as the Oil Rivers. After the establishment of the Colony of Lagos the remainder of the Bight of Benin became added to these trading rivers and the British protectorate established there was named the Oil Rivers Protectorate in 1889. This excluded the Cameroons area which became a German Protectorate. This British Protectorate changed its name in 1893 to the Niger Coast Protectorate. In 1906, on amalgamation with Lagos, it became the Colony and Protectorate of Southern Nigeria and in 1914 it was amalgamated with Northern Nigeria to become part of the Colony and Protectorate of Nigeria.

<h4 style="text-align:center">5. PERSONAL NAMES</h4>

It was customary from an early period for kings, chiefs, and other important Oil River persons with whom Europeans traded to have an English as well as an African name.

In Old Calabar the majority of these names were English transliterations of the Efik word—Afrom and later Ephraim for Effiom, Hogan for Okon, Henshaw for Nsa, Cobham for Akabom, Archibong for Asibong. On the Rio Real there was little attempt to approximate to the African name and most chiefs and notables were given or assumed purely European names. In the time of the Barbots (late seventeenth century) those who were the heads of their communities were given the honorific title of king, chiefs who claimed to be of superior rank received that of duke, while chiefs of lesser status and heads of smaller villages were referred to as captains. By the beginning of the nineteenth century, when the English records continue, most of these titles had disappeared except in houses which had survived from this period. English titles apart from king were no longer used and in the Eastern Delta the English names of chiefs and prominent traders were obtained in a number of different ways. Some like Jumbo, John Bull, Jack, Tom, Dick, Harry, George, Will, and Rich were straightforward English nicknames or proper names; some were fairly literal translations into English of Ijo nicknames e.g. Big Fowl, or of African proper names e.g. Strong Face; some were English transliterations of Ijo proper names, Yellow for *Iyala*, Queen for *Kweni*, Grand Bonny for *Ubani*, Cookey for *Kuki*, Pepple for *Perukule*, or of Ijo nicknames—Braid for *Mbre* (Brother); some were Ijo or trade English transliterations of English words, for example Annie, which later became Arnie, for Hand; some came from the firms with whom the chief traded, like Horsefall, Stewart and Tobin (later corrupted to Toby), and some were obtained in ways that are no longer remembered, for example Anna, Don Pedro, and West India.

Both on the Rio Real and the Old Calabar rivers it was customary for the chief of a house to be known to Europeans by the name of its founder. Thus James Barbot refers to a Duke Afrom in 1699. Antera Duke to another Duke Ephraim in 1785 and early nineteenth century writers to the Great Duke Ephraim who died in 1834. This custom was extended during the nineteenth century to some of the royal dynasties established in these states, the king keeping the name of the founder of his dynasty and being distinguished by a number, for example, Eyo Honesty II, or Amachree IV. In the Kalabari and Bonny houses the names of the chiefs did not remain as constant as in Old Calabar, and there was a period in the middle of the century when the names of some houses and of their chiefs changed from those of their founders to those of the chiefs who had re-established or reformed them. Thus the house founded by Ibolu, the eldest son of King Pepple I, became known first as Indian Queen, and then as George Goodhead, who were two traders who succeeded to its chieftancy. In the majority of cases, however, the name of a chief on a treaty or convention was also the name of the house or group of houses which he represented. The names on those treaties are thus of considerable historical and anthropological value, since they provide a relatively clear indication of the structure of the community at that time. There are more than eighty of these documents available, mainly in Foreign office records, and in Hertslet. A selection of them is given in Appendix B.

III

Traditions and Records

I. ORAL TRADITIONS AND PREH'STORY

T HAT part of a community's traditions which refer to the recent past may provide valuable historical material when used in conjunction with other written European records. But when we leave the recent past for the centuries that precede it these oral traditions cannot help us. They are no substitute for history and are best regarded as systems in which a very limited number of items are manipulated to explain or justify existing institutions and social groups. Some of the items may well be historic facts, for instance the foundation of the community, its conquest by or its assimilation of another group. Some of these events are perfectly feasible and could quite well have happened. There are, for example, Nembe fishermen who, on their fishing expeditions, are still travelling from the Ijo country to the Rio del Rey and back again, as their Andoni forebears are said to have done. Others again are quite obviously fiction, like the tree that crushed the people of Ke or the Benin army that founded Nembe or Lagos.

It is of course possible to construct a hypothetical history using such items as would appear to support one's conjectures, but it would be quite impossible to prove it, unless corroborative archaeological or documentary evidence could be obtained.

Lists of kings

An attempt to provide some kind of time sequence, which has been used by some ethnologists,[1] is to collect a list of kings or chiefs and to seek to provide dates for events associated with the names of particular chiefs by counting backwards from a chief whose dates are known, estimating the reign of each of his predecessors at an average of from ten to twenty years. This method in combination with the historical data available seems to have been used by Talbot in regard to Kalabari history, and his chronological list of Kalabari kings is

---

[1] e.g. Ellenberger and Macgregor.

given in Table 2 together with comparable data from Bonny and Nembe.

There are some Nigerian communities, notably Benin, which are interested in recalling the names of their kings. The Ijo and other peoples of the Eastern Region are not. We can assume, therefore, when we encounter such a list in the delta, that it has been produced to satisfy a European demand or in response to European stimuli. The lists collected and set out in this table derive from Leonard and Talbot, both of whom were government administrative officers, from unpublished reports on Bonny and Nembe written by other administrative officers, and from communications sent to me in 1956 when I was engaged on a government commission of enquiry. Leonard's data were collected about 1896, Talbot's between 1914 and 1916 when he was District Officer, Degema.[2]

Unlike Bonny, Kalabari has never given any official list of kings, their dominant political group maintaining that they had no proper kings before Amakiri. Thus the names produced for the Kalabari report[3] and given to me in 1956 were not a list of kings but a streamlined genealogy, and have not been included in the table.

These lists tell us practically nothing and if anything obscure rather than elucidate the historical perspective, particularly in the case of the Kalabari. This provides a good example of the way in which a place name and a founder's name can be interchangeable, and it also illustrates a process seen more obviously in the Bonny list, whereby the names of the founders of different segments of a community can be listed as a succession of kings. Opu-koro-ye was the founder of the Korome Ward, Owerri Daba, his son Mangi and grandson Suku are three other names from this ward, the rest are from the Endeme ward and represent the last and the penultimate dynasties of chiefs of this ward. Igbessa is the same person as Ngbesa and present-day tradition prefers to consider Amakiri the son of Daba and to make Daba the son of Brembo a son of Ende, the founder of the ward.

It is only when one tries to relate the names on these lists to things still existing, to living people and to the social groups to which these living people belong, that they begin to make sense. In other words when we turn them from lists of kings into genealogies, and this has been done at the foot of the Table. In polygamous societies there is always a tendency for junior sons to be very much younger than

[2] Leonard, p. 47; Talbot, Vol. 1, pp. 238–75; Webber and Dickinson.
[3] Kelsey, 1935.

TABLE 2. LIST OF KINGS OF BONNY, KALABARI, AND NEMBE

KALABARI (Talbot)	BONNY (1895)	BONNY (1956)
1. Owoma	1. Alagbariye	1. Alagbaria
2. Opukoroye (his son)	2. Okparaindole	2. Okpara Ndoli
3. Owerri Daba c. 1600	3. Opu Amakubu	3. Opu Amakubu
4. Igbessa c. 1620	4. Okpara Ashimini	4. Okpara Asimini
5. Kamalo (? King Robert)	5. Ashimini	5. Asimini
6. Mangi Suku (son of 3)	6. Edimini	6. Edimini
7. Igonibaw (1st son of 5) c. 1720	7. Kamalu	7. Kamba
8. Ngbesa (son of 5)	8. Dappa (Great or Opu)	8. Kamalu
9. Omuye (son of 5)	9. Amakiri	9. Opu Dappa
10. Bokoye (son of 5)	10. Appinya	10. Amakiri
11. Daba (son of 5)	11. Warri	11. Apia
12. Kalagba (1st son of 11) c. 1750	King Holliday (Owsa), Igbani, Bupor and Ipor (short quartumvirate)	12. Warri
13. Amakiri (slave and adopted son of 12) c. 1770	12. Perekule	13. Awusa (Halliday), Egbani, Bupuor and Ipuor
14. Amakuru (Amakiri II) c. 1790	13. Foubra (Agbaa)	14. Pelekule (Capt. Pepple)
15. Karibo (Amakiri III) died c. 1870	14. Foubra } sons of 13	15. Fubra
16. Abe (Amakiri IV) died c. 1900	15. Opobo	16. Opobo
	16. Bereibibo	17. Bereibibo
	17. Dappa (William)	18. Dappa (William)
	18. George	19. Agba Fubra
		20. George

BONNY GENEALOGY (Numbers refer to the 1956 list)

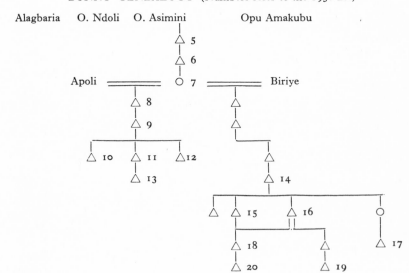

TABLE 2—*continued*

NEMBE

(1933)		(1956)	
Ogbo			
Kala Ekule		Ekule	
Nembe			
Opu Igula		Igula	
Amein		Nembe	
Owagi		Owegi	
Kala Igula			
Ogbolo			
Opu Basuo			
Ogio			
Peresuo		Peresuo	
Obia and Ekutia (regents)		Opu Basuo	
Kala Basuo		Obia	

A	B	A	B
Mingi	Ogbodo	1. Mingi	1. Obodo
Gboro	Gbolowei	2. Gboro	2. Gbolowei
Ikata	Warri	3. Ikata	3. Okiriyai
Kulo	Dede	4. Kulo	4. Tamuno
Amain	Tamuno	5. Amain	5. Aladede
Kien	Kariyai	6. Kien	6. Mein
Ockiya	Arisima	7. Ockiya	7. Duguruya
Koko	Ebifa	8. Koko	8. Arisima
Rev. A. O. Ockiya	Albert Igwira	9. Revd. Ockiya	9. Ebifa
	Ben Warri	10. F. Alagoa	10. Albert Ogwara
			11. Ben Warri

A. Ogbolomabiri kings.   B. Bassambiri kings.

NEMBE GENEALOGY

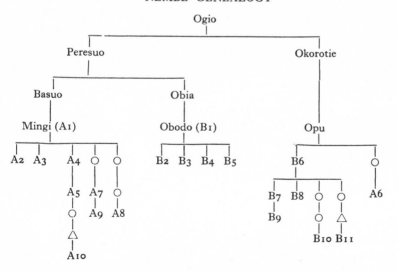

their elder brothers and to be nearer in age to the generation that succeeds these elder brothers. Thus in the Nembe example Mein belongs to the generation that succeeds Mingi and Obodo, while Ben-Warri is of the same generation as Francis Alagoa. Provided it is realized that these lines of brothers are not horizontal but decline considerably as one moves to the right, the series of generations can be taken as more likely to be historically correct than the list of kings. But this is true only of the first four generations (reading from the bottom), which are still associated with a sufficient number of living or recently deceased persons to be reasonably accurate. Beyond this level they become increasingly legendary until by the time we have reached the seventh generation almost all contact has been lost with their living descendant and descent groups. The names become purely mythical, the only ones remaining constant being those of the actual founders of a community or of some of its surviving sub-divisions.

What is interesting in both the Bonny and the Kalabari 'lists of kings', and in the genealogies from which they are derived, is the presence of Ibo names. Both have a King Kamalu. Now Kamalu was neither a typical Ndokki nor Southern Ibo name but is the Cross-River Ibo name for the spirit of lightning and the sky, which the Isuama Ibo call Igwe and the Southern Ibo, Amadioha. Kamalu or Kalu is a very common personal name among the Aro and other Cross-River Ibo tribes and its presence in both Bonny and Kalabari genealogies is not without its significance when one remembers that by the nineteenth century it was people of the Aro tribe who controlled the slave trade of the hinterland.

Patterns of Dispersion

These Ijo, Ibo, and Ibibio traditions do not of themselves provide any coherent historical perspective; all that they can offer when taken collectively and comparatively is a very broad and vague sequence of events or pattern of dispersion and this only when they are considered in conjunction with geographical, cultural, social and political data against which the statements in the legends can be checked and one's general hypotheses tested.

The best that can be attempted in the case of the Ibo, Ibibio, and Central Ijo traditions is to produce a broad pattern of migration and dispersion within the present areas occupied by these peoples, in other words to formulate a system which does for the whole region what the particular traditions of its various tribes and local communities seek to do for their respective groups.

a. *The Ijo pattern*

The delta traditions of origin give a broad and generalized picture of a movement of Ijo peoples from the Benin Aboh hinterland into the heart of the delta, possibly of a succession of movements, the first being the 'Tubatoro' dispersal in the north of the delta referred to in the Azuogu tradition, the second being the Mein and Obiama and similar expansions into the present Brass and Forcados divisions, the third being the Iselema movement.

The expansion of the Nembe tribe was east and south into uninhabited territory; beyond it lay a region between the Santa Barbara and the Andoni Rivers containing a number of small widely dispersed communities of obscure origin—Kula, Ke, Okpo, Tema, Ifoko, and Iyankpo on the coast; Bukuma, Ilelema, Minama, Angulama, Soku, and Idama further inland. Many of these, including Bile, were settled on the northern margin of the delta and preserve traditions relating a gradual movement southwards towards the coast. Beyond them again were the Andoni, who claim to have come from the central Ijo dispersion area and to have moved eastwards to the Cameroon boundary before recoiling back again through the Ibibio (Efik) region to Egwerede on the Andoni river, where they became differentiated as the Ibibio-speaking tribe of this name and whence they expanded westwards towards the Rio Real, eastwards towards the Kwa Ibo River. The Kalabari, Okrika, and Bonny legends tell of small groups from the central Ijo area who migrated east and northeast to settle, not in the true delta region but on its northern margin, and, in the case of Kalabari and Bonny, in contact with the Ibo and near the navigable limits of the two rivers which led from the Rio Real into the Ibo hinterland. It was from these early settlements on the Calabar and Imo rivers that Kalabari and Bonny moved downstream into the Rio Real to emerge into history as the dominant states in this region.

As far as a time sequence is concerned we can probably distinguish three successive stages. Firstly, the gradual expansion of Ijo-speaking people into the central delta; secondly, the expansion of some of them eastwards to become differentiated there into the communities with which this book is concerned; thirdly, the movement of three of the communities, Bile, Kalabari, and Bonny, in this order, from their up-river sites down into the delta.

It is quite impossible to attribute any historical dates to these stages. All that can be said is that the first two probably happened before the middle of the fifteenth century. It is possible that Bonny, or for that matter Kalabari, moved down into the delta during the Portuguese period (1450–1550), but it is equally probable that they had moved down before this time. We can assume that the production of salt, the large canoes, and the trade with the interior antedated the Portuguese period, and this regular internal trade in salt and provisions would provide quite as good a reason for a movement into the delta as that of the overseas trade with Europeans, which must at that time have been very sporadic and uncertain. It is also not possible to correlate these early Ijo movements with corresponding movements among the Edo-speaking peoples of the Benin region since no study has yet been published of Edo or Bini enthnology.

b. *The Ibo pattern*

The Ibo traditions of origin, when analysed in conjunction with other demographic, geographical, structural, and cultural features, suggest an Ibo centre or core in what is now the Awka and the Orlu divisions and a dispersal outwards from it, mainly to the south and east. Traditions are silent about it but one can assume an early dispersion from this centre to the Nsukka-Udi highlands in the east and an early drift southwards towards the coast. The descendants of the latter are known as the Oratta, Ikwerri, Etche, Asa, and Ndokki tribes and like the communities of the centre they have lost any traditions they may have had of migration from elsewhere. One can more positively distinguish a later and more massive dispersal which traditions do refer to, and which was mainly south-eastwards from the Ibo centre into what is now the Eastern Isuama area. From this subsidiary dispersion area there was one movement south-south-east into the Aba Division to form the Ngwa group of tribes, and another movement east into the Umuahia area and thence to the Ohaffia-Arochuku ridge, with an offshoot that struck north to become isolated in the heart of the eastern plains and to develop into the North-Eastern Ibo.

There were also lesser movements from the Awka region westwards across the Niger and an expansion of the people of the Nsukka Udi highlands, first westwards towards Awka and later eastwards into the eastern plains until they came up against the westward expansion of the North-Eastern Ibo.

The expansion to the Arochuku ridge was followed by an Ibo recoil northwards up the ridge by the present Ada and Item group of tribes and by a similar recoil westwards up the Enyong river by Ibibio-speaking groups from the Arochuku area. The traditions of most of these groups depict this movement as a flight from the raids of white-eyed dwarfs, who came up the river armed with muskets. The most important community to develop out of the Ibo and Ibibio remaining there was the tribe of Arochuku.

In addition to this general expansion outwards from a particular centre, there are a few Ibo tribes and villages which preserve traditions of migrations into the Ibo territory from elsewhere, notably the Umunri group who came 'from Idah' and the Umuezechima and Onitsha groups who came 'from Benin'.

c. *The Ibibio pattern*

Most contemporary Ibibio traditions tell of an original dispersion from a place called Ibom or alternatively of descent from a founding ancestor called Ibom.[4] A study of the present distribution of Ibibio tribes suggests an early scatter of Ibibio over an area extending from Arochuku in the north, Ika in the west, and Oron in the south. This was followed by a massive dispersal north and south from a centre somewhere between the present Abak and Uyo government stations, and a differentiation into Anang (Western) and Ibibio (Eastern). This dispersion is clearly preserved in the tribal traditions, all but a few tribes[5] in the extreme north, south and west tracing their origin and present territorial distribution to this movement. Memory of any earlier movement has been lost, except for the name Ibom. There is, however, an Arochuku village of this name and Arochuku commercial and ritual interests are distributed throughout Ibibio country. The modern tendency is therefore to locate the Ibibio Ibom in Arochuku and to associate it with the expansion and dispersal which is preserved in the tribal tradition. But the structural lay-out of the various tribes does not support it and points to an area further south. This area is surrounded by a ring of villages, each the parent village of a different tribe, whose expansion is directed away from this centre. The Efik of Old Calabar is one of the tribes which probably originated from this second movement. They claim that their ancestors moved from the Uruan area to the Cross River where they split, one part moving north to become the Enyong tribe on the river of the same name, the other moving south and expanding into the riverside villages of Ikot Offiong, Ikonetu, and Ikot Itunko (Creek Town). The last-named developed into the group of villages

---

[4] There is no mention of Ibom in the Government Reports of 1930–1940.
[5] Namely the Northern Ibibio, the Oron and Eket tribes, and the Ika in the extreme west.

known to Europeans as Old Calabar, namely Creek Town and its
offshoots Obutong (Old Town) and Atakpa (Duke Town).

d. *Contact between Ibo, Ibibio and Ijo*

In their second phase of expansion the Ibo and Ibibio eventually
came into contact, and the traditions of the Ibo groups along this
boundary indicate an absorption of and fusion with the earlier Ibibio
groups they found in their path, and of hostility and fighting with
the later Anang expansion. For example, the traditions of the Ngwa
say that they result from a fusion of two different groups one Ibo
(Ngwa) and the other Ibibio (Mboko); but their present eastern
boundary with the Otoro (of Anang) is still defined by a wide 'no
man's land', where it is safe for either tribe to farm but not to settle.

Both Ijo and Ibo traditions are silent about any contact between
the two groups, apart from the Azuogo Ndokki, and Kalabari legends.
Talbot[6] attributes the Kalabari movement from Obu Amafo to the
delta to 'pressure from south-driving Ibo', but there is no reference
to this in Ikwerri tradition nor do the demographic data appear to
support this hypothesis. The Ikwerri, and for that matter the
Ndokki area, is the most sparsely populated part of the southern
(Owerri) Ibo territory and there is no evidence to suggest that it was
any denser in the past. It is the same in the central delta in regard
to Edo and Ijo contact. There was certainly a drift of Edo-speaking
tribes southwards towards the delta, but the density was always very
low and today the most densely populated areas of the Warri (Delta)
and Benin provinces are those inhabited by Ibo-speaking tribes,
who have moved into this uninhabited area from the Awka region.
Whatever the reasons for the Ijo movement 'from Benin' into the
delta, pressure of population was not one of them.

2. THE PROTOHISTORIC STAGE

When the historical records are studied in conjunction with the
traditional material discussed in the previous sections, the chronicle
of these Eastern Delta states can be seen to fall into three main
stages. There is a prehistoric stage referred to only in the native
oral traditions and which has already been discussed; this is followed
by a protohistoric stage about which native traditions are largely
silent and where our main information comes from the three 'descriptions' and this again is followed by an historic stage in which both

6 Talbot 1, Vol. 1, p. 238.

written and oral material gradually become more abundant and supplement one another so that it is at last possible to write a coherent historical account of their development. Each of these stages can again be subdivided into a number of sequences or periods.

THE DESCRIPTIONS

Our knowledge of the protohistoric stage falls into three periods:

(*a*) That of the description of the *Esmeraldo*, when the Rio Real was an important trading river in the Portuguese Empire, and which can be dated to between 1450 and 1550.

(*b*) That of Dapper's *Description*, when the dominant traders on the Rio Real were the Dutch and the Kalabari, and which can be dated to the early and middle seventeenth century.

(*c*) That of Barbot's *Description*, when the Dutch were still the principal foreign traders there, but when Bonny had begun to challenge the trading dominance of Kalabari and the English had become seriously interested in the trade. This can be dated to the end of the seventeenth century.

We have little reference to this stage in the native traditions. The *Esmeraldo* and the *Description de l'Afrique* fill in a gap which in the Kalabari 'authorized tradition' is one of over two hundred years, between the 'time of Owame' and the 'time of King Amakiri'.

a. *The Esmeraldo de Situ Orbis*[7] is based on information obtained at the end of the fifteenth century. It gives a very accurate description of the Rio Real estuary and describes the two passages across the bar and how to use the east one to make a safe anchorage. It describes 'a very large village' of some 2,000 inhabitants engaged in making salt near the anchorage and says that the people of this river are called Jos (Ijo) and are warlike cannibals 'rarely at peace'. They are 'naked, wearing only copper necklaces, an inch thick; they carry daggers like those of the white Moors of Berbery'. Like every succeeding description the *Esmeraldo* is very impressed by the size of the canoes, 'the largest in the Ethiopias of Guinea'; some of them are large enough to hold eighty men, and they come from a hundred leagues or more up the river bringing yams in large quantities; they also bring many slaves, cows, goats and sheep. They sell all this to the natives of the village for salt and our ships buy

[7] Tr. G. H. T. Kimble, 1937, pp. 131-2.

these things for copper bracelets, which are here prized more than brass ones, a slave being sold for eight to ten of such bracelets.' The *Esmeraldo* then continues its description of the coast line, referring to a small river three leagues beyond the Rio Real and called the Rio de San Domingos. 'Four leagues beyond this is another river very small, called after Pero de Sintra, three leagues farther on are two very small rivers, but as there is no trade there I will not name them'.

This description of the coastline on the Eastern Delta shows that it was substantially the same as today; it gives no name to the 'very large village'. It could well be the town of Bonny; but it could also be the village of Iyankpo, the traditional home of Tombia which became the Finnema of history. It is not so likely to have been the village occupied by Abalama whom the Bonny emigrants drove away, as the site which Bonny still refer to as Abalamabie is further inland and away from the anchorage.

The *Esmeraldo* shows that the slave trade was already well established. The description also implies that it was communities other than the coastal village which were engaged in this trade. 'They come from up this river and sell to the natives of the village'. This could refer to the Kalabari either at their Obu Amafo or Elem Kalabari site, as both sites would be 'from up the river'. It could also refer to the people of Bonny, but it might equally well refer to the Okrikans, who were the traditional suppliers of yams and similar food crops to the Bonny people, or to the Andoni who provided them with livestock.

The Rio de San Domingos is usually called today the Andoni river, while the one beyond it is the estuary immediately south of Opobo which Burton later referred to as the Kom Toro. Nobody has yet identified the two small rivers 'which have no trade' and are therefore nameless and it is at this point that the *Esmeraldo's* description of the coast line ceases. It passes straight on to the Serra de Fernam do Poo and thence to the Rio dos Camarões and it omits any reference to a hundred miles of coastline including the large estuary of the Cross River. It is clear that the Portuguese did not trade with the Cross River estuary and the Rio del Rey area, and the name of the former river does not appear in the sixteenth century maps. By the seventeenth century, however, the name Calabar had become firmly attached to the Cross River area and to the Efik tribe which controlled its estuary, who were thenceforward called the Old Calabar to distinguish them from the Kalabari of the Rio Real, who became the New Calabar.

Pereira's description shows us that at this period Bonny, or the village that preceded it, was already a local trading centre of some importance, having not only a developed trade in salt and provisions with the interior but an external trade with Europeans as well. Slaves from the interior were traded for copper in the form of manillas (bracelets) and copper was used locally for making necklaces or torques of considerable size and weight. The Rio Real by the end of the fifteenth century already had by African standards a well developed system of distributive trade.

The reference to the people being warlike cannibals rarely at peace, naked and carrying daggers could equally well have been applied to some of the more remote and conservative tribes of the Eastern region five hundred years later. Their only distinctive feature was the wearing of torques made from copper imported from Europe. The statement that they were rarely at peace does not necessarily mean that they were perpetually at war, but rather corroborates the native traditions and shows that their political system was of a segmentary, uncentralized type depending to a very considerable extent upon the perpetual readiness of individuals and small groups to defend themselves and their rights.

Apart from these few points the *Esmeraldo* and the other contemporary records raise more queries than they answer. They give no names of villages or people in this area, they omit all reference to the Cross River and they leave us guessing why, in contradistinction to the Gold Coast, only one commodity—brass or copper manillas—should be exchanged for slaves on the Rio Real, and for that matter at Huguatoo (Gwatto Benin) and at the Rio de Laguo (Lagos), and whether these manillas were an article of barter or a genuine currency.

The oral traditions have very little to offer with which to fill the gap between the Portuguese and Flemish descriptions. Andoni and Bonny legends suggest a salt-boiling industry in the Bonny area before the arrival of the European traders, and they imply an early pattern of slave-raiding and slave-stealing followed by the extension of the slave trade to the inland markets. They also indicate a time sequence in which primacy in the slave trade belonged to Kalabari with Bonny coming on the scene later and learning the trade from them while depriving Andoni of their share in it. The uncoordinated traditions for the Kalabari area also refer to local slave raids and associate it with the dominance of Bile under its King Agbaniye Ejike, while in the Bonny traditions the development of the Kalabari slave trade is associated with the name of Owerri Daba and the Bonny with that of King Asimini. We can assume that the dominance of Kalabari occurred in the sixteenth century if not earlier, since, by the time of Dapper, Calabar was the name given to the Rio Real area as well as to the Efik, who were distinguished as Old Calabar.

b. Dapper's *Description de l'Afrique*. (1686)

Dapper,[8] though he tells us nothing about the Efiks or why they should be called Old Calabar, clears up most of the other problems raised by the *Esmeraldo*. He names and gives the geographical locations of the five principal communities in the Rio Real area as well as of the unidentified people of Moko, showing that at this date the principal communities were already situated in their historical positions. He refers to the village of Ifoko, 'called Wyndorp by the Dutch on account of the amount of wine produced there', and his description of the palisaded village of Calabarie, 'where the Hollanders do most of their trade', shows that the site has altered very little since then. He refers to Belli (Bile) 'where they also trade in slaves but the business is not so good as to the east of the Calbarie river'. He also describes the district (*province*) of Okrika (Kriké), about twenty miles (*vint milles*) from the coast up the Rio Real[9] and which borders that of Moko on the north-west— a region where they make a kind of iron currency, each piece about the size of the palm of the hand with a tail a span in length. South of Moko is the district of Bani, (Bonny) whose chief village is Culeba, which has nine or ten others under it and whose territories extend from the west of the river Calabarie to Sangma [a village to the west of Cape Formosa].

The district of Moko probably refers to a southern Ibo community, possibly to the Isiokpo or Okpo-mbu-tolu tribes who occupy the area to the north-west of Okrika and bordering the New Calabar river, and whose markets on the left bank of this river were referred to in later nineteenth century treaties as the Obiatubo markets. The statement about business being better 'to the east of the Calabarie river' than at Bile may refer to these markets or to those of Bonny, for Dapper also uses Calabarie as an alternative name for the Rio Real. Culeba is one the local names for Bonny and although its claim to rule all the territory traditionally regarded as in the political spheres of Nembe and Kalabari can be dismissed as an idle boast, it at least indicates that Bonny felt strong enough to challenge the dominant position formerly held by Kalabari in this area.

---

[8] Dapper, p. 315–16. This French edition is a free and slightly shortened translation of Dapper's original work published in 1676 by Jacob van Meurs.

[9] Which in this case is the Bonny river.

After describing the country of Calbarie the *Description* passes on to the River Loitomba, 'called S. Domingos by the Portuguese', three leagues from the Rio Real with quite a large village at its mouth on the east side. There are plenty of negroes there who trade in slaves but who have to get them very far from the coast. The Cross River and the Efik people are dismissed in a single sentence—'After Loitomba comes the River of Old Calbarie or Calborg'—and the description then passes from Old Calbarie to the Rio del Rey. The people who live far back at the source of this river were called the Calbongos and were 'a bad and deceitful nation, so lacking in good faith that parents sold their children and husbands their wives. The great business of this river [presumably still the Rio del Rey] is in slaves which they exchange for copper rods, thirteen or fourteen rods weighing twenty-two pounds in all, being given for a slave in good condition. They also import grains of coral and copper basons which one cannot sell on the Gold Coast'.

The *Description* makes it quite clear that on the Rio Real there was a well organized system of trade with the interior.

'All the slaves which they sell to the Hollanders are not prisoners of war. There are many more which they bring from their neighbours and these neighbours in their turn buy them from people removed still further to the north. They also bring provisions by canoe; yams, bananas, palm oil, pigs, deer, poultry etc'.

The merchandise which the Hollanders bring to exchange for slaves are bracelets of grey unpolished copper, which are used locally for currency, and small polished copper rods each a cubit and a quarter long and weighing five '*carterons*'. Fourteen to fifteen of them will buy a slave in good condition. The rods were beaten out and plaited into bracelets and torques (colliers). Whatever may have been the position in the Portuguese period there were now two local currencies in the Rio Real, the iron currency of the hinterland in the form of a conventionalized hoe blade, and the bracelets of grey copper of the delta, while the copper rod had become the medium of exchange for the European trade both on the Rio Real and in the Cross River delta. The village at the mouth of the River Loitomba was probably an Andoni community and the reason for its people having difficulty in obtaining slaves was not the distance they had to go, for the markets accessible to them were those used by the Bonny traders who had to pass through Andoni territory to reach them. The inference is rather that it was precisely those communities which had contacts with the hinterland peoples and access by water to their

markets which were being most successful in this trade; these
were the Kalabari with their connections with the Ibo communities
on the New Calabar river and Bonny with its Ndokki kinsfolk on the
Imo. A possible reason for the Hollanders doing most of their
trade at Kalabari and for the primacy of the Kalabari in this trade
was the accessibility of their Ibo markets; they could reach Isoba or
Amafo or Okpo-mbu-tolu on a single tide and come down on the
following one, whereas it took the Bonny canoes a week or more to
visit the Ndokki markets.

Like Pachecho Pereira, Dapper's informants were struck by the
size of the Rio Real canoes and he gives a very complete description
of them; fifty to seventy feet long with twenty 'rowers' (paddlers)
on each side, each with his shield and bundle of throwing spears
(*trousseau d'assagayes*), these people always being at war with each
other. The canoes can carry sixty to eighty people, are pointed at
both ends and six foot wide in the centre, the thwarts are planks 'as
large as one's open hand'. Each canoe has its own hearth for cooking
and the master can lie down at full length. There are holes in the
thwarts for carrying forked poles which support a mat awning
beneath which they can shelter should they have to spend a night
on board.

c. *John Barbot's 'Description'*

John Barbot made two voyages to the Rio Real and he claims that
his account is based on such information as he could gather between
the years 1678 and 1682, together with additional material which he
was able to collect 'from creditable travellers till the year 1706'. It
contains two separate accounts, a general description bringing Dapper's description up to date and an abstract of a voyage made by
James Barbot to the Rio Real in 1699, with additional information
supplied by Mr. Grazilhier, who continued visiting it up to 1704.

John Barbot's general description[10] is mainly a paraphrase of
Dapper with suitable amendments and with additional sailing
directions, information about the weather, advice on obtaining
provisions, and notes on the slave trade. Ships were already observ-
ing the nineteenth-century practice of riding at Ifoko and not going
as high up as New Calabar Town.[11] Dapper's descriptions of New
Calabar town is repeated and the town is said to contain three hundred

---

[10] Barbot, pp. 379–384.
[11] 'For it is much better to ride at *Foko* which is not so much molested with the
mosquettoes as *New Calabar* town'.

and nine houses. Belli is said to be ten leagues up country and west of New Calabar and governed by a captain, but in contrast with Dapper's time it now 'affords little trade to *Europeans* in some few slaves'. The territory of Crike is placed

some leagues north north-west of *Rio Real*, and borders towards the south on that of *Moko*, which lies near the sea, as well as that of *Bany* another territory, where is a large village call'd *Culebo*, and eight or ten smaller villages in the compass of about four leagues, all of them under the government of a captain; as are also the other territories above mention'd; though such chiefs or captains are now generally allow'd the title of kings by the *Europeans*, all over *Guinea* . . . but are at best such kings as the two and thirty that *Joshua* defeated at once, mention'd in holy writ . . .

The iron currency of Moko is described as having the shape and figure of a thorn back, [sting ray] flat, and as broad as the palm of the hand, having a tail of the same metal, of the length of the hand . . .'

John Barbot is clearly not very happy about the site of Moko and of the identity of Bany and Culebo, and passes on to his own description of Great Bandy (Bonny) apparently assuming it was another place. It consists of

about three hundred houses, divided into parcels, stands in a marshy ground, made an island by some arms of the river from the main: it is well peopled with *Blacks*, who employ themselves in trade, and some at fishing, like those of *New Calabar* town, in the inland country, by means of long and large canoes, some sixty foot long and seven broad, rowed by sixteen, eighteen or twenty paddlers carrying *European* goods and fish to the upland *Blacks*; and bring down to their respective towns, in exchange, a vast number of slaves, of all sexes and ages, and some large elephants teeth, to supply the *Europeans* trading in that river. Several of those *Blacks* act therein as factors, or brokers, either for their own countrymen, or for the *Europeans* who are often obliged to trust them with their goods, to attend the upper markets, and purchase slaves for them.

Then he continues, quoting again from Dapper, that the slaves were not prisoners of war but bought from their inland neighbours who buy them from 'other nations yet more remote'.

He then describes the currency.

The principal thing that passes in *Calabar* as current money among the natives, is brass rings, for the arms and or legs, which they call *Bochie*. The *English* and *Dutch* import there a great deal of copper in small bars round and equal, about three feet long, weighing about a pound and a

D

quarter, which the *Blacks* of *Calabary* work with much art, splitting the bar into three parts, from one end to the other, which they polish as fine as gold, and twist the three pieces together very ingeniously, like cords, to make what sorts of arm-rings they please.

After the Rio de San Domingos John Barbot refers to 'another river which falls into the gulph call'd by the *Hollanders Rio de Conde*; but I have not heard anybody say it is a place of any trade'. He also refers to the Cross River and the Old Calabar River,

where *Europeans* drive their trade with the *Blacks*, who are good civiliz'd people, and where we get, in their proper seasons, as at *New Calabar*, all sorts of eatables, yams, bananas, corn, and other provisions for the slaves, which we barter there, as well as elephant's teeth. . . Trade goes on there very slowly, several ships being observed to stay eight or ten months according to the circumstances of the natives, making fast their ships to large trees on the bank of the river, to save their cables. The air in this river is very malignant and occasions a great mortality amongst our sailors that make any long stay.

Barbot also gives another reason why the Hollanders and other peoples prefer not to visit it and which may account for the Portuguese not going there.

The tide almost continually runs with great violence towards *Camarones* river, in the circular part of the bight, north from all the coast round it.

He ends by giving a list of goods imported into Old Calabar which are much the same as later lists with the significant omission of guns and gunpowder.

The *Blacks* there reckon by copper bars, reducing all sorts of goods to such bars; for example, one bar of iron, four copper bars; a man slave for thirty-eight, and a woman slave for thirty-seven or thirty-six copper bars.

The Abstract of a Voyage to New Calabar River, or Rio Real, in the year 1699,[12] by his brother James Barbot, describes their arrival off the bar in bad weather. They sent in their long boats to get a pilot to take them to New Calabar, but the King of Bonny sent two or three of his pilots with certificates from several English masters of ships and these men piloted them in to 'Bandy River'. They had protracted discussions over the terms of trade with King William and with Pepprell, the king's brother'. When these were settled the king 'ordered the publick cryer to proclaim the permission of trade

[12] Barbot, pp. 455–465.

with us, with the noise of his trumpets, being elephants teeth . . .
we paying sixteen brass rings to the fellow for his fee'. They then
made the usual presents to the king and his principal chiefs and
advanced them and other traders goods on trust which they took to
exchange for slaves in the up-river markets.

While anchored at Bonny, James Barbot and Mr. Grazilhier made
many voyages in their sloop to New Calabar and in their long boat
to Andoni, buying slaves at both places. James Barbot remained
ashore at New Calabar village, staying in the king's house. He was
there at the end of July in the height of the rains and he describes
the town as being 'seated in a marshy island, often overflowed by
the river, the water running even between the houses, whereof
there are about three hundred in a disorderly heap. The king's is
pretty high and airy, which was some comfort to me during the time
I stayed there'. He found King Robert 'a good civil man about
thirty years of age'. Their common food was yams boiled with fish
and palm oil, and every evening

they club together at one another's houses, by turns, providing two or
three jugs of palm wine, each of them containing twelve or fifteen gallons,
to make merry; each person, man and woman, bringing their own stool to
sit on. They sit round and drink to one another out of ox's horns, well
polished, which hold a quart or more, singing and roaring all the while till
the liquor is out.

James Barbot was also struck by their religious devotion.

Every house is full of idols, as well as the streets of the town. They call
them *Jou-Jou*, being in the nature of tutelar gods. Many of them are
dried heads of beasts, others made by the *Blacks* of clay and painted,
which they worship and make their offerings to. Before the king goes
aboard a ship newly come in, he repairs to his idol house, with drums
beating, and trumpets sounding, all his attendants bare-headed. There
he makes abundance of bows to those puppets, begging of them to make
his voyage prosperous; and then sacrifices a hen, which is tied alive by
one leg to the end of a long pole, and has a brass ring on the other leg,
leaving the poor creature in that condition till it starves to death.[13] Every
time their small fleet of canoos goes up for slaves, and when they return,
they blow their horns or trumpets for joy; and the king never fails, at
both those times, to pay his devotions to his idols, for their good success,
and a short voyage.

[13] A comparable ritual in Bonny in 1826 is described by Dr. Jackson. Jackson, pp.
75–77.

On his visit to Andoni James Barbot found they had plenty of cattle, hogs and goats and a prodigious quantity of palm wine. The King of 'Dony' was a very good-natured civil man who spoke Portuguese; he was absent having gone to sell some slaves to them at Bonny. Barbot spent the night in the King's house, awaiting his return. It was

near his idol house, which they call *Jou-Jou*, and are kept there in a large press, full of the skulls of their enemies killed in war, and others of beasts; besides a quantity of human bones and other trash, some of them moulded with clay, and painted as at *Calabar*.

It was forbidden to touch these things and Barbot adds that

besides those idols, they worship bulls, and a large sort of lizards, called *Gouanes* in the *French Caribbee* islands, as their prime gods; and it is not less than death to kill them.

He has little to say about Bonny.

The town of *Great Bandy* is seated in a little island, as that of *Calabar*, being a marshy swampy ground, and somewhat larger, but like it in buildings, and the inhabitants of the same manners, temper, and religion so that it will be needless to say more of them.

He also refers to a large timber building on the Kalabiama side of the river which contained twenty-five or thirty dried elephant heads set up round the house on boards, 'which are the idols of the country, the *Blacks* resorting thither to pay their religion worship'.[14]

James Barbot's abstract is supported by a chart of the estuary which he calls the Calabar River, compiled by him and by Grazilhier, giving the soundings on the bar and marking the positions of the villages of Ifoko, New Calabar, Bandy, and Dony of the New Calabar River and of the 'Old Calabar River' which in this case refers to the Bonny river. He also adds an engraving of New Calabar cutlasses and daggers, these weapons being made by the Hackbous (Ibo) Blacks.

The abstract also gives details of trading at Old Calabar (Efik) by the ship *Dragon* in 1698. In addition to listing the goods exchanged there for slaves and giving the value of the latter in copper bars, it also records the names of a number of chiefs who supplied the ship with game and with baskets of plantains.

[14] The house is shown on his chart as 'The Grange' and may represent the seventeenth-century shrine of the deity referred to in the nineteenth century records as Jew Jew Tiger. Elephants were not sacred animals in the nineteenth century and it was customary to display their skulls as trophies in ju-ju houses.

3. THE HISTORIC STAGE

When we reach this stage we are at last on reasonably secure ground, and can make a more exact and intensive study of the political and economic development of the principal Eastern Delta states.

If we are considering economic development we can distinguish three periods which can be equated very broadly with the eighteenth, nineteenth, and twentieth centuries. The eighteenth century was the heyday of the Rio Real slave trade, when the English were the principal traders and when the political system of the Oil River states assumed its distinctive form, and Bonny and Kalabari established their monopoly of the overseas trade, with Bonny as the dominant state. During the nineteenth century the main exports of the Eastern Delta changed from slaves to palm oil, the principal oil-exporting ports moved inland from the coast to Opobo and Abonnema on the northern margin of the delta and the area came under British protection. The third period, which is outside the scope of this book, developed fully only after the first world war. Trade left the Eastern Delta and the rivers which fed it almost completely, and the trading 'beaches' followed the railway and later the roads into the hinterland. The Eastern Delta states were left derelict, their trade monopoly finally broken, their poorer members reverting once more to fishing for their livelihood, their wealthier and more enterprising being drawn off to the new commercial centres to compete—but this time on level terms—with business and professional men from the trading communities of the hinterland.

If we study political development we are concerned mainly with the rise and fall of the Pepple and Amakiri dynasties in Bonny and Kalabari, and with the political and structural changes that took place in these states during this period which straddles the eighteenth and nineteenth centuries. The political systems established by these chiefs came into being in the eighteenth century and came to an end in the nineteenth century. The Pepple and Amakiri dynasties were revived during the twentieth century but the monarchy is now shorn of all its former powers and prerogatives.

James Barbot's abstract gives us a description of conditions just before the beginning of the eighteenth century, and by comparing it with the accounts of Captain Crow and Captain Adams, who visited the Rio Real at the end of the century, we can see the changes that took place during this period. The Bonny and Kalabari oral

traditions associate these changes with King Pepple and King Amakiri and tell us how, but not when, these changes occurred.

James Barbot's abstract establishes clearly that the system of
trading was the same as that of the nineteenth century. The main
difference was that in 1699 this trade was not the jealously guarded
monopoly of Bonny and Kalabari which it had become in the nineteenth century. James Barbot anchored at Bonny and paid 'comey'
there, but he visited and bought slaves from both Kalabari and
Andoni, and the King of Andoni was able to bring slaves and sell
them to the vessels lying in the Bonny roads.

The end of the seventeenth century was obviously a time of peace
in the Eastern Delta. John Barbot repeats Dapper's description of
the great Ijo canoes armed with shields and throwing-spears. But
whereas in the former description each 'rower' has his shield and his
trousseau d'assagayes, these people being always at war with each
other, John Barbot tones this down to 'they commonly hang at the
head of the canoe two shields, and on the sides some bundles of
javelins, as defensive arms, in a readiness to repulse any attempt
that may be made on them in their voyages along the rivers, being
generally at variance with some neighbouring nation or other'.[15]

James Barbot's unhampered movements in the Rio Real area and
his description of the friendly convivial atmosphere in Kalabari
contrasts very markedly with the situation of intense rivalry, fighting
and bloodshed which the Kalabari traditions attribute to the period
'before Amakiri', when each of the seven sections were prepared to
fight every other and each had its own *Ebeka* (war trophy stand).
Barbot had plenty of time to see all there was to be seen on the very
small and congested acre or so of drier land that was Elem Kalabari.
He saw dried heads of beasts and other 'Jou Jous' but he saw no
human trophies whatever. He met them in Andoni in the 'large
press full of skulls of their enemies', but not apparently in Bonny,
a people or village which he dismissed as being the same as Kalabari.
The only head trophies the Barbots noticed in Bonny were the
twenty-five elephants' skulls in the juju house they called 'the grange'.
By contrast, in the nineteenth century the Bonny juju house with its
pyramid and platform of human skulls was a feature which impressed
itself on everybody who visited the place.[16]

The beginning of the century was a period of relative peace, as
was the end when Captain Crow was there. But the Pepple and

[15] Barbot, p. 382.
[16] Vide Hope Waddell, p. 271.

Amakiri dynasties came into being in a period of warfare and of political changes accomplished by or as a result of warfare. This was true not only of the Eastern Delta but of other parts of the Bights of Benin and Biafra. The eighteenth century saw the conquest of the Slave Coast ports by Dahomey, and on the Cross River the climax of the struggle between the Efik communities of Creek Town, Duke Town, and Old Town. It is not suggested that this period of warfare was continuous or that it happened at the same time in all these places. A more satisfactory hypothesis is that it was progressive, moving down the West African coast from the Gold Coast to the Bight of Biafra and being correlated with very considerable increases in the imports of gunpowder and firearms. In the Gold and Slave Coasts these were traded to the powerful hinterland kingdoms of Ashanti and Dahomey, enabling them to overthrow and conquer the states that had previously controlled their trade with the coast. In the Eastern Delta states and Old Calabar it led to local warfare among these coastal communities to obtain the control or the monopoly of this overseas trade, the warfare being civil in Nembe and Efik, intertribal on the Rio Real. If one takes the lists of trade goods which John Barbot gives as imports for the Gold and Slave Coasts and compares it with the extensive lists given by Dapper, the most conspicuous omission from the latter is gunpowder and firearms. This suggests that the commercial import of these goods occurred after Dapper's time, that is, after 1670. Dapper mentions no trade demand for them and describes the arms used in the Gold Coast, namely cutlasses, swords, assegais, and bows and arrows. Firearms were known, of course, and he records that at Little Ardra on the Slave Coast they were among the conventional presents made to the king by a merchant on his departure—'either two muskets and twenty five pounds of powder' or 'Indian stuffs to the value of nine slaves'.[17] Both were commodities being introduced to the coast and not yet in regular demand. By the time of John Barbot, that is in about 1680, firearms were in demand on both coasts, the Gold Coast negroes had become 'very expert in their use' and 'an aboundance of firearms, powder and ball are sold and are a very profitable commodity'.[18] On the Slave Coast their use appears to have been more recent as only 'some few of the soldiery' of Fida were armed with them[19] while at Ardra, although 'they are commonly armed with

[17] Dapper, p. 300 and p. 306.
[18] Barbot, p. 264.
[19] Ibid, p. 336.

muskets' this applies only to 'those that live near to the coast', the rest being without them. Further east the soldiery of Benin had no muskets only bows and arrows and various types of spears and knives.

If one goes on to compare James Barbot's lists of trade goods for the Rio Real and Old Calabar with those given by Captain Adams[20] and Lieutenant Bold[21] at the beginning of the nineteenth century, the same pattern is repeated. There is no mention of guns and powder in Barbot's lists. Firearms were still a novelty and, with fine hats and coats, formed suitable presents for the kings and chiefs of the Eastern Delta. We can conclude therefore that the extensive use of firearms began on the Gold Coast in the seventeenth century and probably after 1670 and not until a century later in the Niger Delta and on the Cross River. Their extensive use on the Slave Coast can be placed in the first quarter of the eighteenth century, since Snelgrave and Atkins give the year 1727 for the Dahomey conquest of Whydah (Fida). There are no dates for the Kalabari and Bonny wars but we can assume that they occurred later in this century. It is possible that the immediate result of the fall of the Slave Coast states was an increased demand for slaves in the Bight of Biafra, and one can also assume an oscillation of this trade between the Rio Real and the Old Calabar river, depending on which happened to be at peace and able therefore to engage in trade. Captain Adams says that Old Calabar had lost her market for slaves to Bonny because of the exorbitant comey demanded there—£250 as against £150 in Bonny—but cessation of hostilities on the Rio Real would have been a far more potent reason.[22] Kalabari and Bonny were in a position to supply slaves more speedily and in greater numbers than any other Oil River port.

The Bonny and Kalabari traditions both describe this period of warfare through which and out of which their two heroes led their people in triumph and they stress the cost of these wars. Perukule and Amakiri had to have not men but money. Money to buy the arms and ammunition with which to wage these wars, and money to buy the food to feed their people while their trade was interrupted, and, for that matter, money to buy the people to repopulate the devastated Elem Kalabari. They detail the methods of warfare, namely raids, ambushes, and battles in which fleets of canoes manoeuvered, and these canoes were no longer armed with shields

---

[20] Adams, 2, p. 253.
[21] Bold., p. 80-1.
[22] Adams, 2, p. 243.

and assegais, but with muskets and with a cannon lashed to the thwarts at the bow and the stern.

But although the Kalabari legends describe Amakiri and his people as being engaged in warfare against all the surrounding peoples, the particular enemy over whom the Kalabari people ultimately triumphed was not Bonny but Okrika. Similarly, the people with whom Bonny fought their hardest battles were not the Kalabari but the Andoni. It is necessary to underline this as the nineteenth century European tradition implies a Bonny and Kalabari struggle culminating in the defeat of Kalabari by Bonny. Bonny and Kalabari were indeed rivals for the European trade, but this trade was large enough to contain them both and by the eighteenth century each had its established trading organization with the hinterland and European trading vessels decided whether they traded with Kalabari or with Bonny. But both communities were dependent for their survival on their trade with these hinterland markets, which were up the New Calabar River for the Kalabari, up the Imo for the Bonny. Okrika lay on the east flank of the Kalabari route up river and between them and their markets, while Bonny had to pass right through Andoni territory to reach the Imo. These were not their only markets but they were their main and traditional ones.

We can also with some certainty attribute to this period the changes in their political systems and in the organization of their houses, since both the Bonny and Kalabari traditions maintain that they came about this time. Before then the structure of their houses, and the relationship of these houses to each other, was similar to that of other delta communities. But in order to survive during this period of intense warfare, a much greater degree of centralized authority had to be accepted so that the war leaders who became their kings became, temporarily at least, all powerful. It was also during this period that these kings broke down the last discrimination against slaves and those of stranger origin by recognizing the ablest of them as chiefs, that is, as heads of houses. The qualifications needed to become a chief, that is, to found a house, or to succeed to the chieftancy of an existing house, were changed. They ceased to be based on descent, that is, to be limited to those who could trace their ancestry to the founder of the community, and were based on military and economic prowess alone. The candidate for the honour had to give proof of his qualities of leadership by being able to man and maintain a war canoe.

We can regard the eighteenth century then as a period of political change. The pattern of foreign trading had already been established by the beginning of the century and continued relatively unaltered; what did change was the political system and the method of warfare. The use of firearms was introduced during the century; their introduction either stimulated a period of intense conflict between the various communities, or, more probably, this conflict stimulated their import and the change from native weapons. The states that emerged most successfully from this conflict were those whose wealth enabled them to make the greatest use of these new arms. But they were only able to achieve this by placing greater power and authority in the hands of their kings and by revolutionizing the social structure, so that, while still retaining the 'house' structure, the most complete social mobility was possible within it and the strongest incentive to acquire wealth through trading was offered to all its members. It is this reformed structure that is described in the succeeding chapters.

Part Two

POLITICAL AND ECONOMIC ORGANIZATION OF THE OIL RIVERS IN THE NINETEENTH CENTURY

IV

Kinship and Social Status

I. THE EASTERN DELTA HOUSE

THE characteristic political and social unit of the Eastern Delta is usually referred to both in official records and by the Ijo themselves as a house. This term, besides being used officially for those political groups we have already called wards or village-sections, is also used in the delta for any and every subdivision of these groups. The Eastern Ijo word for a house is *wari*, which stands for a dwelling-house and by extension for the people living in it, a family or household. By further extension it stands for the unilineal descendants of such a household, either all of them or those living together as a corporate group, and including any other relatives, strangers, and slaves who may be attached to it.

As so defined it might be thought of as corresponding to the corporate kin group, which among the Ibo and Ibibio is referred to as a family or a lineage and which among the Efik is also known as a house (*ufok*). But the composition of an Ijo house differs considerably from a normal Ibo or Ibibio lineage, as will be apparent as soon as one examines the Ijo system of marriage and descent.

They recognize two forms of marriage, referred to locally as big and little dowry, dowry in the local vernacular English meaning bridewealth. In the Kalabari dialect these forms are called respectively *eya* and *egwa* and, to avoid confusion, these terms will be used in this discussion. The marriage rituals are the same in both forms, but in *eya* a considerable sum of money is paid as bridewealth by the groom to the bride's people, while in the *egwa* system only a negligible sum is required. Under the *egwa* form the groom acquires only conjugal rights over the bride, under the *eya* her children become the property of the groom and his house. Under the *egwa* form divorce, that is to say, termination of the marriage contract, is said to be frequent, under the *eya* form divorce is not permitted, though in Bonny a husband could forego his conjugal rights and his wife could, with his permission, form a temporary or permanent conjugal union with another man.[1] Where a couple resided was a matter of convenience and was affected by economic and other considerations, for example, the age of the spouses, whether it was the first marriage of the bride, or whether she was a divorcée. This, at least, is the position today and the little evidence there is suggests that, in Kalabari and Bonny at least, it was also possible in the nineteenth century for a woman, whether married under the *egwa* or the *eya* form, to change her domicile to suit her own or her husband's or her relatives' convenience. Such changes did not, however, carry with them any transfer of rights over the woman. She and her children and other persons attached to her household belonged to her husband and his group in an *eya* marriage and to her natal group in an *egwa*. An *eya* wife did not entirely lose her connection with her natal family, she remained a member of that family and in Kalabari, for example, they retained the right to bury her.

These *eya* and *egwa* systems are common to the Central and Eastern Delta except in some of the marginal areas. The Andoni area is a transitional one in which the Western and Central Andoni villages follow the *eya* and *egwa* systems, while the eastern villages and the Ibeno tribe follow the normal Ibibio system with a single high bridewealth form of marriage. The chief local differences in the rest of the Central and Eastern Delta lie in the incidence of the two forms of marriage. Speaking generally, more *eya* marriages occur in the wealthier communities, fewer in the poorer. In some of the more remote of these, for example, Akassa, the *egwa* form has become the preferred form. *Eya* marriage is equated with wife purchase or slave marriage and no free-born woman is expected to submit to it. Similarly, a man's sister's son is regarded as his rightful heir.

Jeffreys writing of the Western Andoni[2] saw the *egwa* form as a matrilineal survival but it could be explained more simply as the institutionalizing of a practice accepted by most patrilineal societies of Southern Nigeria. If this is done it ceases to be a matter of matrilineal and patrilineal succession, but one of jural as opposed to natural paternity.

In all patrilineal societies in Eastern Nigeria it is recognized that a child born before the bridewealth has been paid, or before a contract to pay such bridewealth has been made, belongs to the mother's

---

[1] This custom is enshrined in the Bonny legend of Queen Edimini ba Kamba her husband Apoli and her lover Biriye.
[2] Jeffreys, Unpublished report on the Andoni. 1930.

family and lineage. The child's jural father is the mother's father and the actual father, the genitor, has no right over the child.

Whatever its origin, the *egwa* system of marriage is very well suited to the fishing communities of the Delta. It enables a young man to obtain a wife who will be maintained by her natal family while he is away for long periods fishing and accumulating the gear, canoes, and other capital goods he needs for his work. As he advances in his profession his wife may accompany him on his fishing expeditions or if she remains behind he is responsible for the maintenance of his wife and family and, should he fail to supply the money for this maintenance, she can divorce him and become attached to another husband who is capable of doing so. Similarly, in the wealthier trading states the *egwa* system, in addition to providing for the poorer fishing section of the community, also provided a very convenient form of marriage for male slaves, strangers, servants, and other members of a wealthier man's household. They were married in this fashion to his daughters and grand-daughters or to his female slaves and their daughters. Indeed, the Kalabari, according to Horton[3] recognize three forms of marriage, *eya*, *egwa* and *waribiosime*, marriage within the house, that is, of people who though not closely related were members of the same house.[4]

The lineage and the house

In theory those communities in which *egwa* had become the normal form of marriage should have developed from patrilineal into matrilineal societies, their wards becoming matriclans which sub-divided into a number of matrilineages. In fact, however, this does not seem to have taken place since unilineal descent is only one of a number of social and economic factors which affect the situation.

When one examines Ijo houses and Ijo marriages, one is concerned with kinship at two very different levels of the social structure, which can be distinguished as political and domestic.

Kinship at the higher level is political and symbolic rather than actual. The group is depicted in myth as a domestic unit, the family of the founder of the unit and existing members of the group believe themselves to be an extension of this original family and its unilineal descendants.

[3] Though not according to Newns, 1947.
[4] Eastern Ijo custom forbids marriage of cousins, i.e. of those who can trace a common grandparent, and of those who can trace their descent to a common patrilineal ancestor. Efik custom, on the other hand, permits the marriage of any kind of cousin.

At the lower level we are dealing with domestic units, with households or expanded households whose core is a single family or a unilineal extended family. At this level unilineal kinship is actual and jural and carries with it rights over the property and persons of the unit. Among Ibo and Ibibio most of the males and the unmarried females are the patrilineal descendants of the founder of the unit. Among the Ijo the domestic unit can be more bilateral and heterogeneous.

Among the hinterland peoples patrilineal kinship carries with it considerable economic advantages, for example, rights over agricultural and residential land. It is therefore economically as well as politically advantageous for men to live together in patrilineal units. Most of these advantages are absent in the delta fishing communities. They have no farmland and many of them lack even enough dry land on which to build their houses. Most of their male members have to be absent for long periods at distant fishing grounds, where they build their own temporary huts or enter into residential associations with unrelated groups in the neighbourhood. Similarly, their adult women may live in houses built for them either in their own natal home or in their husband's. They may accompany their husbands on some of their fishing expeditions, taking some of their children with them or leaving them with cognatic or agnatic relatives or even with unrelated friends. Thus the composition of an Ijo household may be much more heterogeneous. It may lack either permanently or for limited periods some of the members who would normally be present in a hinterland household and it may contain temporarily or more permanently many members not normally found in them.

This was even more the case with the households in the trading states of the Eastern Delta in the nineteenth century, when a wealthy man could expand his household, not only by marrying *eya* wives but by buying slaves of both sexes and of all ages and by incorporating other persons attached to him by kinship, economic, or political ties.

It is thus probably wiser to refer to the corporate kin groups of the delta as houses rather than lineages. In the hinterland, as in the delta, groups of this order regard themselves as the unilineal descendants of the household of their founder, but whereas in the hinterland the household was normally a minimal patrilineage, this was not necessarily the case in the delta. Indeed, in the nineteenth century delta states the blood descendants of the founder of a house often formed a minority of its members and, in some cases, where, for example, the founder and his wives were sterile, they might even be non-existent.

The ward

In its widest extension the term house (*wari* or *ufok*) is applied to the primary village section which has been called a ward. Among both the Efik and the Eastern Ijo a ward is known by the name of its reputed founder to which is added in Ijo the suffix *-biri* or *-polo* when referring to it as a place of residence, *-ama* or *-ame* when thinking of it as an autonomous community like a town or village, or as a group of people derived from such a community.[5]

Among the Efik a ward segmented into a number of major and minor segments which were coordinated by a genealogical charter of descent from its founder. Eastern Ijo wards, though they cherished a tradition of agnatic descent from a single founder, had no such clearly defined pattern of segmentation. As we have already shown, their personnel was more heterogeneous and it also tended to be more fluid. Many of a ward's members could and did maintain relationship with more than one ward.

The canoe house

We have so far been describing the structure of the traditional house as it existed in Bonny, Kalabari, and Nembe before the changes which tradition attributes to the time of King Pepple and King Amakiri. The type of house which replaced it has been distinguished as the canoe house.

By comparison with the traditional house, the canoe house was a compact and well organized trading and fighting corporation, capable of manning and maintaining a war canoe. The canoe was a large dug-out, similar in construction to those described by Dapper and John Barbot, but it was now armed with cannon fore and aft which were lashed to the thwarts and it occasionally carried another on a swivel amidships. The fifty or more paddlers now carried muskets in place of their 'bundles of assegais'. The captain and helmsman was the house chief unless he was too old, and one or more drummers conveyed his commands to the men and provided the rhythm for their movements. Besides being its war leader the chief was also the manager of its trading organization and of its

---

[5] Thus in Elem Kalabari the ward of Endeme (Ende-ame) was otherwise known as Kalabari-polo, and the ward founded by Opu-koro-ye was called Korome (Koro-ame). Sometimes the two suffixes were combined as in Ogbolo-ama-biri, the senior moiety of Nembe.

house funds derived from a system of house taxation, the work-bars and custom-bars described in Chapter VII. By the judicious administration of these funds he was able to maintain and expand the house and should he fail to do this he could be deposed by the members of the house and another more able chief appointed in his place.

Formerly only kings and those of royal or of chiefly descent could found a new house, but in the case of a new canoe house any member of a canoe house who had become wealthy enough and acquired a sufficiently large following to be able to man and maintain a war canoe could be presented by the head of his house to the king, chiefs and other elders. If they were satisfied that he had 'filled his canoe' he was allowed to perform the rituals which made him a chief and founder of his own canoe house, a house which was independent in its commercial business but subordinate politically to the house from which it derived.

Canoe houses in Kalabari and Bonny in the historical period were of two main types, those of long ancestry which could trace their origin to a founding ancestor of the distant past and those of more recent establishment. The first type, which were the surviving remnants of former wards which had become converted into canoe houses, were called in Bonny *duowari* and were relatively poor in wealth and small in size. The latter, which included most of the important houses, were further differentiated in Bonny into *opuwari* and *kalawari*. An *opuwari* was the founding house, the great or main house, of a canoe house group, a *kalawari* was a house derived from it and subordinate to it.

The canoe house group

In comparison with the traditional house, the size of the canoe house was much more closely defined, as was its personnel. It was smaller and it took care to assert its rights over all its members.[6] Expansion in the case of the traditional house might or might not be met by a segmentation into a number of sub-houses. Expansion in the case of the canoe house was met by carefully planned segmentation into one or more new canoe houses. The personnel of the expanded canoe house, was apportioned between the original or main house and the new canoe house and although it was economically independent the new canoe house remained politically subordinate to its main house. For in nineteenth-century Bonny and Kalabari

[6] Apart from the old and infirm and other persons who were merely liabilities.

a canoe house could only be politically effective when in combination with other such houses. These combinations were the result either of the expansion of a single house or of the association together of a number of unrelated and formerly independent canoe houses.

2. THE STATUS SYSTEMS OF THE EASTERN DELTA STATES IN THE NINETEENTH CENTURY

In other Ijo communities, as in those of the hinterland, age and descent were the cardinal determinants of a man's status. Only a man who was of advanced age could aspire to the headship of the house or lineage and then only if he were a lineal descendant of its founder. Social mobility existed but it was a slow process, a matter of several generations before the descendants of slaves and of strangers became accepted as full members of the lineage or house. In the principal Oil River states, on the other hand, social mobility became so rapid that it was possible for a bought slave to become the founder of his own canoe house and for some of these to become first the chief of a group of houses, and eventually the most powerful chief in the state, for example, the two Braid brothers and George Amakiri in Kalabari, and Jaja Anna Pepple in Bonny. Indeed, the majority of the *opuwari* houses were founded by slaves of this type.

Although in ritual matters descent still counted and priests of ritual cults still had to be lineal descendants of the patrilineage that 'owned' the cult, it ceased to be a prerequisite for social advancement in political and economic spheres and was replaced very largely by other qualities, particularly those of administrative and business ability. With this exaggerated emphasis on wealth and economic leadership went a rather different status evaluation which, as it was never properly appreciated by nineteenth century Europeans and has been partly forgotten or misrepresented in contemporary local tradition, will have to be examined in some detail.

People in these states were classed or ranked by a number of different and frequently conflicting criteria which can be seen as belonging to two very different systems—a traditional one based primarily on descent and a newer one based mainly on wealth. The traditional system probably indicated where power resided in the past, the new one very clearly showed where it lay in the Eastern Delta in the nineteenth century.

The traditional system distinguished two main categories, namely, slave and freeborn with a superior class of freeborn, royalty. The last categorized the king and the princes, that is, freeborn persons who were direct lineal descendants of the founder of the dynasty. They were distinguished from other members of the community by the fact that they alone were eligible for the office of king. The eighteenth- and nineteenth-century Bonny and Kalabari monarchs were blessed with very few children,[7] and thus, throughout this period there were very few people who could claim to be of royal blood and never enough to constitute an aristocracy or similar specially privileged class of persons.

The categories freeborn and slave were used in the nineteenth-century historical sources but they did not carry the same meanings in the delta as in Western European society nor did they provide the same clear-cut division. Freeborn always carried a sense of superiority and slave one of inferiority and this was enhanced by the weight given to such ideas by the European visitors to the Rio Real. But in the Eastern Delta and in its hinterland no man was free in the accepted European sense, every freeman and slave was a member of a corporate group, a house. They enjoyed the same political rights as its members as against members of other houses, while within the house the rights they enjoyed depended mainly on criteria other than those of descent. They were both equally the property of the house and, in cases of necessity, both could be sold by it to meet its financial commitments. The real distinction in Eastern Delta society between freeborn and slave was based not so much on political and legal criteria as on values which, for want of a better name, will have to be called ritual. A true freeborn was a person whose ancestor had founded the place. He was a person who belonged there by right of kinship, of descent. A stranger was inferior in that he did not belong, but he could at least return to the place where he did belong. A slave was a stranger who had the stigma of having lost his right to belong to his own community and who belonged to his master's house by right of purchase by this master. But, in course of time, the slave came to be regarded as belonging more and more completely to his master's community. A slave born in the place belonged to it by right of birth and it was felt in the Eastern Delta that any person born in a place should not be sold out of it, and, as elsewhere in the region, the descendants of such a slave formed a minor descent group and eventually came to be regarded as freeborn though not to the same degree as those in the direct line of descent. Thus there was always a potential or

[7] Conditions in Nembe were very little better.

actual division of the category of freemen into those of superior and those of inferior descent and only the former were originally eligible to succeed to the office of head of the house. We can refer to the superior ones as nobles and the rest as commoners and where, as in the Delta states, the kingship of the community came to be vested in a particular dynasty we can distinguish a further differentiation of these nobles into princes, those who alone possessed the right to succeed to the kingship, a right which could descend through a daughter as well as through a son. It was possible, in default of any suitable heir, for a collateral line to succeed to the kingship but not for a slave or a stranger.[8]

Similarly, within the category of slaves there was an equivalent differentiation into superior and inferior, the former being those born in the place, the latter those born elsewhere who were distinguished as 'bought slaves'.

Thus the full range of categories descended from royalty through princes to noble freeborn and commoner freeborn, thence to locally born slaves and then, finally, to bought slaves.[9]

The second system divided delta society into the king, princes, chiefs, gentlemen, and niggers. It was essentially a classification based on power. Power, in this context, was the right to command the support of others and this right in the eighteenth and nineteenth century delta states was dependent to an overwhelming degree upon wealth. A gentleman was a person who could command the support of other people, a nigger was one whom others could command. A chief was a gentleman who was the head of a house and could therefore command the support of all persons in that house. A king was a person who had the resources, economic, political, and ritual, to command the support of the whole community. There is a passage in Smith's memoirs which brings this out very clearly.

---

[8] Hence the efforts of the rival contemporary political groups in Kalabari to prove on the one side that King Amakiri was freeborn and a direct descendant of the founder while the Kamalu dynasty were descendants of an Ibo, and on the other side, that Amakiri was of slave, and Kamalu of Kalabari descent.

[9] Below these again in the early nineteenth century was a further category of people, the slaves who were bought for resale to the European traders. But these could hardly be considered members of Delta society, they were merely goods or chattels in transit from the Nigerian hinterland to the New World. The cost of feeding them and other factors saw to it that their stay in the delta ports was of the shortest possible duration. There were occasions when the British Naval blockade made the Rio Real too hot for slavers and left Bonny and Kalabari with such slaves on their hands. Consular reports say that in such cases the slaves were left to die of starvation but it is more probable that economic incentives would lead to the more able-bodied of such slaves being absorbed in the category of bought slaves into the houses which had bought them.

After rating a great man for being so tardy in meeting his payments, he called me a 'white nigger' as a set off for my having called him a 'black nigger'. 'What way' said I, 'you call me a nigger. I be free-man. I be gentleman in my own country'. 'Chi' said he. 'What way you call yourself gentleman? Who them ship belong for? He be yours?'. 'No' I replied 'the ship is not my property'. 'Well then, you be white nigger, suppose you no be nigger, you bring your own ship and no 'tother man's ship'.[10]

Nigger then as now was a derogatory word which could be used as an insult and its polite equivalent was 'boy', a servant or employee.[11]

The essential difference from the traditional system was that every one of these positions could be acquired and could also be lost. It was also very much a competitive system. A king, if he lacked the resources associated with kingship, could find himself deposed. A nigger of the lowest category if he possessed the requisite capacity could rise to the rank of chief of a main house, and, in the case of Jaja Anna Pepple, to the rank of king.

The traditional and the new systems came together at the top and at the bottom of the scale. The two highest categories of king and and prince corresponded. The terms nigger and slave could also be said to correspond, at least at their lowest level, and European traders certainly regarded them as more or less inter-changeable. But gentleman and freeborn could not be brought together, for most of the more important gentlemen and chiefs were slaves. The European traders were concerned mainly with people in the two extreme forms of gentlemen and of niggers, that is, with the house chiefs and other trading members of their houses on the one hand, and with their canoe boys, labourers, and servants on the other. A gentleman to them was primarily a trader, a person who made money by trading with them and with this money supported his niggers, that is, the people of whom he was the master. They tended to evaluate such gentlemen by the volume of their trade and to denigrate those whose claims to the rank rested on their being the freeborn head of an ancient though commercially insolvent house, as 'Parliament Gentlemen'.[12] The consuls, on the other hand, particularly those who like Burton tried to understand the political and social organization, found themselves at a loss for a term under which to classify the ordinary Bonny or Kalabari citizen who was, in

[10] Smith, p. 196.
[11] E.g. Article XII of the Bonny treaty of 1854. 'Any King, chief, trader or boy coming armed to the court—shall be fined in 50 puncheons of oil'. Appendix B 3.
[12] Smith, p. 163.

the consul's estimation, neither a gentleman nor a nigger. Freeborn was the category that should have intervened between gentlefolk and slaves but the difficulty was to determine who, if any, were really free. For the term nigger or slave could be applied by a person of higher rank to anyone who was financially and politically dependent upon him. Thus a chief could refer to the gentlemen and other members of his house as his niggers, the chief of a main house could describe the chiefs of all houses subordinate to it as his niggers, while the king of Bonny could and did refer to all the people of Bonny as his slaves. Even if the term slave was taken more exactly as meaning a person who had been bought or the descendants of such a person the position was still far from clear, for owing to the vagaries of fortune in their various houses, a considerable proportion of those who were born in Bonny and Kalabari of ancestral stock had either been sold by their ancestral houses to meet their house debts or were the descendants of persons sold in this way and thus were technically slaves.

What the European observers failed to grasp was that these various status categories did not build up into a simple stratified society of upper (chiefs and gentlemen), middle (freeborn), and lower (slave) classes, but constituted two alternative systems of status valuation whereby a person could rank himself and be ranked by others. A poor freeman could take comfort in the superiority of his birth, he could engage in traditional occupations like fishing, in in which he did not have to work for other people, and he could regard himself as ranking above the enterprising young trader whose greater wealth could be cancelled out by the fact that he was a slave and had a master. The trader, in his turn, could rank himself as a gentleman, superior to the fisherman whose occupation was the menial one of a canoe man ('Pulla boy').

Those people who possessed neither birth nor wealth could fall back on the superior status of the household and of the house to which they belonged, or had formerly belonged, for status valuation applied to groups just as much as to individuals. Houses ranked themselves according to the same alternative systems; those of long establishment, the *duowari*, were able to forget their dwindling assets in contemplation of their superior pedigree, and to look down upon the parvenu though powerful *opuwari* and their recent and often servile origin. The status of the house in turn affected the status of its members; an inferior member of a superior house could, for example, rank himself above a superior member of an inferior house. The head of a *duowari* might be a bought slave but the members of his house could rank him as a chief whose status was superior to any *opuwari* chief by reason of the antiquity of this *duowari*.

But the *opuwari* houses and chiefs in their turn could despise the *duowari* for their lack of wealth, of people, and therefore of power and it was these political criteria more than any other that determined a house's actual position in nineteenth century delta society. Similarly, within the house what mattered most to each of its individual members was not his birth or origin but what particular household or household group he might belong to, and what was the quality of its leadership. These were the factors that most affected a man's career. A potentially able young trader in a declining *duowari* house would find his career blocked; the decline in the quality of the house's trading meant the loss of those contacts with the Europeans and with hinterland traders which can be included under the term good-will and, instead of financial assistance from his house funds towards his trading, he could expect to find himself obliged to contribute from his own capital to meet the house's debts. By contrast an able young Ibo slave incorporated into the household of an *eya* wife of an able *opuwari* chief, would begin his career as a gentleman and receive a sufficient start to enable him in a large number of cases to establish his own canoe house early in his life and in due course he could be elected, either to the chieftancy of his late master's house or to the chieftaincy of a satellite canoe house of his own. A man's fortunes were thus bound up with those of his household and his canoe house and could not be pursued independently. This will be seen more clearly when we examine the patterns of expansion of canoe houses in Chapter X.

V

The Eastern Delta state
at the beginning of the nineteenth century

THE political systems of the Eastern Delta states during the period we are studying were in a condition of fairly rapid change. But throughout this period they shared a number of common features which, when taken together, distinguished them from other political systems of the Eastern Region and which justify their being considered as a special type peculiar to the Eastern Delta. The simplest way to describe this type is to examine the characteristic institutions which distinguish them from other Eastern Nigerian communities, in particular the Efik, indicating where necessary particular variations in the different states.

I. TERRITORIAL STRUCTURE

The territory over which the state maintained political and economic rights was of two kinds, which will be referred to as its tribal territory and its 'trading empire'. The former was a compact area of estuaries, creeks and waterways, together with fishing grounds and mangrove and other forests. It contained in its principal estuary ('river') an anchorage for ocean-going shipping, where all European traders who wished to do business with the state resided in their trading vessels.

The population of the state was distributed over this tribal territory in a number of towns or groups of villages and in smaller settlements. The dominant one which gave its name to the state can be called its capital. The others were attached to it by ties of varying strength. Those adjacent to it were virtually incorporated into the capital and formed sub-communities of it. Those which were more distant were less closely attached and some might claim to be politically though not economically independent, that is, although they might claim to rule themselves without reference to any outside authority, they could not trade direct with Europeans but only through one or other of the canoe houses of the state in whose territory they lay.

64   POLITICAL AND ECONOMIC ORGANIZATION

The capital and its sub-communities was organized into primary segments, which were composed of either a single canoe house or a group of such houses and which have been described in the preceding chapter. The members of a canoe house lived partly in an area which belonged to the house in the capital or sub-community, partly in adjacent villages, and partly in small settlements (plantations) within the tribal territory on land which belonged to their particular house.

Thus the villages in the Nembe tribal territory fell into three separate groups; the coastal villages (Okpoma, Ewama, Twon, Beletiama, Egwema and Liama); the central area occupied by the capital and its plantations; and the northern area lying between it and the Niger river. Civil war in the eighteenth century had divided the capital into two residential and political moieties, Ogbolomabiri and Bassambiri, each with its king, its general council and its Ekine lodge, but with Ogbolomabiri ranking as senior. The coastal villages considered themselves offshoots of and part of Nembe and were organized into canoe houses in the same manner. The northern villages were of different linguistic and cultural origins; they had their own social and political organization but were considered a part of the state and within its tribal territory.

The Kalabari tribal territory was the largest in population and the most heterogeneous of the Eastern Delta states. Its tribal territory comprised the area between the Santa Barbara and the New Calabar rivers, as far north as the delta margin and the Kalabari dominance over the various communities in this area[1] which maintained a semi-independent existence had been reasserted during the later years of the first King Amakiri. Bile might maintain its autonomy and marry its *amayanabo's* daughter to the King of Bonny but it was too small and isolated to be able to oppose the Kalabari state. Elem Kalabari, the capital, and a number of smaller village communities adjacent to it—namely Ifoko, Tombia, Ido, and Abalama— were so closely interrelated that they formed a single political group and, like Elem Kalabari, they each sub-divided into a number of primary sections which were composed in the larger communities of canoe house groups, and in the smaller of single canoe houses. The more distant and poorer villages retained their original structure.

The limited area of dry land at Elem Kalabari prevented most canoe houses from accommodating all their members there, and an ever increasing number lived either in plantations further inland, or in the adjacent communities or even in the more distant ones. Many

[1] Listed in Chapter II table I, p. 12.

people in these villages, particularly in the adjacent ones, were closely connected with particular canoe houses of Elem Kalabari and a large number of their men had a dual allegiance, being considered members both of a particular house in their own community and also of another house in Elem Kalabari.

The state of Ubani or Grand Bonny, as it was called by Europeans at this time, was the smallest in area and in population of all the Eastern Delta states. But its wealth and therefore its power was by far the greatest.

It was composed of the town or large village of Bonny, together with a few lesser villages adjacent to it, and a number of plantation settlements further afield. These villages were to all intents and purposes a part of the capital. The most important of them was Finnema (Juju town) which lay near to the coast and which, like the corresponding villages of Ifoko in Kalabari and Twon (Brass), in Nembe provided pilots for vessels crossing the Bar.

The trading empire of a state consisted of a number of waterways leading into the hinterland and of the markets to which they provided access. The state made no claim to political jurisdiction over these rivers or markets, but it maintained an exclusive monopoly of the trade between these markets and the European traders. Any trade with the outside world had to pass through its middlemen and not through those of other Delta states.

The territorial structure of the Efik state followed a similar pattern. Its tribal territory consisted of the Cross River estuary. Its capital was a community living at the junction of the Old Calabar and the Cross river which had expanded into the three villages of Creek Town, Old Town and Duke Town, while its trading empire covered the whole of the Cross River and its hinterland. Its social and political organization however differed considerably, more especially in the structure of its primary political segments (wards), and in the political role of its secret society (Ekpe).[2]

2. THE MONARCHY

Under the earlier political systems the office of head of the community is said to have been one for which the chief of any of its houses (wards) was eligible.[3] Under the nineteenth century system this office was vested in a particular lineage and passed from founder

[2] For a fuller description of it see Jones, 2.
[3] E.g. in Bonny, Okrika and Kalabari.

to sons (provided they were able enough) and then to sons' sons. This office originally carried with it little additional authority except in ritual matters, the community head ranking as little more than the senior of a number of ward heads and performing the function of presiding over village council meetings and similar public gatherings. With the advent of European trading vessels the office which was now dignified by the European title of king developed into one of considerable power. The king represented the community in its external relations with other powers and he was the person to whom the Europeans looked to arrange the conditions under which they traded and to whom they paid trading dues or comey, which, in the early nineteenth century, amounted to a very considerable revenue. An able king could use his position to obtain favourable trading concessions from these Europeans, and so add to the wealth of his canoe house, and he could manipulate the distribution of comey in ways that would secure the maximum of political support from the heads of other houses. Although there was a royal lineage there was no royal house. The son who succeeded to the kingship was already the chief of his own canoe house. While his father was alive, this canoe house was a subordinate house in the group which looked to the king's house as its main house. When the father died this group broke up and the new King's house expanded and became the main house of a new group of houses, which were derived from this house and not from his predecessor's.

3. THE GENERAL COUNCIL

Local traditions do not distinguish between the formal conciliar organization of these governments and their administrative and executive machinery. During the nineteenth century the distribution of power between the different parts of the system changed very radically so that by the end of the century most of it lay with chiefs of the dominant canoe house groups. This situation was then consolidated by the British consular government, which constituted a council consisting of the chiefs of main canoe houses as the local administrative and judicial authority. My informants were very much aware of this change but they tended to over-simplify it by saying that in the colonial period it was the chiefs who ruled, while in the period before it was the secret society, Ekine. It seems clear, however, that in internal matters each canoe house, and each canoe house group governed itself; that in ordinary administrative, executive, and judicial business involving inter-house activity and co-operation the house-heads and other leaders of the houses involved met together and settled things wherever they could. Where they could not, and in the case of legislative, judicial, and other business affecting the whole community, the matter was dealt with at a general council meeting and where necessary its decision could be executed by members of the Ekine society. This society also provided an effective tribunal for hearing and deciding civil cases between litigants who belonged to different houses.

This general council was composed of a general meeting of the men of the community, assembled together according to their canoe house groups. Its business was managed by the heads of these groups together with the priests of the principal religious cults, the heads of Ekine, and any other elders whose counsel was valued. It had its spokesman and was generally presided over by the head of the community—the king. As such its form was the same as that of the general councils of other Delta communities, but the distribution of power among these council members was very different and much more of it rested with the king and with the chiefs of the more powerful canoe house groups.

4. THE EKINE SOCIETY

This society in most of the Eastern Delta communities had two names, *ekine*, its proper name and *sekiapu* (the dancers), the name by which it was more generally known and which referred to its playing and dancing. The masked players in these dances were said to represent the water spirits, *owu*, to whom the society ministered and who were brought to the town by the society in the season considered suitable for such festivities. They appeared, miming and dancing in the special plays which belonged to them, and at the end of the season or of the cycle of plays, they were returned by the society to the waters where they were said to live. There were special masks which belonged to the whole community, others which belonged to particular houses, and others again which belonged to particular chiefs and which could be 'played' by that chief's descendants.

In Nembe and, according to my informants,[4] in Kalabari also, the society was divided into a number of sections or divisions, each responsible for the maintenance of particular masks and for the production of the special plays associated with them. Members—

---

[4] Horton could find no reference to such divisions in Kalabari.

and they included practically all the able-bodied men in the community—were drafted as they joined the society into one or other of these divisions regardless of the house to which they belonged. In most of the Kalabari satellite communities and in Okrika this sectional division was absent and the society was organized on a ward basis. Bonny had no Ekine society. Its equivalent, *owu ogbo*, is said to have been of minor importance and concerned only with the production of masked dances.

In all Ekine societies initiates remained in a subordinate grade of novices until they had mastered the dances, songs, miming and interpretation of the drum signals and had been tested in this. They passed into *kala sekiapu* which was directly responsible for the performance of the current cycle of Owu plays. Those who had completed the cycle became *opu sekiapu* though they could and very often did take part in the succeeding productions particularly if they were the possessor of a personal mask. Considerable prestige accrued to those who were specially gifted in these arts and men who were skilled performers might continue in their roles until they were too old to play them and, if they happened to be chiefs or other important leaders, might be permitted by the society to introduce a new mask of their own. Most of the active part in the playing was performed, however, by younger men and the society thus divided into two main grades. The lower, *kala* (little) *sekiapu* being the younger men, the higher, *opu* (big) *sekiapu* their seniors. This latter grade divided once again into those who were the heads of the societies and those who carried out their orders. As in the Efik secret society of Ekpe, chiefs of houses were not necessarily or usually the heads of divisions or grades of the society, but, unlike Ekpe, Ekine did not rule the community. In the Efik state the two king's were the first head and second head of Ekpe, the members of its senior grade its councillors, judges and law-makers, those of its second grade were its executive officers, and those of lower grades wearing their network disguises were their agents. Ekine was never the formal government of any Eastern Delta state. But it did bring together into a single association all the men who mattered in the community and provide them with a forum for the private discussion of political and judicial matters. In its junior members it possessed agents who could carry out its orders and it could also enforce its authority by placing its seal on the property of anyone who had offended it. Although it might divide for dancing purposes into subdivisions, it formed a single unit in which canoe houses and their special interests were unrecognized.

5. PRIESTS AND RITUAL INSTITUTIONS

The role of priests and of religious cults did not differ from those of other Eastern Delta communities. Most communities had a particular tutelary deity (*oru*) whose welfare was particularly associated with that of the community. Its people could expect help and protection from their deity provided they conformed to its 'laws'. They could also expect its vengeance should they fail to do so, for the deity's prosperity was bound up with that of its worshippers and failure to conform to these 'laws' was harmful to the deity as to the community. There were also other local spirits or deities (*oru*) associated with the tutelary deity and with the community and these were able to confer fertility, protection, success in war, and various other benefits, while each canoe house had an ancestor or founder's cult (*duen fobara*) associated with the founder of the house which provided a religious focus of unity within the house, and a sanction for conformity to its rules.

There were again special cults associated with warfare and with the *peri* society in which captives were killed and eaten before the shrine of the deity associated with warfare and their skulls and long bones exhibited on a stand beside it (*ebeka*).

The political roles of priest were important in these Eastern Delta states. They were members of the general council. They were able to invoke their deities to provide and maintain peaceful discussion in their meetings and to sanction decisions that were just and in the public interest. Situations where the political system was in danger of breaking down through excessive rivalry among political leaders or through a deficiency of adequate leadership were remedied to a considerable extent by the intervention of priests and other ritual specialists. Such men could invoke religious sanctions against bloodshed and civil strife and they could through divination give expression to the voice of more disinterested public opinion in the guise of the oracular revelations of tutelary deities or ancestors. These deities could be represented as being 'vexed' by the behaviour of their people and about to wreak vengeance upon them unless they followed a particular course of action. External cults, in particular the Long Juju of Arochuku, were also used in a similar manner to confirm controversial decisions or to judge politically dangerous cases in which rival leaders were involved. The decision to refer to such external super-natural agencies secured an immediate relaxation of the tension. The meeting was adjourned, the members of the council dispersed, tempers were able to cool and more moderate councils had a chance of being heard.

The Okrika war deity was Fenibeso who was regarded as the spirit of a warrior who feared neither god nor man.[5] The Nembe war deity was also its tutelary deity Ogidiga. Kalabari differed from all the other states in having a female tutelary deity, Owame Akaso, who prohibited homicide within her community. Her cult thus provided a very powerful sanction against civil disturbances. This did not however deprive it of a war deity—Okpolodo, or of a *peri* (warrior) society, or prevent its members from killing and eating prisoners captured in war, but these had to be despatched before they came in sight of the town. The priest (*so alabo*) of Owame Akaso was accorded very high status. The cult of Akaso belonged to the former Korome ward and only members who could trace their descent to this patrilineal kin group were eligible for the office of *so alabo*. The Korome ward had also introduced the cult of the Arochuku, 'Long Juju', to Elem Kalabari where it was known as *suku obiama*. Considerable use was made of this cult during the nineteenth century. The traditional and documentary sources indicate that the invocation of this deity was being used as a political weapon, prominent men being accused of treason and of sorcery and challenged to prove their innocence by invoking *suku obiama* to support their denial of the charge. The principal rival leaders were too powerful for attack in this way; the charges were levelled against one or other of their main supporters. Such a chief's wealth might be sufficient to secure a favourable answer from the 'oracle' but he would have sustained heavy financial losses in clearing his name.

The principal tutelary deity of Bonny was Simingi. He was the local deity of Bonny Island and belonged to the community originally known as Iyankpo which split into Finnema village of Bonny and Tombia village (New Town) of Kalabari. Tombia took their cult of Simingi with them to New Town, Finnema continued the local worship of Simingi and provided its priests. Two other tutelary deities and their cults also existed at Ayama and Peterside—villages on the opposite side of the river to Bonny, which belonged to the canoe houses of Sunju (Shoo Peterside) Wilcox and Tolofari. One of these was Otuburu, the tutelary deity of the Ibo village of Azuogu Ndokki, whose cult was brought there by Apoli the legendary chief of this village when he came to join his Bonny wife Edimini ba Kamba.

[5] For details of the Fenibeso legend see Talbot, 2, pp. 80-88.

The other was Ananaba, a female deity concerned with fertility in women and with fortifying warriors before battle. This cult belonged to the Shoo Peterside house. There was also a fourth important cult located in Bonny town, that of the war deity Ikuba introduced from Ayangala village of Andoni. The iguana was sacred to and associated with Ikuba who was represented in his juju house in the form of a bronze iguana. European and Bonny traditions record that the monkey was originally sacred in Bonny but neither tradition can recollect the name of the deity it was associated with. It would also appear from European tradition that the 'tiger' (leopard) was sacred to one of the deities on the other side of the river, possibly Ananaba.[6]

The European records of this period bring out very clearly the important political role of priests in Bonny as members of the general council, in judicial matters, and as mediators in civil disputes. Finnema, because of the power of its deity, was a sanctuary to which any person or group who felt themselves in danger could remove, and where they could remain unmolested until their troubles had been settled. Fish Town (Ayama) was also a sanctuary at this time; but it is uncertain which deity made it so for European sources considered Ayama a part of Peterside. The priests of the major Bonny deities were considered persons of sufficient importance for their signature to be recorded on the earlier treaties.[7]

---

[6] Crow, p. 210: 'The second grand Jue Jue man lives at a place called Fishtown, between three and four miles from Bonny, on the opposite side of the river. There the tiger is worshipped as the chief idol.'

[7] The mark of 'Jeu Jeu Guana' occurs on four treaties (1837, 1841, 1844 and 1848). 'Jew Jew Peter' (1841) and 'Jew Jew Tiger' (1846) probably refers to the priest of Ananaba. 'Jeu Jeu Tompson' (1837) may refer to the priest of Simingi, 'Jew Jew Telefar' (1846) may represent the priest of Otuburu.

F

VI

European Influences during the nineteenth century

LIVING on these rivers and closely associated with the African community that controlled the rivers trade were a small but influential number of Europeans. Their organization in relation to the African community and their effects upon it form the subject of this chapter.

Before the nineteenth century contact between European traders and the trading communities of the Oil Rivers was limited to the bare minimum needed for trading. They maintained no factories ashore and the trading vessels which visited these rivers sought to remain there for as short a time as possible. Their influence therefore upon the development of these trading states was mainly economic in character. The development of the overseas slave trade brought increased wealth to the whole region and with it increased dependence upon overseas imports, and the control of this trade brought considerable wealth to these coastal states. This wealth also gave the more favourably situated the superior arms they needed to complete their local monopoly of this trade.

In their negotiations with the Oil River states European trading vessels were at a disadvantage. They were competing against each other and they could not afford to wait. A prolonged stay in the Bight of Biafra resulted in heavy mortality among their crews from blackwater fever, yellow fever, and other deadly tropical diseases. With the nineteenth century conditions changed and the governments of the Oil River states had thenceforward to reckon with a gradually increasing interference in their political affairs by the Europeans and by the British Government.

First came the abolition of the British slave trade and a blockade of the West African coast, which became increasingly effective until it brought the slave trade from the Bight of Biafra virtually to an end by 1840. Then came the use of the British Navy to support the rights of British palm oil traders, and to obtain the signature of treaties abolishing the slave trade and fixing the conditions of 'legitimate

72

commerce'. Then to supervise these interests more adequately came the establishment at Fernando Po of a consul for the Bights of Benin and Biafra and the organization of the European trading establishments into communities under a uniform system of government— the court of equity under the jurisdiction of the consul. Finally in 1884 came the establishment of a Protectorate over the Niger coast and its hinterland.

The Oil River states were also faced with a changed outlook among the people of Great Britain that was associated with liberal, evangelizing, and expansionist attitudes towards tropical and other 'backward peoples' and these attitudes were accompanied by a determination to put an end to the more barbarous and 'obnoxious' customs of these people and to bring to them the blessings of Victorian civilization, in particular Christianity and Free Trade. This determination found expression directly in missionary activity, indirectly in the organization of pressure groups to influence British foreign policy.

In the economic sphere these states had to adjust to a change-over in the principal export from slaves to palm oil. This change meant among other things that the Aro people lost their monopoly of the hinterland trade. The internal slave trade remained in their hands as did the import trade in the more valuable imports, cloth, tobacco, gunpowder and muskets. But in the marketing of palm oil the Aro were at a disadvantage as against the local producers and their trading relatives. The oil could be produced by anyone who had access to the trees and traded in by anyone who could find the cash to buy it or who could obtain it on credit.

Although the palm oil trade started with a boom, competition from mineral oil put an end to this by 1862. Transport difficulties prevented much of the hinterland oil from reaching the delta, and prevented the delta states from increasing the volume of their trade to compensate for the fall in oil prices. The result of this in the Eastern Delta was competition between the different states to secure the control of their rivals' principal oil markets which culminated in warfare between them, accompanied in the case of Bonny and Kalabari by a withdrawal from the coast to the northern margin of the delta to be closer to these markets. At the same time the customs duty due from European trading vessels ceased to be a matter for bargaining and was firmly defined by treaty in terms of a depreciating currency, the iron bar. Any attempt on the part of the delta states to increase this duty was sternly resisted and regarded by the cons u a a breach of treaty obligations.

I. THE EUROPEAN COMMUNITIES
OF THE OIL RIVER PORTS

European and Non-Native population

The change from slaves to palm oil also affected the European population of these ports, not only in their numbers but also in the duration of their stay there and in their organization. It took much longer to collect a cargo of palm oil than one of slaves. Captain Crow was able to turn round with a full cargo of slaves in from one to three months.[1] But the average time spent in the Bonny river by vessels in the palm oil trade between 1832 and 1837 was five months and six days.[2]

By the time of consul Beecroft that is by 1850, Messrs. Charles Horsefall and Co., and following them other trading firms, had found it more profitable to maintain in each Oil River port a permanent establishment consisting of an agent, and his European assistants, together with coopers, and other craftsmen and a number of African seamen and general labourers—'pull away boys', who were Kru tribesmen recruited on the Leeward coast. They all lived on board a 'hulk', that is, a dismasted sailing vessel, and they kept the oil they bought for their firm in a 'cask house' on a 'beach' set aside for their firm by the king, shipping it to Great Britain by the sailing vessels their companies chartered or owned.

During the middle of the nineteenth century, the European population of these Oil River ports was considerable by West African standards. Consul Burton listed the European population of the principal Oil River ports when he visited them in 1862 as, Bonny 278 New Calabar 278, Brass varying from 15 in 1862 to about 100 in 1864, with a maximum of about 300 in Old Calabar, and an average number of 350 in Bonny. The bulk of this population was made up of European seamen on the vessels visiting the ports. Mortality was always high and reached staggering figures whenever there was a yellow fever epidemic. For instance, 169 out of the 278 given for New Calabar died of this disease.

The number of hulks at this time were 7 in Bonny, 4 in New Calabar (some had just been gutted by fire), 10 in Old Calabar. In Brass three agents lived in quarters ashore and two in hulks.[3]

After 1869 the number of sailing ships visiting these ports declined rapidly in face of competition from the two steamship lines. These

[1] Crow, pp. 43, 61, 67.
[2] Table given in Inclosure 5 in Despatch no. 1 PP. 1847/8. Vol. LXIV.
[3] F.O.84/1221. Burton's letter of 15.4.64.

supplied a regular service of five vessels a month and secured most of the carrying trade. The European population of the ports dropped considerably and Livingstone in his 1873 report for Old Calabar, which covered the Oil Rivers of the Bights of Benin and Biafra, gave the white population in commercial employment on the rivers as 207. These were employed as the agents, clerks, and mates of 26 firms that maintained 55 trading establishments which employed 419 negro coopers, carpenters, cooks and stewards recruited from British settlements at Accra, Cape Coast, and Sierra Leone, and 2,000 Kroomen from Cape Palmas. There were no longer any European craftsmen. The high mortality rate among the whites led to their replacement by West Africans as soon as these acquired the necessary skills.

Social organization of the European community

In the time of the slave trade each ship that visited the coast normally constituted a separate political and economic unit, negotiating its own terms of trading separately with the king, and competing against any other ship that it found there. There was little scope for concerted action by the captains of these vessels and little need for it as long as the government of the local community was strong enough to maintain conditions favourable for trade. If it was unable to do this, there was no alternative but to visit another river with a stronger government. There was however, at least in the case of the British slave trade, a number of vessels which made regular visits every year to a particular river and which sought to establish more enduring relationships with its government and between themselves as against other 'interlopers'. The change to the palm oil trade resulted in the development of larger and better organized companies in Britain which provided regular and more continuous contact and residence in the river, and which eventually consolidated this position by the establishment of a permanent agency with its own hulk and its beach. It was difficult, once the boom in palm oil eased off, for newcomers to cut into this trade, but there were always a number of interlopers and newcomers prepared to enter into it, particularly in the Old Calabar river, and it was only in exceptional circumstances that the European traders were able to combine together and gain a monopolistic control of the river's trade. They were however able to combine for political, recreational, and other social purposes, and from the middle of the nineteenth century onwards the principal oil rivers ports contained two separate communities, British and African, in a condition of symbiosis who together monopolized the trade of the river. Each community was independent of the other, they were separated territorially, and contact between them was limited as far as possible to trade. In the first quarter of the century coordination between the two communities was supplied by the king or the kings of the African community, in the second quarter it was supplied by the leaders of the European community, in the third by the court of equity and the consul.

The structure of the two communities was in some respects very similar. Both were organized into a limited number of trading houses, usually not more than ten or less than seven in the case of the British community. The British like the African houses were completely independent in their internal management. The power of the agent, the head of a British house, was considerable. He controlled the disposal of far greater wealth than the chief of an African house but he was normally an employee and not the 'owner' of the house and the influence which he could build up for himself locally was circumscribed by the briefness of his tenure of office. The government of the British community was thus of the same segmentary character as that of the African with each house the political equal of every other.

There were a number of cultural, political, and commercial interests which kept these houses united and in opposition to the other community, and other interests—mainly commercial for the British houses, both political and commercial for the African houses—which kept them divided against each other. There were also common interests which the two communities shared as against other trading communities, and particular interests which brought together particular houses in the African and British communities.

The degree to which the European community remained united or divided depended partly on the quality of its leaders, partly on the stability of the African community, and partly on other external factors. In Old Calabar, for example, the Efik community lacked any formidable leaders, and its political system remained very stable, whereas in the European community there was a greater number of houses competing against each other for a much smaller production of oil. The European community was rarely able to unite for any length of time, and the consul had to spend an unduly large part of his time trying to settle disputes, between particular agents, between the agents and the Scottish mission, and between particular agents and particular Efik chiefs.

In Bonny, on the other hand, there were fewer British houses and less local competition between them, and the constant anxiety of the British community was the political instability of the African community. The British captains and agents remained united throughout the period and found themselves constantly having to intervene in the civil disturbances of the African community in an attempt to restore order and with it a resumption of trade.

On the New Calabar river the war against Nembe and Okrika kept the African community united, competition between British houses was the same as in Bonny, and cohesion between them as great. On the Brass river, leadership in the African community was weak, competition between British houses less, and their agents were able on occasions to combine for economic as well as for political action.

The British community of Bonny was the most important and the first to become organized, and its structure became the pattern which the British communities in the other rivers came to follow—partly on their own initiative, partly under pressure from the consul.

Its principal institution was a general council which, when it had received consular recognition, became dignified with the name of a 'court of equity'. It met in a building ashore which also served the purposes of a club and a church for the Europeans.[4] All European agents were members of this court and it was extended to include the king and the chiefs of the African community.

A combined general council of 'all and every English Captains with the King and gentlemen of Bonny' for the purpose of settling disputes between members of the two communities was an institution which had come into existence at least as early as the period of the interregnum, and was first defined in the Treaty of 1836.[5] But the court of equity was never a body which combined the general councils of the African and European communities. Its president was the senior agent on the River, that is the one who had served longest on that river,[6] and it remained an instrument of the European community into which were incorporated the king and house heads of the African community whenever it was dealing with matters in in which the African community or members of this community were involved.

Its decision was by a simple majority vote, the president having

---

[4] Until this building was destroyed in the disturbances following the death of King Dappo in 1855.

[5] Appendix B 1.

[6] Which meant that the office was held in rotation. Later in New Calabar the office was held by each agent in turn for a month at a time.

two votes. Punishments imposed by it were in the form of fines paid in puncheons of oil and appeal from its judicial decisions lay to the consul. The revenue from such fines was divided, half going to the king of the African community for 'the revenue of the country', the other being expended on the clearance of open spaces in the African town and on other public works there. The court had administrative and legislative functions as well as judicial, its president for instance was also harbour master, and it was used to discipline British traders and to make them conform to any rules it might make to regulate marine, commercial, and other matters affecting the European community. But from the point of view of the British consul its main functions were judicial. In the words of Consul Hutchinson, 'the general design upon which the court of equity was founded was, for the purpose of keeping commercial transactions between the European and the Native traders on a proper basis of justice and honesty as well as to nurture friendly feelings between both parties. In the absence of any international codes of jurisprudence, such a court was considered by its founders necessary to hold the natives true to the principles of fair and honest dealing, and the more so, as there was no tribunal of appeal in this country for the recovery of debts due by the native traders to the supercargoes ... By black traders, as well as by white, its utility to the healthy conditions of their commerce was universally allowed'.[7]

Consular authority before 1884

Thus far the structure of the British and African communities was very similar, both were segmentary in character, both were equally dependent on trade and had a common interest in the maintenance of conditions favourable for it; each could use the withholding of its trade as the most effective sanction for bringing the other community to terms. But the British houses were branches of larger trading corporations, which maintained such agencies in most of the principal rivers, and controlled them from head offices in Liverpool, Glasgow, and elsewhere; and the members of the British community were subjects of a wider political system whose government after 1848 was prepared to intervene in their support if it could be convinced that their 'legitimate commercial interests' were being obstructed. This meant that there was now behind the British community the power of the British government, a power which the British community could invoke through its local representative, the British consul

[7] Hutchinson I, p. 108.

stationed at Fernando Po. The consul was able to mobilize and apply British naval power should he consider it to be necessary. It never was necessary, the threat of it was sufficient. But both European traders and consuls remained convinced that such a display of force was necessary and that 'a consul's moral force without a ship of war was a moral farce in these regions'.[8] The consul's principal weapon for enforcing his will, however, was the economic one of an embargo on trade, a sanction which he, unlike the councils of the African or European communities, had no difficulty in enforcing as the European traders accepted it without question.

The consul, however, was not the head of the various British communities of the Oil Rivers. His office was rather a tribunal to which they could appeal when the local government broke down, that is, when their trade was endangered. He had been appointed to regulate the 'legal trade' in the Bights of Benin and Biafra. He was stationed at Fernando Po, an island off the coast and adjacent to the Cameroons, he had no transport of his own and had to borrow from the commander of the West African Squadron or hire any private transport that might be available.[9] His visits to the Eastern Delta rivers were thus very infrequent and his objective and that of his government was to regulate trade in each river on the basis of a treaty concluded with the government of the African community,[10] and so to organize the British community that it was able to manage its own affairs and its dealings with the African community without reference to him. The court of equity seemed an admirable instrument for achieving this and the consul urged its adoption on all British trading communities which had not got one. Not only did it provide for the local government of the British community, but, with the inclusion on its bench of the heads of the African community it provided a tribunal for dealing with those matters most calculated to bring the two communities into conflict, namely trade disputes and the collection of debts.

This was a radical change from what had happened previously. In the time of King Opobo integration and co-ordination between the two communities had been provided by the king who took care to establish a personal relationship with the captain and supercargo of every trading vessel. The British traders were prepared to accept his authority because they regarded him as the supreme

---

[8] Hutchinson, quoted by Burton. F/O 84/1221.
[9] This was a sore point with the consuls and there was considerable correspondence about it. FO 84/1265.
[10] e.g. Appendix B 2, 3 and 4.

authority in the area. It was the same in Old Calabar at this time where an appeal to the King of Duke Town as head of Egbo could also mobilize the agents of this secret society for the collection of a trader's debts.[11]

At Bonny King Opobo's successors had not the capacity or authority to perform these functions and the court of equity was expected to perform them instead. But the Bonny court of equity, though it served as a tribunal for determining trade disputes between individual European and African traders, was not able to act as a co-ordinating body between the two communities. Its authority was never fully accepted by the African community. This was partly because supreme authority over the British community lay not with the court of equity but with the consul, but mainly because the British community and their court became involved in the internal politics of the African community.

As long as the government of the African community was stable the British community could remain aloof from it. But when, as in Bonny, the government broke down the British community was bound to intervene in an effort to restore order, a condition which was vital for the economic survival of both. Whenever this stability was endangered the British community was appealed to by those leaders of the African community who wanted peace, as for instance in Old Calabar, where disputes over the succession to the kingships of Duke Town and of Creek Town were referred to the supercargoes for settlement, or as in Bonny when the Anna Pepple house had refused to accept the authority of the new King William Dappa Pepple. On this and subsequent occasions, when two rival parties had come to blows, it was the senior members of the British community who came ashore and sought to negotiate a truce. But when, as in Bonny, this political rivalry crystallized into two permanent political associations of the principal houses, each association sought to enlist the support of the British community, and, having once obtained it, tended to keep it. The Manilla Pepple group was from the first able to place its rivals in the position of a rebel group which was opposed to the government of Bonny as represented by the 'Bonny parliament', and which had resisted by force of arms this parliament's attempt to make it accept its decision. The Manilla Pepple group therefore tended to receive the support of the British community and to appeal to this community for its intervention. This meant that the Anna Pepple leaders were able to represent

[11] Holman, Vol. I, p. 392/3.

themselves as the champions of native African liberties and the Manilla Pepple group as those who had betrayed these liberties to the British government. This did not mean that the commercial relationship between individual British houses and the Anna Pepple houses suffered. They sold as much if not more oil to them than did the Manilla Pepple houses; but it did mean that whenever the British community intervened in the African community, the Anna Pepple group felt bound to resist its authority and that of the court of equity. As a result, the consul had always to intervene to support the court against the Anna Pepple group.

But although he could restore order, he was not in a position to maintain it. The parties involved in the fighting submitted to the authority of his court and were duly fined and bound over, the consul returned to Fernando Po, the British members of the court of equity retired to their hulks and the struggle for power continued until the Anna Pepple group produced a leader who was able to bring it to a successful conclusion.

It was the same in the wars between Kalabari and Will Braid, between Kalabari and Bonny, and between Bonny and Opobo. The British government was not prepared to use force to end them, and the consul's intervention was limited to offering to mediate and to arranging a submission to arbitration. Not until the parties had agreed and submitted to arbitration could he use his powers of an embargo on trade to enforce compliance with the settlement which had been made.

Conclusions

The consular power was thus not absolute and the choice of whether or not it accepted his authority still lay with the African community. Its political development during the nineteenth century was determined by the African community and its leaders, and this despite the efforts made by the British community to modify or prevent it. The principal British contribution to this development was the provision of additional and supplementary institutions and sanctions, which could be counted upon to operate when the government broke down, and to which the leaders of the warring parties or states could turn when they wished to come to terms with one another.

Apart from the exceptional case of Brass in 1863[12] the British community was never able to dominate the other or to impose terms

[12] Referred to in Chapter VII, p. 98.

upon it. But the African community still could and did. Whether they liked it or not the European traders had, for example, to conform to the African trading organization. To take the case of Kalabari, there was no reason why British trading firms should maintain separate agencies for the Bonny and New Calabar rivers, the two anchorages were barely seven miles apart. But the Kalabari state was not prepared to trade through Bonny and any Europeans who wished to trade with it had to use the Kalabari anchorage. All the consul could do was in 1850 to insist upon this traditional site off Ifoko being maintained when the Kalabari tried to move it nearer to Elem Kalabari. At the end of the period in 1882 the Kalabari state far from being weaker in its relation to the British community, was able to dictate terms to it. With the new port of Opobo taking a large part of the Bonny trade, European firms were no doubt trying to adjust to this by merging the staffs of their Bonny and Kalabari agencies. Hence the letter of 1882[13] reaffirming the principle that 'this river (the New Calabar) is distinclty separate both in trade and natives to Bonny' and insisting that 'we require our agents to (be) the same' (i.e. separate). When, soon after, the Kalabari people removed from Elem Kalabari to Degama the European traders had to abandon the New Calabar river and establish themselves on the Sombreiro river at Abonnema.

The structure on which the Kalabari were insisting was one that ran counter to the British government's principles and policy but one that was accepted and supported by European traders and even by the consul. It preserved the monopoly of the up-country trade on the river to the African state and of its overseas trade to the European trading community established at the river's port. The European traders paid dues to the African state for the right to the trade of the river and neither was expected to trade outside this organization.[14] Each community lived separately and superior ritual status was given to Europeans which enhanced this separation, their persons were 'jew jew'. It was a structure that suited both parties and which both wished to see enforced. The Brass court of equity fined the King of Ogbolomabiri when he traded outside the organization. The Bonny agents were solidly behind the Manilla Pepple group (i.e. the Bonny majority party) in pressing the consul to force Jaja Anna Pepple to return to Bonny.

[13] Appendix B 10.
[14] Kalabari traders could not sell to Bonny agents, or vice versa, and other African communities like Okrika or Engenni had to sell and buy through the African traders of the state which had the monopoly of their trade.

Jaja himself was careful to adhere to the same pattern when he founded Opobo. He moved there with supporting European traders who became established at Egwanga higher up and on the opposite side of the river to the African town.

Will Braid was unable to find this European trading support, and thus could not maintain his independence. He could with Bonny support remain independent like Okrika or Andoni, but only by ceasing to trade directly with Europeans. If he wished to continue trading with them he had to become either a part of the Bonny or of the Kalabari state. When Bonny and Kalabari had agreed to settle their differences a peace was made between Will Braid and Kalabari in which he was returned to the Kalabari state, and when he tried to ignore this treaty he found that his trade with Bonny was blocked by consular instructions to the Bonny agents.

Consular authority after 1884

After 1884 the British government policy changed and with it the power of the consul who was now recognized as responsible for maintaining law and order, and for giving effect to the British policy of opening up the hinterland to free trade. The consul and vice-consuls became the government of the Oil Rivers. They began by recreating the court of equity as a 'governing council'. But these combined councils soon disappeared and with them any political organization of the European community. In the African community the kingship ceased to carry any political value, and the consul or his assistants reorganized its government on the same lines as the European community had previously been organized, with a council of chiefs who were heads of houses,—the native council, which later became a native court, and with a code of rules prepared under the house rule ordinance which defined their position and their powers.

2. EUROPEAN INFLUENCE ON RITUAL INSTITUTIONS

The consul and the European agents could justify their intervention in the political affairs of these Oil River states on the grounds that civil war was a breach of their treaty obligations, and that if the government of the state was unable to maintain order they had a right to enforce a return to order. The consuls and their government maintained that they had no right to meddle in any way in the 'social laws, prejudices or customs of the natives'[15] and they and the

[15] Hutchinson in F.O. 84/1030.

European supercargoes were under the impression that they did not interfere with them. But European influence upon, for example, the ritual institutions and beliefs of the Oil River communities were far more overwhelming than upon their political organization.

At the beginning of the nineteenth century the members of these trading states were all 'heathen'; by the end of the century the Niger Delta Pastorate was the 'established' church of the Eastern Delta, and the Church of Scotland that of Old Calabar, while the indigenous cults where they still survived were discredited and looked down upon alike by Europeans and progressive Africans. [King Opobo when he visited European vessels was accompanied by his 'jew jew man' whose rituals and medicines were required to fortify and protect the king. His successors King William Dappa Pepple and King George Pepple were Christians.

The attitude of African communities in the Eastern Region towards religious and magical beliefs was and is open-minded, empirical, and eclectic. As a result their religious cults were more unstable and liable to change than some of their other institutions. A cult was subject to popular feeling, that is, to fashion and when it had 'lost its power', that is, when most people had ceased to believe in it, it tended to disappear and to be replaced by another more fashionable cult. This inherent instability rendered these religious beliefs very vulnerable in periods of rapid cultural change like the nineteenth century.

In addition to those people who were attracted to Christian ritual, there were many more who felt that there were considerable political and economic advantages to be gained by acquiring European religious cults, and missionaries were invited by the chiefs in most of these Oil River states to come and establish churches among them. They did so at Duke Town and Creek Town in 1846 and soon after in the Cameroons. Bonny was negotiating for a mission in 1849[16] and got one in 1864.

Indigenous ritual institutions and their priests, doctors, and other ritual specialists performed important political functions, some of them integrative some of them cathartic. Christian missions did none of these things. Even more than the British trading community they sought to maintain their aloofness from politics, and their Christian teaching was based on the separation of the things of God

[16] Vide the Treaty of 2.12.49. 'I King Pepple engage to use all my influence and power to abolish human sacrifice to Jusse (Jew Jew?) in consideration of the promise Commander Cumming, H.M.S. *Rattler*, has given me to endeavour to send missionaries and teachers to aid me in the matters'. Hertslet, Vol. IX, p. 18.

from those of Caesar. When they did become involved the results were to divide rather than unite. In Old Calabar the consul had to disentangle disputes between European traders and the mission, between Duke Town chiefs supported by the mission against the British traders, or between British and Efik traders against the mission. There and elsewhere a division developed in the African community between 'progressive' (pro-mission) and 'conservative' (anti-mission) elements, which in Nembe for example resulted in civil strife. Christian missions also afforded rival political parties and groups yet another means of emphasizing their rivalry. In Old Calabar, King Eyo II of Creek Town embraced Christianity and championed the Scottish Mission. The Duke Town king remained a 'heathen' and out of sympathy with the mission. In Nembe one moiety, Ogbolomabiri, acquired a mission in 1867, the other Bassambiri remained 'heathen'. Kalabari, during the period we are considering, had no mission, possibly because Bonny and Nembe both had them. When Christianity was accepted by this state its strongest supporters were in Will Braid's village of Bakana, and in the former Barboy houses at Abonnema. In the following century, when the religious revival associated with the prophet Garrick Braid of Bakana swept the Eastern Delta, Buguma, the anti-Braid stronghold, alone among Kalabari villages seems to have remained almost unaffected by it.

In the field of education Christian missions were able to provide something that was superior to anything the indigenous religious institutions could offer, while in the political field the sanctions formerly supplied by the indigenous cults and their priests were being supplanted by those provided by the political institutions of the British community. In addition to this, however, these indigenous cults found themselves under continuous attack throughout the century because they were considered strongholds of the traditional way of life and thus responsible for human sacrifices and other 'obnoxious customs' which Europeans of all kinds as well as progressive Africans wished to see eliminated.

The decline of these cults is best documented for Bonny and Old Calabar, the former being more typical of the region. Here, as elsewhere in the Eastern Delta, the priests of the principal cults had considerable authority at the beginning of the century. Their persons were 'jew jew', that is sacred and inviolable, and their villages (when they were separate from the main community) were sanctuaries. Any attack upon them was an attack on the divinity they served. But in 1847 Awanta the priest of Simingi could not be disciplined by the Bonny government and when he became associated with the murder of British seamen, the British Navy intervened and deported him. The Bonny priests were also superior members of the Bonny council and their signatures appeared on all early treaties with the British government. After 1846 they disappeared and in 1856, when the Consul had to intervene in a dispute between the British and African communities over wood-cutting, the status of priest had already deteriorated, and the agents were able to refuse any kind of recognition to 'jew jew' priests and their 'religious tomfooleries'. The dispute over wood-cutting was settled to the satisfaction of both parties, not a word was said about either the compensation or the punishment of the priest of 'Jew Jew Peterside', whose sacred grove had probably afforded the most easily accessible target for Kroomen sent out on wood-cutting operations, and who precipitated the dispute by instigating attacks upon these wood-cutting gangs. It was the European traders whose persons were now said to be 'jew jew' when they went ashore in Bonny, and their vessels which were considered sanctuaries.[17] As for the Bonny priests and their former right to visit European vessels and be given a 'dash', the traders reaffirmed their refusal 'to recognize the jew jew men aboard any of their vessels' and the consul and the Bonny chiefs and elders accepted this refusal.[18]

The next stage was the establishment in 1864 of a mission church in Bonny itself, on the site of a 'jew jew grove', which was followed by the disappearance of the sacred iguanas which, like the sacred monkeys that had preceded them, found themselves slaughtered as soon as their protective deity had lost its power.[19] The Bonny juju house likewise disappeared, though not the cannibalism associated with it.[20] What became of Jew Jew Tolofari and Jew Jew Peterside is not recorded. Finnema, although its deity had become discredited, remained a political sanctuary to the end of the period.

By contrast, in Kalabari the decline in the indigenous ritual institu-

---

[17] Provided the refugee could get there unaided. The Bonny people's dispute with Captain Witt in 1855 was that he had rescued Yanibo and Isacco in his own gig.
[18] F.O. 84/1001.
[19] It should be noted that the reaction against the iguanas of the Ikuba cult did not come only from Christians and 'progressives' but was supported by the whole community. There was a similar reaction in 'heathen' Kalabari about the same time against the sharks which had formerly been under the protection of the Owu Akpana deity.
[20] In 1873 the Bonny chiefs admitted to the consul that they were not in a position to return some of King Jaja Anna Pepple's wives as they had been eaten.

tions was very much slower. The power of the deity Owame Akaso and the authority of her priest the *so alabo* remained for most of the period. In 1856 Consul Beecroft was called by the European community to insist on adherence to the terms of the treaty of 1850 which the Kalabari government was seeking to change by demanding an additional comey for the *so alabo*: in 1859 when a madman killed the *so alabo*, the Kalabari general council decided that the murder must be expiated by the killing in the same manner of the entire lineage of the murderer, while in 1863 the dispute over the succession to King Karibo Amakiri was settled by local oracular revelation confirmed, according to Kalabari tradition, by reference to the Arochuku oracle.

In Old Calabar, on the other hand, the power of the tutelary deity Ndem Efik and of the domestic deity Ekpenyong had already been supplanted before the beginning of the century by the Ekpe secret society, which had acquired a great deal of the ritual authority formerly vested in these and other cults. European influence was therefore directed first towards getting Ekpe to pass laws banning obnoxious customs which were older than Ekpe, for instance human sacrifices, the exposure of twins, and the poison ordeal ('chopping nut'). Only when the authority of Ekpe had been success-fully challenged by the 'slave revolt' was European influence directed against the 'obnoxious customs' introduced by Ekpe,— namely the 'Egbo floggings' and the 'Egbo sabbath', which confined everyone except Egbo members (and Europeans) to their houses every week on Aqua Offiong day.

VII

The Trading System of the Eastern Delta States

POLITICAL supremacy in the Eastern Delta could not be separated from economic supremacy. Wealth was needed to maintain favourable commercial and political relations with political leaders in the communities that controlled the up-river markets, it was also needed to buy the men who manned the trading and the war canoes, and the muskets, cannon and gunpowder with which to arm them if Bonny, Kalabari and Nembe were to maintain their monopoly of the overseas trade from which this wealth was derived. Wealth was equally necessary to rise to positions of political leadership within these states. The successful politician whether he was the king of Bonny or the chief of one of its houses was also a successful business man, and it was from the ranks of its successful traders, whether slave or freeborn that a house selected its chief. Before we can proceed to a detailed examination of their political history it will be necessary to describe the economic basis of these trading states, in particular their system of trading with European visiting merchants as this developed during the eighteenth and nineteenth century.

I. IMPORTS

Before the nineteenth century European merchants trading on the West Africa coast were mainly engaged in commerce. They brought the goods of one area and sold them to another and a great number of these commodities came from outside Europe, many of them from other parts of Africa. The industrial revolution brought a greater concentration on British goods and a much closer association between the West African trading firms and British manufacturers. During the nineteenth century Manchester cottons, originally direct copies of Indian cloths, captured the West African cotton trade and other British products began to compete there successfully, not only against those of other foreign countries but against those of the delta itself. The most notable of these was salt. Local salt produced by boiling sea water could not compete with Cheshire salt brought out from Liverpool in ballast, and salt-making virtually ceased in the delta. Similarly the tools and weapons produced in the hinterland were replaced by these made in Birmingham and elsewhere and by the end of the century Western Europe was able to compete with the main product of the delta, namely dried fish. Norwegian dried cod, locally known as stockfish, became one of the standard varieties of dried fish in Ibo markets.

The general trend of the import trade was not to create more luxuries but to convert former luxuries into necessities, for example, spirits, tobacco, beads, guns and gunpowder, and to make the people of the region dependent on this overseas trade for a large range of necessities which they had formerly either produced themselves or had gone without.

There are no satisfactory figures of the value or the volume of this import trade. We know however that these trade goods were exchanged directly for exports, first of slaves and yams and then of palm oil. The price of palm oil varied from year to year, but if we take Burton's estimate of tonnage[1] and £20 a ton as an average price we obtain the following very rough figures for the annual value of the Oil Rivers trade.

Bonny and Kalabari	£320,000
Brass	60,000
Old Calabar	90,000
Cameroons	40,000
	£510,000

2. THE EXPORT TRADE

These imports were paid for first in ivory and slaves, later in palm oil, later still (after 1870) in palm oil and palm kernels. By the time of James Barbot the export of ivory had ceased; he reports that it cost more in Kalabari than on the European market. The export of slaves and of yams to feed the slaves increased and went on increasing till the early part of the nineteenth century. It was replaced by the export of palm oil which began soon after the abolition of the British slave trade in 1808. The general pattern of this export trade was a

[1] Burton. F.O. 84/1221.

gradually expanding trade in slaves during the eighteenth century, which reached a peak in the Rio Real of about 15,000 to 20,000 annually in the first quarter of the nineteenth. Thereafter the British naval blockade reduced it and after 1839 brought it to an end. With the nineteenth century there also developed a trade in palm oil which followed a different course. It reached its peak both in price and in volume about 1855, thereafter the price declined while the quantity exported remained almost unaltered till the end of the century. The reason for this was the difficulty of its transport. It was heavy, semi-solid or fluid;[2] its containers, whether native pots or British casks, were also heavy and only suitable for transport in bulk and this was only possible on waterways which were navigable for canoes. Not until the Protectorate government improved communications did the volume of oil exports increase appreciably. The loss from the fall in prices was counteracted to some extent however by the development of a new export, palm kernels, which began about 1870. This presented less difficulty in its transport and continued to increase in volume steadily to the end of the century.

3. THE TRADING SYSTEM

European traders and consuls insisted on referring to the system of trade in the Bight of Biafra as one of barter.[3] Technically speaking they were wrong. There is no evidence that the system of trade in this region was carried on by barter and in the time of the slave trade if not earlier there were not one but a number of different European and Native currencies recognized on the Slave Coast and on the Oil Rivers. In addition there was in each particular trading area a special currency accepted by European and African traders as the one on which their trade was based, which I have distinguished as the 'trade currency'.[4] Both European and African traders had their own national or regional currencies but neither found it convenient to acquire and use the others' particular medium. The one side wanted slaves the other trade goods, and they only needed currency to enable them to convert trade goods into slaves. The simplest way to do this was to accept a convenient import or export as a unit of trade currency. All exports and imports could then be valued in terms of this unit.

[2] Depending on its method of preparation.
[3] For example Beecroft to the select committee on the slave trade PP. 1850 Vol. IX, p. 238, or Hutchinson in his trade report for 1856 PP. 1857 Vol. XVI.
[4] See Jones. 3.

In course of time the units of these trade currencies either became, like the manilla and the copper rod, accepted as the local native currency in place of the original local currency units, or, like the iron bar, they lost their original value and disappeared. In the latter case they were replaced in the trade currency either by a fictitious unit of valuation like the pawn of the Benin river trade, or by a more convenient trading commodity—the puncheon of oil of the Eastern Delta, and the crewe of oil of the Cameroons.

The system of trading is first clearly described by James Barbot in 1699. After about a weeks' bargaining with the 'king and his principal men' to determine the price to be paid for slaves

we fetch'd the king from shore, attended by all his *caboceiros* and officers, in three large canoes; and entring the ship, was saluted with seven guns . . .

We had again a long discourse with the king and *Pepprell* his brother, concerning the rates of our goods and his customs. This *Pepprell* being a sharp blade, and a mighty talking *Black*, perpetually making sly objections against something or other, and teazing us for this or that *Dassy*, or present, as well as for drams, etc. it were to be wish'd, that such a one as he were out of the way, to facilitate trade . . . Thus with much patience, all our matters were adjusted indifferently, after their way, . . . The king order'd the publick cryer to proclaim the permission of trade with us, with the noise of his trumpets, being elephants teeth, made much after the same fashion, as is used at the *Gold Coast*, we paying sixteen brass rings to the fellow for his fee . . . We gave the usual presents to the king and his officers; . . . We adjusted with them the reduction of our merchandize into bars of iron, as the standard coin, *viz.* One bunch of beads, one bar. Four strings of rings, ten rings in each, one *ditto*. Four copper bars, one *ditto*. One piece of narrow *Guinea* stuff, one *ditto*. One piece broad *Hamborough*, one *ditto*. One piece *Nicanees*, three *ditto*. Brass rings, *ditto*. And so *pro rata* for every other sort of goods. The price of provisions and wood was also regulated. Sixty king's yams, one bar; one hundred and sixty slaves yams, one bar; for fifty thousand to be delivered to us. A butt of water, two rings. For the length of wood, seven bars, which is dear; but they were to deliver it ready cut into out boat. For a goat, one bar. A cow, ten or eight bars, according to its bigness. A hog, two bars. A calf, eight bars. A jar of palm oil one bar and a quarter.

We paid also the king's duties in goods; five hundred slaves, to be purchased at two copper rings a head.

We also advanced to the king, by way of loan, the value of a hundred and fifty bars of iron, in sundry goods; and to his principal men, and others, as much again, each in proportion of his quality and ability. To Captain *Forty*, eighty bars, to another, forty, to others, twenty each. This we did, in order to repair forthwith to the inland markets, to buy yams for greater expedition; they employing usually nine or ten days in each journey up the country, in their long canoos up the river. All the before regulations being so made, the supper was served . . . After having drank and eat till they were ready to burst, they returned ashore, being again saluted with seven guns.[5]

This was no primitive method of bartering but a well developed system of trade with its own specific currency, the iron bar in which all the commodities exchanged were valued, with an elaborate credit system, and with a specific trading tax or duty, namely comey, paid by each ship that called at the Rio Real for purposes of trade. Before any commercial business was allowed the king and his officers had to 'break trade' as it was called, that is they had to be received on board with due ceremony, to assess and receive this comey and to fix the value of the commodities being traded. Only when this had been done and when the King and his principal men had received 'the usual presents' was the vessel publicly declared free to trade.

Breaking of trade, comey and the iron bar currency system were institutions which continued to the end of the period, that is, until the introduction of British Colonial Rule. The credit system and the dash survived well into the twentieth century. The only institution not mentioned by James Barbot was the 'Work Bar' and the 'Customs Bar', taxes which in the nineteenth century were paid to the heads of each canoe house.

The currency

Portuguese trade in the Rio Real area consisted of the exchange of copper in the form of bracelets (manillas) for slaves. It is not clear whether these manillas were currency in the accepted sense or merely a medium of trade, as no other European commodities were traded there. By the time of Dapper and the Dutch monopoly, manillas were specifically described as the local currency and copper rods were also traded for slaves. By the time of James Barbot there were two currencies, the trade currency in which the unit was the iron bar or the copper bar and the native currency used in market transactions between coastal traders and the people of the hinterland. This native currency consisted of cowries in the Western Delta manillas in the Eastern Delta.

We do not know what the original Portuguese and Dutch manillas were like. The 'king' and 'queen' manillas one sees today are more

[5] Barbot, John. p. 459–460.

like the torques described by Pereira and Dapper than bracelets.[6] By the time of the Barbots manillas had become conventionalized in their modern reduced form and were beginning to become standardized. They were too small to encircle any human wrist and James Barbot describes them more accurately as rings. There was no clash between the trade and native currencies in the Eastern Delta as there was on the Slave Coast where European traders wanted the iron bar and the native traders demanded cowries. The native currency of the New Calabar and Imo River markets remained the manilla. The iron bar continued as the trade currency of the Eastern Delta and accepted the manilla as a lower unit valuing it at forty manillas to the bar and the currency of the trading states of the Eastern Delta during the nineteenth century was this combined native and trade currency, which with the change to palm oil acquired a third and highest unit—the puncheon of palm oil. The ratio of forty manillas to the iron bar continued apparently throughout the eighteenth century; Adams and Bold writing in about 1820 both repeat it and value the iron bar at 2/6. The iron bar depreciated steadily during the nineteenth century. Its value dropped to 1/– in the 1840's. Baikie valued it at 7d. when he was in the area in 1854; Consul Burton, writing in 1864, says that it averaged 8d. and that comey at 5 bars per ton amounted to 3/4 a ton.[7] By 1869 its value dropped to 6d. By the end of the century its place had been taken by the case of gin, a more accommodating medium which not only formed a unit of higher value than the depreciated bar but also subdivided conveniently into twelve bottles each worth 1/–.

In contrast to the cowrie the manilla seems to have appreciated during the nineteenth century. Consul Hutchinson, writing in 1856, refers to 'manillas which cost threepence and twenty of them amounting to five shillings signified a bar in the olden times'. Consul Livingstone in his trade report for the year 1873 speaks of 'the manilla a bronze coin from Birmingham worth about sixpence'.[8] By the end of the nineteenth century the gradual fall in the price of palm oil had reduced its value in the case of the standard type to five to the gin bottle.

The copper and brass rod ceased to be used as currency in the Eastern Delta, though it continued in Old Calabar and moved

---

[6] For illustration see Talbot (2) Plate facing p. 238.
[7] 'The above mentioned chiefs received 1/– for each customs bar'. From an account of Customs Bars given by King Pepple to the chiefs and natives to Bonny 'since he came up King' F.O. 84/1161. Baikie. p. 356. Burton's letter F.O. 84/1221.
[8] P.P. 1857, Vol. XVI and 1873, Vol. LXV.

inland to become the native currency of the Cross River and its hinterland.

The manilla, brass rod, iron bar and the puncheon and crewe of oil were not the only trade currencies used in the Oil Rivers during the nineteenth century. The Spanish and Portuguese slave traders of the early nineteenth century were unable to secure enough of the requisite trade goods and paid for their slaves partly in goods and partly in Spanish doubloons and dollars and the payments to the kings who signed the Anti-Slavery treaties were also specified in dollars—though the actual payments were made in trade goods.

Breaking of trade

Breaking of trade continued throughout the eighteenth century. No details are available in the case of Brass or New Calabar. At Bonny it was the king alone or his representative who broke trade in the nineteenth century, and kings like Opobo developed it into a ceremonial visit followed by a dinner given by the ship's captain to the king, and reciprocated before the ship sailed by an invitation to dine ashore extended by the king to the ship's captain and officers. Increase in the volume of trade had by this time caused prices very largely to fix themselves without the necessity for special negotiations and bargaining for each separate vessel, while any delay on the part of the king in making his ceremonial visit was becoming increasingly irksome and costly. After King Opobo's death therefore, attempts were made to regulate matters by a treaty which defined the amount payable as comey and which enabled a vessel to begin trading after the lapse of a week, should the King or his deputy fail to break trade.

Comey

It is clear from James Barbot's account that comey was assessed on the capacity of the vessel. In the eighteenth century the unit of capacity was the slave. James Barbot's vessel, the Albion frigate of 300 tons, was assessed at 500 slaves, and it paid comey of 1000, manillas or 25 iron bars. It actually shipped 648 slaves.[9] British slavers a hundred years later were only carrying between 300 and 500, depending on the size of the vessel. The number was regulated by government ordinance and Thomas Tobin's ship the '*Molly*' of 301 tons was allowed to carry 438 slaves.[10] With the boom in the slave trade the amount paid as comey increased considerably.

[9] Which may have been one of the reasons why most of them died before reaching the West Indies, 'which rendered the so hopeful voyage of the Albion abortive and above 60% of the capital was lost' Barbot, p. 465.
[10] PP. 1847–8, Vol. XXII.

Captain Crow estimated that in 1792 his vessel had to pay a comey amounting to about £400 but this is probably an exaggeration. Captain Adams, referring to the period of the early nineteenth century, estimated the value of the Bonny comey at about £150 a vessel compared with £250 at Old Calabar.[11] With the change from slaves to palm oil the unit of capacity changed in New Calabar and Bonny from the slave to the puncheon of palm oil and then to the registered tonnage of the vessel, and was assessed at 2½ bars on each puncheon or 5 bars on each ton. Taking the value of the bar in sterling at 1/-, this amounted to a comey of £75 on a 300-ton vessel or £100 on one of 400 tons. In Brass comey was assessed on the masts of the ship, a two-mast vessel paying two puncheons worth of goods, and a three-mast vessel three puncheons worth of goods to each king. This would make the Brass comey considerably less than that of the Rio Real, as there are just under three puncheons to the ton of oil and the value of a ton of oil in Brass in 1855 when the commercial treaty was signed was probably not much more than £19–20. With the change from sailing to steam vessels came a change in the methods of shipping oil and from about 1870 the bulk of it was carried by steamship lines, which provided a regular transport and passenger service to and from the West Coast. Breaking of trade continued for the dwindling number of individual trading ships visiting the river, but could not be applied to the trade carried by these regular services. Comey was changed from 5 bars per registered ton of each vessel calling for trade to 5 bars on every ton of oil shipped from the river and was made payable by the trading company that shipped it. The bar was now worth 6d so that comey amounted to an export duty of 2/6 per ton of oil.[12] With the establishment of the British Protectorate comey came to an end, being replaced by customs and other duties paid to the Colonial government, and by subsidies paid by the government to 'the native chiefs who have been already in receipt of comey'. These subsidies were fixed at £450 for Bonny, £500 later reduced to £399 for Opobo and £400 later increased to £420 for Kalabari.[13]

Comey was not only shared between 'the king and his principal men'. The foreign records bring out clearly the dependence of the trading and political systems of these Eastern Delta states on the

---

[11] Crow, p. 43. Adams, 2, p. 245 and p. 248.
[12] 'As trading ships have nearly ceased to come to Bonny and Old Calabar the Kings demanded and the agents agreed to pay half a crown for every ton they shipped by steamer'. Consular letter F.O. 84/1308, dated 3.12.69.
[13] Newns, 1949.

payment of tolls, subsidies and other gifts to the leading men in other communities, which could control or at least interfere with and interrupt the trade with the hinterland markets. By the middle of the nineteenth century it was accepted that such expenditure was a proper charge against the revenue from comey.

By this time the English merchants' view was that comey constituted a payment which guaranteed to the ship that paid it the right to do business, secure from any interference, molestation, or stoppage of trade.[14] The British government supported this view and it was duly incorporated in the various Treaties of Amity and Commerce, and the subsequent additional articles signed by the three Eastern Delta states. This view was in due course expanded so that warfare and civil disturbances could be held to constitute a breach of the contract implicit in the payments of comey.

The trust system

Breaking of trade, comey, and the iron bar and manilla currency were institutions that derived from European culture or that arose out of contact with it, while the system of having a fixed price for everything that was bought or sold ran counter to the indigenous system which was one of bargaining. But in granting credit, and handing over goods on trust, the European traders had to defer to the indigenous system which still to this day depends on credit, discouraging any forms of hoarding and providing strong social incentives for the giving out of goods on trust and for the distribution of any savings as advances and loans to others. The European traders never liked giving trust at any time and the consuls, reflecting their government's attitude, constantly inveighed against it while pointing out that the European traders had only themselves to blame for their difficult position. Consul Livingstone's trade report and other consular references, however, tend to give a rather false impression of the position, as they regarded the trust system as an evil common to the whole region (the Bight of Biafra), while their examples of its abuses come almost exclusively from Old Calabar where, for various reasons, the system got completely out of hand during the nineteenth century.[15] It is obvious from the records, however, that conditions were very different in the Eastern Delta

[14] Vide Article V of Treaty of 1850 and Article XIV of Treaty of 1856. Appendix B, 2 and 4.

[15] In 1856, for example, Consul Hutchinson estimated that in Old Calabar there were 9,000 to 10,000 tons of Palm Oil owed to supercargoes while the yearly production of that river did not exceed 4,000 tons. P.P. 1857, Vol. XVI.

and there are a number of probable reasons for this. In the first place the European supercargoes seem to have shown greater discrimination in giving credit. They gave for example to those traders whom they found they could trust 'books', that is to say 'characters' or 'references', most of them on paper, others in the form of the ivory bracelets described in chapter I. Conditions varied again in the different trading communities. These differing situations found expression in the three commercial treaties. In Bonny article V of the Treaty of 1837 reads, 'That no master of a British vessel shall in future except at his own risk, give out any part of his cargo upon trust to the native chiefs . . . as the King will not hold himself responsible for the payment of such goods'. In New Calabar article XI of the Treaty of 1850 reads 'That the King shall not nor shall he permit any of his chiefs to demand or enforce any trust from any of the ships upon any pretext whatever'. In Nembe article VIII of the Treaty of 1856 reads 'That it shall under no circumstances be compulsory on the master or supercargo of a vessel to give goods on trust, but when trust is taken, that it shall be incumbent on the Kings and chiefs and those to whom comey is paid, to see that no losses accrue to British supercargoes from defaulting debtors'.[16]

Fixed prices and bargaining

The European merchants had to accept the indigenous system of trust, but they were able to use their own system of fixed prices in place of the indigenous one of bargaining. Recent unpublished studies[17] of buying and selling in Eastern Nigerian markets have shown that although everything for sale has a value which can be ascertained very rapidly by buyer or seller and which is ultimately determined by normal economic laws of supply and demand, bargaining maximizes the profit that a skilful buyer or seller can make, for it introduces, in addition to the more obvious factors of time, place, and demand, a wide range of other factors, some economic some more purely social in character, which can modify the price paid one way or the other. But it was obviously to the advantage of the local trading community to sacrifice the potential advantages their members might obtain from individual bargaining for a negotiated trading agreement with a foreign trading vessel, based on an accepted list of fixed prices. These would not only facilitate negotiation for trust, but would make

[16] Hertslet, Vol. VII, p. 1; Vol. IX, p. 24, Appendix B4. This does not mean however that these articles were adhered to. Trust continued to be given everywhere.

[17] Made by the Agricultural Department Umuahia and myself during the last war.

it more difficult for the supercargoes to play off one African trader against another. With the increase in trade which marked the end of the eighteenth century, business was so continuous that there was no question of negotiating a new set of prices with each ship as it arrived. Prices were fixed by the market, and though both foreign and local traders might try to fix them in their own favour, they were seldom able to do so, at least in the nineteenth century when records become available. Competition among Europeans as among local traders was normally too keen to permit much combination or the formation of price rings. The Brass supercargoes in 1863 did combine and forced the Nembe traders to lower their prices for oil[18] but this merely meant that less oil reached Brass from the Northern Delta oil markets, the Nembe traders being unable to compete against the prices offered by traders from the Niger and from New Calabar and Bonny.

The African traders were even less able to combine than the European for in their case their canoe houses were in political as well as economic competition. The Departmental studies referred to previously showed that in the period 1940 to 1945 competition between African oil traders ('middlemen') was so keen that any profits obtained from the retailing of trade goods in short supply tended to be passed on to the producers in higher prices for their oil. There is sufficient evidence to show that this also occurred in the nineteenth century. For instance, the chiefs of Bonny petitioned against King William Dappa Pepple's misuse of comey, and his other revenue for this purpose so that he was able to undersell and outbid them in the hinterland markets[19] and they demanded that his successor should not be allowed to engage in trade.

Under the indigenous system such profits also accrued through bargaining, and although bargaining was eliminated by fixed prices, a great deal of the essence of bargaining remained in the very careful selection which an African trader made of the trade goods which he bought or obtained on credit, and in the way he kept changing and modifying this selection; J. Smith describes this process very clearly 'Although it is perfectly understood before you begin to hand them their goods, what quantity of each article is to be paid, they torment you almost to death with 'change dis', 'change dat', and take care generally to be on the right side as to value . . .' There was also another item which the African trader could count towards his

18 Burton's letter in F.O. 84/1221.
19 F.O. 84/950.

profits and which until it became standardized could also be bargained for—the dash.

The dash

Continuing with Smith's description; 'Then comes the dash, he first wants a valuable article such as a gun or a piece of high-priced cloth, which if he does not get, nay whether he does or not, he next solicits an article of less value as a knife; then a nightcap, then a mug, afterwards a plate and lastly a tobacco pipe'.[20]

The origin of this institution is unknown; the word itself is said to come from the Portuguese '*doação*', a gift or present, and the practice may derive from European influence and from the system of trade introduced by the Portuguese, who would naturally present gifts to the people with whom they wished to establish trading relations. Certainly the 'trade dash' as developed during the nineteenth century has no counterpart in the indigenous system of trade. The dash, however, accords very well with the traditional usage of the Eastern Region in which it is correct for a small gift or concession to be made to anyone from whom some special social service is required. Such gifts can be made whether or not the service also involves a definite return payment in money, goods or reciprocal service. No stigma is attached to demanding such a present and it can be and often is a matter for bargaining.

By the eighteenth century the dash had become a payment for their goodwill which was demanded from Europeans by any coastal Africans who had any political or commercial dealings with them. To these Europeans it was a very tedious and irritating form of begging and during the nineteenth century they did their best to deprive it of its bargaining element and to restrict it to those with whom they dealt in business. By the middle of this century the dash had become an overall term applied to a number of rather different prestations.

There was firstly the 'trade dash' as it came to be termed, an additional payment of goods of a standardized amount, which marked the completion of any business deal between a European and an African trader or his agent, whether it was a sale, or an advance of trade goods on trust or the purchase of palm oil or kernels. The dash was paid by the European to the African trader and its amount was based strictly upon the size and value of the transaction. Both sides knew what it would amount to and could take

[20] Smith, p. 193.

account of it in their business calculations. For example, in New Calabar at the end of the century a trader could count upon getting on every puncheon of oil which he sold, a 'puncheon dash' which amounted to three pieces of small and one piece of medium madras cotton cloth.

Secondly, there were the presents which the European trader might find it politic to make to a king or influential chief, and which 'Parliament Gentlemen' and other less important persons might hope to wheedle out of him. The most important of these became standardized as 'shake hands', which was a fixed amount paid to the king and to the chiefs with whom they traded by supercargoes and later by agents of trading firms on assumption or resumption of duty.

Thirdly, there was the reward for services actually rendered by canoe boys and other menials. Fourthly, there was, particularly at the end of the century and later, the distribution of largesse or alms which the beachcombers and other coastal riff-raff demanded from any European who ventured to walk ashore.

Canoe house imposts: the work bar and the customs bar

The institution described above were common both to the Eastern Delta and to the Cross River area. The work bar and the customs bar were peculiar to the trading states of the Eastern Delta. Neither of these imposts are mentioned by Barbot and we can assume that they probably arose during the eighteenth century as part of the structural changes that led to the formation of the canoe house. The first reference to the work bar is by Captain Crow, 'with regard to the slaves we had to pay for them a second time for . . . we were called upon to pay what were called 'Work Bars' a few days before the vessel sailed'.[21] Consul Hutchinson writing in 1857 distinguishes between these taxes. 'Besides this comey there are two others demanded here (Bonny). One a 'customs bar' for each puncheon of oil sold which is deducted from the native trader's money and is levied by the chief under whose auspices the supercargo may have placed his ship for trading. The other a 'work bar' of one bar for every twenty puncheon bought and which is claimed from the supercargo by the representatives of the house to whom the trader belongs'.[22]

[21] Crow, p. 216.
[22] General report on the trade of the Bight of Biafra for the year 1856 P.P. Vol. XVI, 1857. Repeated in Hutchinson *Western Africa* p. 258, where 'one bar' (for twenty puncheons) has been replaced by 'three hundred'. In his *Ten Years Wandering amongst the Ethiopians*, he refers only to the 'Bar Comey' or 'customs bar'.

'Work bar' is not referred to in any of the commercial treaties, nor in any subsequent consular or other record.[23] It appears to have continued to the end of the period at least in New Calabar.[24] 'Customs bar' or 'bar comey' is referred to in the New Calabar and Brass Treaties. Article VI of the first stipulates that 'the supercargoes are not responsible to any of the chiefs for the customs bar but it must be collected by themselves and at their own cost'.[25] The supercargoes and the agents who succeed them continued however to collect it, and with the establishment of the Protectorate it became known as 'toppings', which was a 20 per cent rebate on the price paid for all oil sold by a member of a canoe house which the agent deducted and paid to the head of this house.[26]

[23] Except in Article 3 of Agreement of 1869 Appendix B.5.
[24] Newns, 1947.
[25] Hertslet, Vol. IX. p. 24, and Article VI of Appendix B.4.
[26] Consul Johnson writing in January 1886. F.O. 84/1750. Toppings was abolished in Bonny the same year.

Part Three

POLITICAL HISTORY OF BONNY
AND KALABARI

H

DURING THE 19th C

of Treaties and Agr
1860–1870 (4)

ohn Africa N
)ge Africa

`obin or
ack Brown N
`om Brown N
ntonio N

ungo Manilla N

)ublin Green

)ick Tullifari
ack Tulefari N
)eeri Tulefari

`illibo @ Duke No
lack Fubra N

:ing Halliday

ine Bone N

barney

VIII

The History of Bonny

1. PREHISTORY

ACCORDING to tradition, the Bonny people were derived from a section of the Ndokki Tribe living on the Lower Imo river, which claimed to have migrated there from the central Ijo area. They gradually moved down river and into the delta and eventually settled at the mouth of the Rio Real in territory already occupied by two other communities, Abalama and Iyankpo. The latter were probably the first arrivals, since their deity Simingi was considered the tutelary deity of the area. Abalama was driven out and settled in the Kalabari area. Iyankpo split into two groups, one, which became known as Tombia moving to the Kalabari area, the other, which became known as Finnema, remaining and becoming part of the Bonny state.

We have no means of learning when all this happened nor when Bonny developed her slave-trading organization with the interior. Tradition associates this with Asimini, who learnt the secrets of the overseas trade from Owerri Daba of Kalabari and who became the first King of Bonny; and it attributes either to him or to his successor the establishment of firm trading relations with the Ndokki on the Imo through the marriage of his daughter to the chief of Azuogu village; Kamalu, a son of this marriage, eventually succeeded as King of Bonny, and his line continued until King Warri, whose name is associated with the cult of the deity Ikuba, subsequently introduced as a war deity to Bonny. The cult was derived from Andoni and the iguana was associated with it as its sacred animal. This event must have occurred after 1699 as no reference is made to iguanas in Bonny by James or John Barbot.

2. PROTOHISTORY

After King Warri's death Awusa (Halliday), his elder brother's son, reigned with three other chiefs for a year before being deposed in favour of Perukule (Pepple), a descendant of Papa, who was said to be a half brother of King Kamalu. It was a period of general warfare through which King Pepple led his people to victory over all their enemies and it can be dated with some certainty to the eighteenth century and probably about the middle of it.

Bonny tradition maintains that Perukule's English name was Captain Pepple. James Barbot on his visit to Bonny in 1699 gave presents of 'a hat, a fire lock, and nine bunches of beads, instead of a coat' to king William and 'to Captain *Forty*, the king's general, captain *Pepprell*, captain *Boileau*, alderman *Bougsby* my lord *Willyby*, duke of *Monmouth*, drunken *Henry*, and some others, two firelocks, eight hats, nine narrow *Guinea* stuffs'.[1] Another paragraph refers to Captain Pepprell, the King's brother'. The Duke of Monmouth's relationship to Owerri Daba of Kalabari is discussed in chapter IX. None of the other names can be correlated with those in the African oral traditions except Captain Pepprell. But was Barbot's Captain Pepprell the King of the Bonny traditions? Leonard assumes[2] that he was, but if so he must have lived for a very long time. He need not have been an elder in 1699 when he conducted the trade negotiations with James Barbot, for in their dealings with Europeans, these delta states employed as their spokesmen their ablest men and preferably those who could speak a European language; but he must have been at least adult. According to Bonny tradition he was succeeded by his younger sons Fubra and Opobo, and the last named was a young man when he came to the throne in 1792. It is possible, of course, for a chief of exceptional stamina to live to an advanced age in the delta as in other parts of Nigeria. Such a man was chief Allagoa of Nembe who signed the Treaty of 1879 as head of the house of Amain and who died a very old man in 1934. Another, if we accept the Kalabari traditions, was Amakiri. But the Bonny traditions, unlike the Kalabari do not stress their hero king's longevity and imply that he died at a normal age. Leonard in his list of the Kings of Bonny[3] does insert another name 'Foubra (Agbaa)' between Perukule and Fubra.[4] If such a son of Perukule existed, he left behind him no house or other descendants and contemporary Bonny tradition does not recognize this name. Baikie in 1854[5] recorded the Pepple genealogy in the form in which it was given to the writer of the Bonny report in 1931 and to me in 1956. It is possible however,

---

[1] Barbot, John, p. 460.
[2] Leonard, p. 23.
[3] Leonard, p. 47.
[4] A similar name Agbaa Fubra occurs in Andoni tradition as the founder of Bonny.
[5] Baikie, p. 444.

that the genealogy given to Baikie and later to Captain Webber has been subjected to legendary elision and only records names which are structurally meaningful. Papa, the first name on Baikie's list, marks the origin of the line and differentiates it from the descendants of Edimini by Kamalu. Zhidie (Siriye), Baikie's second name, distinguishes it from the descendants of Papa by his other son Kala Igoni. Pelikoli the third name is the founder of this house as distinct from Siriye's other son, Sima, the founder of the Sima (Peterside) house. Any subsequent names, until we reach Fubra the founder of the Manilla Pepple house, are structurally irrelevant. If we accept this explanation and remember that it was customary in these Oil River states for the head of a house to be known by the titular name of its founder we can assume that the Perukule who became King of Bonny was a descendant of the Captain Pepprell who met James Barbot, and that he succeeded to the chieftaincy of this Captain Pepprell's house.

Perukule according to Bonny tradition was succeeded by Fubra. It has little to say about him beyond the fact that he was a hunchback with webbed fingers and toes, but very intelligent and a man of strong character. His reign was said to have been a peaceful one, he was childless and was succeeded by his younger brother, Opobo.

3. HISTORY

King Opobo

Captain Crow arrived in Bonny in 1792 to find that 'Old King Pepple (had) died just on our arrival'. He had to wait three months before the chiefs and priests decided 'on whom they should appoint as regent until the son of the deceased came of age'. Crow completed his cargo of 'about 400 blacks and set sail after a stay of about five months'.[6] It is clear from this account that Opobo had been built up as Fubra's heir and succeeded without question, the only dispute being over who should act as regent, that is, have the right to 'break trade' and with it control the 'comey' that went with this ceremony. It is also clear from Crow's later references to feasting and drinking with him that Opobo, though he may have been a minor when he succeeded, was certainly not an infant.

According to Bonny traditions there was an early war against Andoni which like other Andoni wars ended successfully for Bonny. There was also some kind of minor war with Kalabari as the traditions of both communities refer to it, and associate it with the name of

[6] Crow, p. 43.

Ogoloye Fubra and Orikadibia who were captured and consumed by Bonny. Apart from these episodes, and the fact that Opobo was an able, popular and powerful king, Bonny traditions tell us little about his long reign. The European records tell us nothing about these military episodes but they have a lot to say about the character of this monarch and of the way he had organized his relations with European traders. A comparison of the ceremony of 'breaking trade' as described by Lt. Holman or Dr. Jackson in 1826 with that given by James Barbot in 1699, shows that it had been developed into an institution which emphasized the superiority of the king and which set him above and apart from his chiefs and other subjects. In the words of Holman:

The ceremony of opening the trade with each vessel is as follows: a day being appointed by the King, a dinner is prepared, and his Majesty is entertained by the Captain and his officers on board the trader. The black gentlemen who form the royal suite are obliged, upon this occasion, to trust to chance, and the good nature of the ship's crew, for their share of the feast. In order that no point of courtesy may be wanting, it is requisite to send a boat from the ship to meet His Majesty, as he comes out of the creek in his own canoe. The King upon joining his entertainers, immediately enters their boat: which condescension is acknowledged by a salute of seven guns, fired from the ship. On arriving alongside His Majesty throws an egg at the vessel's hull, he then ascends to the deck, which is usually covered, from the gangway to the cabin, with a piece of cloth; an armchair, covered and ornamented with the same material, being placed ready for his accommodation. The only beverage used by King Pepple is his favourite Membo (palm wine), which is brought on board by his attendants. His Majesty commonly returns about sunset to the shore, when a second salute of seven guns is fired from the ship, and the trade is declared free to all his subjects.[7]

Jackson's account confirms these details and has more to say about the ritual side.

His Majesty was dressed in a pair of Spanish plaid trousers, check shirt and French straw hat of remarkably fine texture and from his neck was suspended by a string tied to its legs a newly fledged chicken ... at his feet sat two little naked Negroes holding a small box and two hens eggs. He was likewise accompanied by a favourite Pointer dog, of the Spanish breed which invariably attends him wherever he moves ... When about five hundred yards from the Kingston, his Majesty took one of the hen eggs from the boys, and after a long preamble in which he was joined by the

[7] Holman, pp. 376–7.

Jujew and Coxswain he touched the different parts of his Body as before described, as likewise my forehead (all whites being Jujews) and threw it with great force into the water. The other egg he dashed against the ship as we came alongside, this constituting the ceremony previous to breaking trade. He was received at the gangway by the Captain and Mates: fine India cloth was laid from thence into the cabin and upon this his Majesty walked to a chair of state placed for him at the upper end of the dinner table, which was already laid out for the repast he was invited to partake of. Boiled corned beef and chickens, roasted ducks and broiled fowls, a fine sheep cooked in various ways, with two large plumb dumplings etc. etc . . . Before he tasted meat, a glass of spirits was handed to him and the same foolery he had practised was repeated here, the box brought with him and placed at his feet forming a receptacle for the liquor. I had the curiosity (unobserved) to look inside and found there were placed in it a stuffed Quanah dried leaves etc. etc.[8]

There were also other rituals performed by the king at the shrine or grave of his father, and at various other jew jew houses before he set off to dine on the *Kingston*.

Breaking of trade in Opobo's time was very different from the businesslike, informal proceeding described by Barbot. The 'chiefs and principal men' who had formerly assisted in the negotiations and shared in the dinner were now excluded. It was reserved for the king and the ships' officers who like him were 'jew jew'. Payment of comey and other business connected with breaking trade had already been completed ashore and this was a purely formal visit made by the head of the Bonny state. But it also brought the king and the captain and supercargoes together in a cordial, relaxed and relatively private atmosphere and this relationship was reaffirmed at a second less formal occasion, when the captain and his officers were invited by the king to dine with him ashore, at his 'palace' or at his 'country estate' at 'Old Bonny' (Orupiri). We are also left in no doubt as to Opobo's capacity as a business man. Dr. Jackson again provides the most detail.

He possesses a shrewed intellect and a most retentive recollection. Indeed when it is considered that without the assistance of the slightest education, he transacts business with thirteen vessels now laying here (and often there are many more) all the concerns of which however minute and complicated he carefully bears in his remembrance never forgetting what he promises to do for them nor omitting to send for what they promise him, and the traffic with them naturally leading to the despatch of Trade

---

[8] Jackson, pp. 76–7. Coxswain was the term given to the particular Bonny man which each vessel employed in Bonny as their agent and messenger.

into the interior, by bartering their merchandise for oil, ivory and slaves, all passing through his hands and under his own observation, one cannot sufficiently eulogise his extraordinary abilities. In fact his generally admitted correctness in all points of business excites the wonder and claims the admiration of all who know him. If you speak of the slave trade and the ships which were formerly sent out from Liverpool to engage in it, name but a vessel and he will instantly recollect her commander, how long she lay in Bonny, how many times she traded there, what number of slaves she carried etc. etc. From enquiries I find that as an absolute sovereign . . . he is admirably adapted for his situation, never wavering but always decisive in his commands, tho' possessing power the most despotic he tempers justice with mercy, altho' a crime never escapes punishment he is kind too, to his people, pitying them when sick and ameliorating their condition. His manners are likewise conciliatory and on the whole he is very well liked, tho' very much feared by the natives.[9]

Jackson was young and romantic, but he was not the only European to be impressed by Opobo, and there is enough substance in his description to explain the secret of his power. Whatever the kingship may have been under Fubra, under Opobo it was a personal monarchy, lacking any inner council of ministers, Egbo society or other stabilizing institution which could operate should the king prove weak or incapable, or should he be removed by death or other cause.

The interregnum

The weakness of the system became apparent as soon as Opobo died leaving no obvious successor behind him. He had few sons; the only two whose names occur in written records were Dappo (or Datu), said by tradition to have been his own son, and William Dappa (Bill Pepple), said to have been the son of one of Fubra's wives whom Opobo inherited, and who could therefore be considered Fubra's jural son, though his actual father was Opobo. Dappo had predeceased his father and was survived only by an infant son.

European records are silent about this period of Bonny history and oral tradition has very little to say about it, beyond the fact that Bereibibo, chief of the Bristol (Alagbaria) house and the son of Perukule's (Captain Pepple's) daughter, was elected king by the Bonny chiefs and almost immediately deposed and William Dappa elected in his stead. It is only possible, therefore, to conjecture what actually happened as the official records do not begin until 1836. Two oral traditions referred to by Dike say that Opobo died in either 1829 or

[9] Ibid, p. 78.

1830, that his son and successor William Dappa Pepple was a minor having been born on 23 August 1817, and that Madu, the head of King Opobo's house, became regent until 1835 when William Dappa ascended the throne.[10] But dates of this sort, when they appear in recent Eastern Delta traditions, are no more reliable than those concocted by ethnologists in reference to the more distant past. None of the contemporary European records gives any date for Opobo's death, and William Dappa, though he may well have been considered a minor by the Bonny chiefs and elders, has quite a different age given to him by the Europeans who met him. He was a young man and a friend of Dr. Jackson in 1826 and J. Smith, who claims to have been in Bonny in 1836, describes him as 'tall and thin, a rather awkward looking man about four or five and thirty years'. The version given to Dike also omits Bereibibo, a name which occurs not only in the current tradition but in data collected by Talbot, Leonard, and Baikie. It is very probable that Maduka, the head of Opobo's house, was left on his master's death the most powerful chief in Bonny and that he was able to secure recognition as the regent. It also looks as though the struggle for power between the Manilla and Anna Pepple houses began with the death of Opobo. They had as their heads two formidable chiefs, Erinashabo and Maduka. William Dappa as the jural son of Fubra (Manilla) would naturally have the support of the Manilla house, while Dappo's death had left the Anna Pepple house with no satisfactory candidate, since Dappo's son was still an infant. The election of Bereibibo looks like a compromise that failed and Maduka and the Anna Pepple chiefs had to accept William Dappa as Opobo's successor, though they could and probably did continue to hold on to the regency by insisting that he was still too young to succeed.

If we accept the evidence given in the *Report of the Commission of Inquiry on the West Coast of Africa* in 1840[11] this period saw a considerable increase in the export of slaves from the West Coast of Africa particularly from the Bight of Biafra. In 1835 the British Navy was at last empowered to seize obvious Spanish slavers before they had embarked their slaves, and in January 1836 H.M.S. *Trinculo* did so without prior notice to the chiefs of Bonny. Maduka Anna Pepple and his chiefs supported the cause of the Spanish slavers and when Lieutenant Tryon and one of the British supercargoes went ashore to meet Anna Pepple and explain the position,

[10] Dike, pp. 68-69.
[11] P.P. 1842, Vol. XII.

he lost his temper and imprisoned them. Their immediate release was demanded by H.M.S. *Trinculo*, Anna Pepple's request to defer this till the following morning was allowed, and on that morning an agreement was made between Anna Pepple, Manilla Pepple, and the British supercargoes in the presence of Lieutenant Tryon, which stipulated that no English subject should thence-forward be detained ashore or maltreated, and which provided for the breaking of trade immediately comey had been paid, and for the settlement of disputes between the 'English captains' and the king or the chiefs of Bonny at a council meeting of the captains with the king and chiefs. The document[12] begins with the words 'It is hereby agreed between the undersigned His Britannic Majesty's Subjects and the King of Bonny' it was signed in 'Old King Pepple's house', but its only African signatories are Anna Pepple and Manilla Pepple.

The Foreign Office correspondence does not mention the internal disturbances at Bonny.[13]

J. Smith however describes a 'war' between the king's house (that is, the Manilla Pepple canoe house group) and Anna Pepple's house very similar to the artillery duels which occurred between the Manilla and Anna Pepple groups in 1859 and 1869, in which he and another supercargo intervened to effect a truce. He also describes a meeting of the Bonny council of chiefs, 'jew jew members' and 'parliament gentlemen' which met a few days later to make peace between them. The fees charged by the council for settling this dispute were two thousand manillas; four thousand were originally demanded and 'almost as much time was occupied in settling about the fees as in adjusting the differences'. Smith adds that the result of this was a complete victory for the king, 'Anna was shorn of his power and emoluments. He took the thing to heart and soon killed himself with drinking'.[14]

King William Dappa Pepple

To the European traders on the river the accession of King William Dappa in 1836 meant an end to a period of anarchy and a return to the system of King Opobo. The interregnum had been a period of very considerable economic competition between traders whether afloat or ashore. The slave trade had taken a new lease of life the palm oil trade was booming and still expanding. There were fortunes to be made in both these trades and an increasing number

[12] Appendix B 1.
[13] F.O. 2/1.
[14] Smith, pp. 159–163.

of ships and supercargoes trying to make them. There were also a still larger number of Bonny traders and would-be traders ready to exploit the situation and take advantage of the easy credit that was being offered to them. Debts and trade disputes multiplied, and in settling them each trader had to fend for himself, and, if he considered it strategic, take the law into his own hands. Trading and social relationships between the Europeans and the African communities were governed by conventions which had been consolidated in the time of Opobo and when necessary enforced by him. They were still adhered to, but there was now no authority ashore capable of enforcing them. What is suprising is not the abuses and breaches of these conventions which occurred, but the fact that despite all these disturbances both the legitimate and the slave trade continued to flourish. As a result of British intervention King William Dappa Pepple had been placed upon his throne, and the conventions giving superior privileged status to Europeans ('British Subjects') which King Opobo had considered it to his advantage to enforce, had been confirmed in the Agreement of 1836. On April 9 1837 this was expanded to cover the conventions relating to the breaking of trade which were modified to enable supercargoes to trade within seven days of arrival, and also to cover innovations in the trade concerned with the marking of casks. This 'Convention of Amity and Commerce' became the model for similar treaties concluded later with the other Eastern Delta states.

The convention was between the King of Bonny and Commander Craigie and others, His Britannic Majesty's subjects, and it confirmed the King of Bonny as the person to whom the Europeans should refer for settlement of their disputes and for the enforcement of other articles of the convention. But King William Dappa lacked the capacity of his father and he had to contend with economic conditions very different from those which had operated in his father's reign. The increased powers of seizure now available to the British naval squadron were bringing the slave trade in the Eastern Delta to an end.[15] The expansion of the palm oil trade was continuing but at a much slower rate.[16] It was a period in which the weaker traders,

[15] Vide Jamieson, 1: 'The export of slaves from the Bonny River is at an end if the same watchfulness be shown by H.M. cruisers'; also Dr. Madden's *Report, of the Commission of Inquiry on the West Coast of Africa*. P.P. XII, 1842 App. 3.
[16] If we take Jamieson's figures, oil shipped from the Bight of Biafra to Liverpool had jumped from 8,000 tons in 1829 to 13,600 tons in 1838 (Jamieson, 2). In the next ten years it increased to only 15,700.

European and African, were being eliminated and the most illustrious of the latter was King William Dappa. Opobo's power derived to a very large extent from his business ability, which made his house the wealthiest and therefore the most powerful in Bonny. King William Dappa could only lose money. His house, though it had some able members,[17] remained small and weak, while his relations with European supercargoes were undermined by the fact that he was, to most of them, a defaulting debtor.

He had hopes of recouping some of his losses from the subsidies which the British Government were holding out to those kings who signed a treaty agreeing to abolish the slave trade in their dominions. Captain Craigie in 1839 had offered 2,000 dollars but this offer was not accepted for various reasons. In 1841 Captain Tucker visited Bonny to try to make the king pay his debts and to negotiate an anti-slave treaty. He succeeded in achieving both objectives. The treaty provided the king with a subsidy of 10,000 dollars which he immediately offset against his debt to Messrs. Hamilton Jackson & Co. But when this firm tried to collect the money from the British Treasury they found that the treaty had not been ratified by the British Government since the amount of the subsidy was considered excessive.[18] After this the naval squadron ceased to intervene in commercial disputes and the European traders were again left to fend for themselves. Relations between them and the king became increasingly strained and in 1844 a 'civil war' which ended in the king's favour, was reported to have broken out between 'the King and the shipping'. Details are inadequate, being mainly hearsay.[19] On this occasion the Navy did not intervene. More serious, apparently, was the constant lawlessness which prevailed on the river and which was directed against British boats plying between Bonny and the New Calabar anchorage. This was associated with Awanta, the priest of Simingi at Finnema, who according to Smith 'had been a great slave dealer and was ruined in consequence of the suppression of the slave trade'. After this had resulted in the murder of British subjects, the Navy was instructed to intervene. The king maintained that the priest was 'jew jew' and therefore outside his control but raised no objection to the Navy dealing with him, so Awanta was seized and deported in 1847.[20] The following year a treaty was finally concluded for the

[17] Fred Pepple (Isacco) had no difficulty in liquidating the house debts once William Dappa had been removed. F.O. 84/1161.
[18] P.P. 1847/8, Vol. LXIV, 5.
[19] Beecroft and Hope Waddell were reporting what they had been told.
[20] Smith, p. 56 and F.O. 2/3.

abolition of the slave trade and for the payment to the king of a subsidy of 2,000 dollars for the next three years.

King William Dappa's relations with his own people were as unfortunate as with the English trading community. Here again his position was difficult. He could count on the active hostility of the Anna Pepple House and its leaders, but, unlike King Abbe Amakiri of Kalabari who was in a similar situation in 1864, he was not prepared to work with the Manilla Pepple and other houses that had supported his accession. Bonny tradition has nothing to say about his relations with the European community, but deals with an episode which European records do not mention—the war with Andoni. According to these traditions war broke out again with Andoni because the Anna Pepple house had captured, killed and eaten some Andoni in the course of King Opobo's funeral celebrations, part of which commemorated that king's victory over the Andoni. The Andoni killed some Bonny people in revenge and the Bonny people decided to go to war with the Andoni. King William Dappa tried unsuccessfully to stop them, and when the fighting went against Bonny they held him responsible for this. Eventually the war was settled in favour of Bonny and a treaty was made and signed between them. This treaty has been preserved[21] and a reference to this war is probably contained in Captain Tucker's report in 1841 of '7 slaves whom King Pepple had permitted to be sacrificed in the town, their flesh openly cooked and eaten by the fetish people and their heads and bones of their limbs publicly exposed opposite the fetish house'.[22] The Eastern Delta people did not kill and eat slaves but prisoners captured in war. The treaty with Andoni is a very interesting document. Its form is the same as the contemporary treaties concluded between Great Britain and African natives states, and it was probably prepared and recorded by the British traders who signed as witnesses to the Bonny and Andoni signatures. It is highly improbable that the Andoni chiefs who signed it knew that under Article I they had ceded their country to the King of Bonny. What they did accept and what they had previously accepted was that they were economically dependent on Bonny and, except in the matter of foodstuffs, they were within the the Bonny 'trading empire'. This dependence was conceded in Article II, particularly its concluding sentence: 'but under no circumstances or pretence whatever shall Young Calabar (Kalabari)

[21] Baikie, p. 414 and, Hertslet, Vol. XIII, p. 13.
[22] F.O. 84/384.

or Creeka (Okrika) country men retail in the Andony'.[23] 'Article VIII Each party (namely) the Andoni and Bonny men mutually agree and bind themselves that for the future they will not eat human flesh' is best interpreted as a modern version of the mutual non-consumer pacts between Eastern Delta groups of villages that are also met with in the early Kalabari traditions,[24] the non-consumers in this instance being Bonny and Andoni. It is clear from the Andoni names in the treaty[25] that a genuine and successful attempt was made to achieve a lasting settlement between Bonny and her Andoni neighbours. Relations between these two communities have remained peaceful ever since, while the relations between the Anna Pepple House and the Andoni became so cordial later that Jaja Anna Pepple was able to withdraw into their territory and to found there his new state of Opobo.

By 1849 the European traders on the river had become fewer and better organized. The more progressive firms were changing over to the 'hulk' system, described in chapter VI, which meant that they maintained a permanent agency on the river. These resident agents became the leaders of the European community and they were able to combine together, at least where 'interlopers' and the African community were concerned. The hardening of the conditions of trading were also eliminating the weaker African traders ashore. The use of 'books', trading tokens, and similar certificates and testimonials helped to eliminate unreliable traders, and, when combined with the control exercised by the head of a canoe house over its trading members, gave the European traders advantages which were not available on the Old Calabar river. It also meant that those canoe houses whose chiefs were honest and reliable traders were able to corner a much greater share of the trade.[26] Commodore Hotham was therefore able to report in 1848 that 'trade was going on quietly and safely with no complaints from the traders.' He also reported that the system of giving out goods on trust had been totally abolished.[27] It had not.

[23] Baikie makes nonsense of this clause by inserting the word 'spirits' after 'retail'; he also bowdlerised Article IV.
[24] The parties 'swearing juju' not to eat one another.
[25] I was able to discuss these signatures at a meeting with representatives of the Andoni (Obolo) tribe in 1956. They represent people who were said to have been the heads and deputy heads of the principal Western Obolo villages, that is of the Ngo and Unyeada (Ayanda of the treaty) sections of the Tribe, and of Nkoro (Corro) a village of Okrika extraction within the Andoni area. The Eastern Obolo villages were not included, and were too far distant to have been in the war.
[26] E.g. The Jumbo Manilla house.
[27] P. P. 1847/8 Vol. LXIV.

By this time the policy of the British government had changed. Lord Palmerston's view of more active intervention had been accepted and a consul was appointed for the Bights of Benin and Biafra in 1849. Beecroft the new consul visited Bonny in 1850 in H.M.S. *Jackal* and convened a meeting of the European and African communities which accepted and signed a revised code of commercial relations, the treaty of October 1850.[28] This reaffirmed the main provisions of the 1837 treaty but also provided penalties for breach of any of its clauses, and it specifically penalized the king should he cause any delay in breaking trade. It also provided new regulations to cover the changes brought about by the consolidation of the palm oil trade.

In May 1852 William Dappa had a stroke and the supercargoes at the request of the Manilla Pepple chiefs and their supporters, recognized or appointed the two head men of his house, Yanibo (Yaniboo) and Isacco (Ishaca alias Fred Pepple) to act for him. The Anna Pepple house refused to accept this, and when it was reported to the consul he came to Bonny and held a meeting of supercargoes and chiefs at which he ratified this appointment and recognized them as agents. But the stroke was only temporary and the king soon recovered from it.

By now he had succeeded in mobilizing the African as well as the European traders against him. According to the Europeans he was compelling African traders to accept goods from him on trust at exorbitant rates before he would allow them to trade in the hinterland markets; according to the African traders he was using the trade goods he received as comey and shake-hands and those from the anti-slavery subsidies to undersell them in these markets.[29] His final blunder was an attempt to trick them into a war against New Calabar by getting them to mobilize their 43 war canoes on the pretext of making a ceremonial visit to Bile, and according to Bonny tradition, the chiefs, realizing they had been deceived returned home, held a general council meeting, and deposed him. According to a petition sent to the consul by the chiefs and traders in the river Bonny, 'on our return to Bonny (from this naval expedition) the whole voice of the country called for his removal and we accordingly declared him no longer King'—The signatures to this petition were the chiefs of all the important Bonny houses and they included Manilla Pepple. In answer to this petition Consul Beecroft visited

[28] Appendix B 2.
[29] Documents attached to Despatch No. 1 of 20/2/54. F.O. 84/950.

Bonny and 'on January 20th', to quote from the consul's journal, he went on shore and convened a meeting of King Pepple and Chiefs. The first point entered upon was Pepple's reason for trying to commence a war with New Calabar, which he denied and said such was never his intention. The Chiefs said it was his intention, and that they accompanied him as far as in sight of Young Town without knowing his intention was otherwise than to visit his mother's country, Billa; and upon arriving there he requested them to lie in wait at a certain point, which the Calabar men must pass on their way to the ships', which they refused, telling him they did not come to war.

The next question was related to whether, if the Consul reinstated him, prohibiting him from all trade and allowing him two-thirds of the 'coomey' for his support, he would remain as King and conduct the Business of the Country as formerly. Upon consideration, he answered he would do so.

The chiefs were then asked if they would keep him as King upon these terms. They answered, they were tired of his rule, and did not wish him to remain King any longer, bringing a series of charges against him, such as oppression and tyranny. The Consul then inquired whom they had appointed for his successor, if he was removed from being King, as he could not allow the country to remain without a headman. They answered, Prince Dappo, the son of an elder brother than Pepple and the rightful heir. The Consul informed them he should draw up certain laws, restricting him from all trade etc., allowing him two thirds of the 'coomey' for his support, and that his whole time must be given to governing the country; to all of which they were agreeable.

Upon Prince Dappo being proposed, Pepple claimed the protection of the Consul and begged to be removed to Fernando Po, to which the consul consented.

Shortly afterwards, the whole of the Chiefs said that sooner than Pepple should be taken away, they would let him be King again, they also said they thought if he was taken away, the Eboe men would not pay either his debts or theirs. It was elicited from them that the chief reason they did not wish him to go was that they might be called upon to pay his debts, and that it was contrary to their jew jew; the Consul explained he was not taking him away, but allowing him to go at his own request, the Chiefs then retired to discuss, and afterwards said they did not care where Pepple went, if he paid his debts first. The whole of this day and the 21st were devoted to hearing palavers and going through the book.

On the 23rd, Pepple was pronounced deposed, and Prince Dappo formally elected King, under the title of King Dappo, the boats of Her Majesty's Ship 'Antelope' firing a salute of 21 guns.[30]

What is clear from these documents is that the chiefs of Bonny

---

[30] Beecroft's, *Journal of Proceedings in the river Bonny* etc., Inclosure No. 1 in No. 48. F.O. 84/950.

when they deposed King William Dappa Pepple had envisaged his removal from office but not from Bonny. Before he could be allowed to leave Bonny there were three questions which had first to be answered. What was to happen about the king's debts? What would be the reaction of the Imo river oil markets? Was the deportation of a native of Bonny not contrary to their customs and forbidden by their religion? It was customary in Bonny for the members of a canoe house group to depose the head of the group should they consider he had mismanaged his office but the debts which he had incurred while in office remained the liability of the group and had to be paid by all the houses in the group. The Bonny chiefs and no doubt the British agents, felt that this convention might be extended to cover the higher office of kingship and all the Bonny houses be held liable for his debts. In regard to the second question King William Dappa Pepple's first wife and queen was an Ibo woman from the Ndokki area and her relatives had considerable influence in the communities which controlled these oil markets. As to the third point, while such deportation may have been contrary to custom, this custom had already been broken on numerous occasions in the past and more recently by the deportation of the high priest Awanta.

The first point was settled by recognizing King William Dappa Pepple's house as solely responsible for the king's debts and by naming his two principal slaves and agents, Yanibo and Isacco, as joint chiefs of this house. We can assume that the Bonny chiefs were reassured by King William Dappa Pepple or his queen that there would be no disturbance of the oil markets, as there was no Ibo reaction there to the king's removal and the amounts owing to him in these markets were collected by Isacco without difficulty. The consul's statement that the king was being removed from Bonny at his own request appears to have satisfied them on the third point.

Before he left for Fernando Po with the deposed king and his family[31] the consul and the Bonny chiefs signed another convention, the convention of January 23rd 1854 which added a number of additional articles to the Treaty of October 3rd 1850.[32] These were intended to provide for the changed political situation and to guard against the abuses of the previous reign. The most revolutionary of them was Article I, which prohibited the king from any form of trading and embodied the consul's conviction that the king should be

---

[31] William Dappa was later moved to Ascension Island whence he was later allowed to come to England. See F.O. 84/1161–4.

[32] Appendix B, 3 and 2.

I

concerned with government and not with trade and that King William Dappa Pepple's downfall was due to his neglect of this principle.

A comparison of the conventions and Treaties of 1837, 1850 and 1854 reveals the decline in the position and authority of the monarchy during King William Dappa Pepple's reign.

The 1837 'convention with the King of Bonny' was signed at the king's house and any complaint by English captains against any of the natives of Bonny was to be made to the king. The 1850 'Treaty with the King and chiefs of the River Bonny' was 'dated at Bonny Town'. Any complaint by a British subject was now to be made to the 'King and chiefs and Masters assembled and they hereby promise to redress all such grievances by punishing the offender', and it is the 'King and chiefs' who in article I pledge themselves not to detain or maltreat British subjects. In the 1837 convention the king might recommend people to receive trust, in the 1850 Treaty the king was barred from demanding or enforcing trust on any pretence. The king was still recognized however as the head of the state, it was he who in article VIII should set apart for the use of trading ships an area of the beach, who in article XI has to deal with and 'adjust' any depredations and plundering committed upon British Subjects, within the limits of King Pepple's dominions, and who was to sell up the property of a defaulting debtor in article XV. The authority of the superior chiefs is also clearly recognized as well as their superior status. They and the king are the only people who are free to walk during the day for the purpose of exercise on the British traders' beach. (Article XVI).

The convention of 1854, signed in the court house Grand Bonny, was not a revision of the previous treaty of 1850 but an addition to it. But these additions reduced the king's status almost to that of principal executive agent of the 'court' and made this 'court' the supreme authority on the Bonny River. Article I barred the king from trading, penalized him should he do so, rewarded anyone giving information against him in this respect, and further penalized the king should he avenge himself upon the informer. It also provided as his emoluments two-thirds of the comey, the other third being reserved for the 'exigencies of the country'. The 'court' was the assembly of 'king and chiefs and masters assembled', referred to in article III of the 1850 treaty. Its venue was the court house built by the European community, and its personnel were the king and chiefs of the Bonny community and the masters, supercargoes and other European traders of the British community. The chiefs like the king were made subordinate to the court and reponsible for carrying out the court's decisions. The king or chiefs were not to assault or arrest any trader (African trader) without the prior sanction of the 'court' (Article II); all future meetings were to be held in the court-house and any supercargo, King, chief or trader who refused to attend without due cause or who came armed or with armed followers was to be fined one puncheon of oil in the first case, 50 puncheons in the second (Articles V and XII).

The new alignment of power was also clearly indicated in article III. That 'the King or chiefs of Bonny shall not go to war with any neighbouring country without informing the supercargoes . . . and should it be thought necessary for them to do so, it is distinctly understood that all debts owing to the ships must be first paid'; and in article VIII 'That in the event of any difficulty arising . . . we may be empowered to draw out such fresh clauses as may be deemed necessary, and which being approved by Her Majesty's consul may be considered the laws of the country'.

'We' in this article presumably meaning the 'court' though only the consul, Lieutenant Young of H.M.S. *Antelope*, King Dappo and nineteen chiefs of Bonny signed the treaty.

There was now no king with any real authority in Bonny, the chiefs were too powerful and disunited to accept the leadership of any of them, and the only stabilizing influence was the European community. 'The court', that is the general council meeting of European agents and African chiefs, was therefore made the supreme authority for the river.

Manilla versus Anna Pepple

With King William Dappa Pepple out of the way the struggle between the two principal canoe house groups in Bonny reached its final stage. These groups, originally the canoe houses founded respectively by Fubra (Manilla) and Opobo (Anna) Pepple before they came to the throne, had, under the management of the able slaves who had succeeded their royal masters as chiefs, expanded into two powerful groups. The Manilla Pepple group had had longer time in which to consolidate. According to the traditions of these houses, when Fubra became king the chieftaincy of his house was offered to Captain Hart (Adango alias Akunnayi), a slave of Captain Pepple's, who had been originally attached to Fubra's household. But as he was already established as chief of his own house he refused and put forward instead Ibani-burufia (Ibani) another superior slave of Fubra's. Under Ibani's leadership and administration the house was expanded into the following group of houses.

Main house	MANILLA PEPPLE
Subordinate houses	BANIGO—(founded by Iringeresibo (alias Erinashabo) though taking the name of his successor William Ibanigo)
	JUMBO MANILLA—(Sinaminabofori Okponkata)
	LONG JOHN—founded by Imo (John Bull) but taking the name of his successor Long John (Amanibieyefori)
	JACK MANILLA—(Gboboitemegha alias Ncheke alias Ntshaka)

In addition to these subordinate houses directly derived from the main or parent house, there were two other smaller houses which claimed to derive from King Fubra's household namely WILSON PEPPLE (Ojuigbe or Nkwere), which was later known by the name of his successor, Jack Wilson (Minabofiango), and FINE COUNTRY, founded by Igwe but taking the name of one of his successors whose native name was Ibiama.

These seven formed the Manilla Pepple group of houses. Against them were ranged the Anna Pepple houses. These had had a shorter time to establish themselves, and whereas some of the subordinate houses of the Manilla Pepple group, notably Banigo and Jumbo, were as powerful and later more powerful than the main house, this was not the case in the Anna Pepple group. Here the main house continued the dominant house, the largest in Bonny, and the subordinate houses were smaller, more vulnerable and more dependent on the ability of the chief who had founded them, while some of them, though accepted as subordinate houses within the Anna Pepple group, were not recognized as separate houses outside it. Those which now survive are

Main house	ANNA PEPPLE (now changed to JAJA)
Subordinate houses	KIEPIRIMA (Toby) later known as ANNIE STEWART
	IBIFA (Boniface) now reconstituted as BRUCE JAJA
	URANTA (Iruanya)

EPELLE

JAJA (changed to ANNA PEPPLE)

while in 1850 there were at least two other houses which are now extinct and whose names survive only in the European records

CALLANADASSA (Kala Ndassa)

TOM TAYLOR

Other houses derived from Opobo's sons which associated with the Anna Pepple group were:

PRINCE DAPPO now known as WOGU DAPPA

STRONG FACE (Fubara Akworo) Founded by a minor son of Opobo.

These ten houses, and possibly others now forgotten, formed the Anna Pepple group.

The other two large houses founded by members of Captain Pepple's (Perukule's household, namely ALLISON and CAPTAIN HART, claimed, if we accept the consular records, to be independent and neutral, but Captain Hart was virtually a part of the Manilla group and Allison also, when faced with a choice between Manilla and Anna, invariably supported the former. On the other hand, the house founded by Captain Pepple's (Perukule's) eldest son Ibolu, variously known during the period by the names of its successive chiefs, Indian Queen, Ukonu, George Goodhead, and now known as UKONU and which had been closely associated with King Opobo during his lifetime, supported the Anna Pepple group. The other Bonny houses and they were many as can be seen from Table 3 were small and lacking in wealth, and though their chiefs at a council meeting might represent a sizeable proportion of the whole council, they were not associated together in any firm political groupings. A few of them like GOGO FUBRA (Duke Norfolk) were firmly attached to the Anna Pepple group, and a few like JACK BROWN of Finnema village supported the Manilla, but most during the time of King William Dappa claimed to be independent and not involved in the political struggle of the Manilla and Anna Pepple Groups.

Ibani had been succeeded as chief of the Manilla Pepple house by Iringeresibo—the Erinashabo of the consular records—who left the chieftaincy of his own house with his slave William Ibanigo .These records confirm that he died soon after King William Dappa's accession and was succeeded by Imo (John Bull) who left his own house to his slave Long John. There is no record of Imo's death; Manilla tradition says that he was succeeded by Ibani's son Ibulu.

Ibulu's management of the main house was disastrous and by the time he died it had become heavily in debt.

It was the same in the case of the Anna Pepple main house. Madu (Maduka) had been succeeded by his two senior sons in turn, first Alali and then Iloli.[33] Like Ibulu, Iloli's management of the main house was bad and it became heavily in debt. In both cases tradition implies that it was the incapacity of the chief that was responsible for this, but the fact that this happened to both main houses at the same time suggests that, at least in times of hardening trade, the chief of a main house was at an economic disadvantage as against chiefs of subordinate houses, who were free to devote more of their time and resources to trade. It was during this same period that Oko Jumbo, the slave successor of Okponkata (Jumbo Manilla), and Jaja Anna Pepple were beginning to accumulate the fortunes and the followers which later made them the dominant chiefs in Grand Bonny.

European records, and following them Nigerian historians, stress the fact that the chiefs of these houses, and for that matter of most other Bonny houses as well, were slaves and most of them 'bought slaves'. Apart from indicating that it was more easy for bought slaves than for other persons to rise to the top in the nineteenth-century Bonny, the fact that they were slaves was, politically speaking, irrelevant. The essential point was that they were not of royal, that is of Perukule descent, they could not hope therefore to succeed to the throne as could the chiefs of many Nembe or Okrika houses. They could become kingmakers but never kings. Maduka tried to go against this by retaining the Regency and refusing in 1836 to accept William Dappa the Manilla candidate as king. He was defeated, and the Manilla group scored their first success. But William Dappa antagonized the Manilla group as he did the other chiefs of Bonny and it was a temporarily united council of chiefs that petitioned the consul against him. The recognition of King Dappo left the Anna Pepple house temporarily supreme, and the Acting Consul Lyn-slagher's reports make it clear that King Dappo was under the control of Anna Pepple (Iloli) and that this chief was not prepared to accept the authority of the court of equity now that Beecroft was dead.

Iloli's first objective was to break the house of William Dappa Pepple. There was immediate trouble over Yanibo, who had been named in the treaty of 1854 as one of the chiefs of the William Dappa

---

[33] No firm dates are available. Dike, p. 69, following a Bonny or Opobo tradition, gives 1833 as the date for Madu's death. But J. Smith claims to have talked with Madu and his 'mate' Itchi after his unsuccessful attempt to retain the regency, that is in 1836, and says that he died soon after. (Smith, p. 161.)

Pepple house. Iloli Anna Pepple claimed him as a member of the Anna Pepple house. When the decision of the court of equity went against Iloli he withdrew from the court, followed by the other chiefs and King Dappo and promoted a hostile demonstration of market women against the supercargoes.[34] The acting consul intervened to enforce the authority of the court of equity, fined Anna Pepple three puncheons of oil, agreed, at the request of the supercargoes, to allow King Dappo to engage in trade, and with their approval and that of the Bonny chiefs recognized Fred Pepple (Isacco), who had almost succeeded in liquidating William Dappa Pepple's debts to the supercargoes, as the owner of any property belonging to William Dappa, that is as the head of the William Dappa Pepple house. This was in January 1855.

On the 13 August 1855 King Dappo died of a chill, resulting from inflammation of the chest according to the English doctor who was asked to treat him, from the sorcery of Yanibo and Fred Pepple according to the Bonny chiefs. This calamity united the Bonny people against the house of William Dappa Pepple. Yanibo and Isacco were accused of having procured his death by sorcery (poison). They appealed to Captain Witt for protection and he sent his boat and brought them aboard his ship, the Ferozopore, whence they were conveyed to the consul at Fernando Po. The people of Bonny then turned upon the other members of the house and, apart from three children of William Dappa who had sought sanctuary in Finnema, massacred them all to an estimated total of 600–700 persons, those who had managed to shelter in the King's house, blowing themselves up with his gunpowder when their supplies ran out. The chiefs then sought to secure from the European community the surrender of Yanibo and Isacco, claiming that they had broken the custom relating to seeking sanctuary by fetching them off in a boat.[35] The Europeans refused to surrender the fugitives and the chiefs then placed an embargo on all trade and on the recovery of all trust that was outstanding and which was estimated at £80,000.

An embargo on trade was a sanction that neither community in Bonny could sustain for long, and bore harder on the Bonny Community than on the British, and when later the consul appeared and called a meeting of the court of equity the chiefs were glad to settle

---

[34] The first recorded instance of women being used for political demonstration in Nigeria.
[35] The chiefs told the consul that the massacre began after Yanibo and Isacco escaped. Other informants said they escaped after it had started. F.O. 84/975.

their differences with the British community and to accept his suggestion of a council of regents, who should act until King Dappo's unborn heir[36] should come of age. They were naturally unable to agree upon the names of these regents and referred it to the acting consul who, after consultation with the European agents, named Anna Pepple (Iloli), Ada Allison, Captain Hart, and Manilla Pepple (Ntshaka), the latter 'being a young man', to consult with William Banigo and Oko Jumbo.[37] On paper these were the heads of the four largest independent houses in Bonny. In fact the Ada Allison, and Captain Hart houses formed one political group with Manilla Pepple while Anna Pepple headed the other group and could be counted upon to oppose whatever they advocated.

By 1858 this cleavage had become clear even to the consul, who reported that Captain Hart had just died, and that Ada Allison was excluded 'as far as comey was concerned'. The 'senior regents' were Ntshaka or Manilla Pepple, the 'head of the most extensive and most powerful house now in Bonny' and Anna Pepple (Iloli), who was reported as 'having taken too much power on himself as well as too much comey and did nothing for it'. Manilla Pepple was already asking for the return of the deposed king William Dappa Pepple from his exile, 'though conscious that from loss of all the ex-king's property and slaves he could only possess a shadow of authority in Bonny at the present time'. The consul gave the council a better balanced division by appointing Wogu Dappa the head of King Dappo's house as a regent in place of the deceased Captain Hart. He also gave Manilla Pepple, who styled himself head regent, a paper of manumission. The next year fighting broke out on 25th of April between the Anna Pepple subordinate house of Oko Epelle, and the Oko Jumbo house. Both parties according to the consular report were fined by the regents at the consul's request, but the fighting was resumed on 22 May, the houses which faced each other across an open square, shooting it out from 9 a.m. to 3 p.m. with pieces of ordinance from 3 pounds calibre up to 34 pounds and some Lancaster guns.[38] The supercargoes assembled and went ashore to arrange a truce, and summoned the consul, who arrived and fined both parties 100 puncheons of oil each. At the request of both sides the fine was reduced to 50 puncheons each on condition that they

---

[36] Three of his wives were said to be pregnant.
[37] Hertslet, Vol. X, p. 25. P.P. 1865, Vol. LXII.
[38] Captain Reuben Hemingway's evidence, in a document dated 29/10/59, a copy of which was submitted to me at Bonny. No trace of the original in Foreign Office Records, and F.O. 84/1087.

undertook[39] not to use guns and cannon again in Bonny town. Iloli at first refused to sign, but on a threat by the supercargoes and the other regents that he should cease to be a regent or be received on board the European ships, he agreed and 'pledged himself to unite with the other regents'. At the same time a petition was submitted by 'the more powerful of the Manilla Pepple chiefs, amongst whom were now included 'Ada Allison, Odge (Oge) Hart, and Ossa and Ominoma Brown (Jack Brown)', which asked for the return of King William Dappa Pepple and stated that 'neither Manilla Pepple nor Anna Pepple were strong enough to rule the country'.

In 1861 King William Dappa Pepple returned to Bonny and Richard Burton became consul of the Bight of Biafra and in December of that year reported that the 'King's greatest enemy Ilola (Annie) Pepple had been stricken with paralysis.' King William Dappa began his new reign by getting on the wrong side of the European community. Claiming that his visit to England had abrogated all existing treaties, he demanded an increased rate of comey (10/– in place of the customary 5 bars which now amounted to about 3/4); he also attempted to sell the rights to trade in the hinterland of the Bonny river, 'which was not his property' to an Anglo-French firm. Protests reached the Foreign Secretary from the Liverpool merchants and the consul was instructed to inform him of the 'illegality of these actions'. He did so by letter but forbore to visit the river with a naval vessel because of a severe outbreak there of yellow fever. The Bonny chiefs knew nothing about the attempt to sell the Bonny river trading rights but they supported the king in his demands for increased comey. When the European traders refused to accept them King Dappa stopped trade on 26 December 1863. The embargo lasted for about two months when the chiefs abandoned it and reopened trade on 19 February 1864. The following month the consul arrived, called a meeting of the court of equity and when the king refused to attend had him brought there by force. The king and chiefs 'could offer no other excuse (for the breach of the treaty of 1850) than they wanted money and must have it' and 'seeing that it was necessary to arrest these disorders and that the King having been abetted by his chiefs will be aided by them in paying the fine' the consul took 'strong measures' and fined King Pepple 240 puncheons of tradeable oil'. The fine was paid early the following year in 1865, when Commander Ruxton, H.M.S. *Pandora*, visited the river and agreed to reduce it by half. Meanwhile Iloli Anna Pepple had

---

[39] 'swore juju', according to Captain Hemingway.

died on April 1862 and, if we accept Burton's account, Jaja was chosen by the 'boys', that is, the 'juniors of the house', as their chief in 1863; but Oko Epelle, who later quarrelled with Jaja claimed that Annie Stewart was first elected and then deposed, while de Cardi has stated[40] that none of the other more senior chiefs of the group were prepared to accept the office because of the debts which Iloli had left his successor. Ncheke, the head of the Manilla main house, had also died 'early in 1863' and 'the well known Oko Jumbo and Will Bannigo' being unable each to witness the rise of the other agreed that one Wogro (Warribo), a 'boy' of 'old Jack Manilla' should 'come up for chief. He cannot expect the deference due to an old man and but for the peril of disunion the party would split into three'. In the consul's opinion there was 'at present an ominous calm in Bonny which will not improbably end in a tornado. The resident inhabitants of Grand Bonny may be 5,000 souls and the floating 4,000 more. Two great houses of slave chiefs now contend for superiority and they are so equally balanced that the present puppet King remains in position. In case of a fight each side could raise 2,500 musketeers, they have an abundance of ammunition, ships, swivels and carronades and when hostilities break out they will be equally bloody to the natives and injurious if not dangerous to the Europeans'.[41]

As soon as he became head of the Anna Pepple main house Jaja set about implementing secret plans, on which, as he later admitted,[42] he had been working for some time. It was clear to him that there was no immediate prospect of the Anna Pepple house becoming dominant in Bonny as the Manilla group was too powerful. Even if the Anna Pepple house did achieve this its head would never be accepted in Bonny as King, as he was not of Pepple or of Asimini or Alagbaria descent. It was also becoming clearer to some of the more farsighted European and African traders that the principal reasons for keeping the trading port close to the sea no longer applied, now that steam was superseding sail and vessels of shallow draft had been developed for use on inland waterways, and now that a prophylaxis against malaria had been discovered to enable Europeans to live in the malarious hinterland. There were considerable economic advantages to be gained by moving closer to the oil markets, and fortunes to be made by those traders who made the first move. For Jaja and

[40] de Cardi, p. 526.
[41] Burton's letter in F.O. 84/1221.
[42] To Consul Hewitt. F.O. 84/1593.

the Anna Pepple group there were political advantages as well. Jaja could become the founder and king of a new community, and if this communtity was established near where the Imo river entered the Delta his people could cut off their Bonny rivals from their hinterland oil markets.

By this time most of the so-called independent houses had become attached to one or other of the Anna Pepple or Manilla houses these attachments being created in some cases, and reinforced in others, by ties of financial dependence. The Anna Pepple house in particular was accused of having paid the debts of some of these houses and advanced money to others for this purpose. Jaja was not yet ready for war and preferred to be conciliatory, and without any consular intervention an agreement was reached in which he and his chiefs signed the undertaking reproduced below:[43]

Bonny Town January 7. 1865

We, Annie Pepple, party chiefs etc. do hereby and for the future agree to give up the following parties viz: Tillibor alias Gogo Foobra, Fine Bone, Sonjo, Black Foobra, Strong Face, Oko Eppelleh, Antonio, Tom Brown, Tobin, John Africa, Jack Tellifare, Warrisoo, Semah Sunju, Young Trader, and Tarribor, to be masters of their own houses, and to have no interference with their house and trade businesses and managements; and they the above named parties also promised not to give or sell themselves or house to Annie Pepple, Manilla Pepple or to any person or persons whatever; but in the event of any disputes arising between any two houses they are to endeavour with the juju men to settle such disputes amicably.

| Annie Pepple | Wogo Dappa | Toby Stuart |
| Annie Stuart | | Uranta. |

The idea behind this agreement, which was later supported by the consul, was that these and other 'independent' houses should form a 'neutral party' which might maintain some kind of balance between the Anna Pepple and Manilla Pepple parties. But whatever the Anna Pepple party may have undertaken to do in this agreement, the majority of the houses named in it remained firmly behind the Anna Pepple house[44] while the independent houses not named in the agreement remained as firmly behind the Manilla Pepple house. Bonny meanwhile had become involved in the war between Kalabari

---

[43] Reproduced in Hertslet's [Treaties Vol. XIII. No record of it in F.O. correspondence.
[44] Exceptions were Antonio and Tobin subordinate houses of Brown group and Oko Epelle whose chief had a quarrel with Jaja. Young Trader and Tarribor houses are extinct and not traced.

and Okrika which is discussed in the chapter following. King William Dappa Pepple was dying and his son George taking his place,[45] but the accepted leaders of Bonny were now Oko Jumbo of the Manilla Pepple faction and Jaja of the Anna Pepple. Warribo had, either now or a little later,[46] been deposed from the headship of the Manilla Pepple house and Oko Jumbo was now so powerful that he could support William Banigo taking over the headship of the main house. Tension between the two groups continued to mount until on March 2nd 1867 it was temporarily relieved by a brawl between members of the houses of Ada Allison (Manilla Pepple faction) and Charley Africa (Anna Pepple) which developed into a 'civil skirmish' between supporters of the two parties and 'soon all the low men in Bonny were fighting with matchets and gin bottles, there being no stones in the town'. The skirmish, which kept within the terms of the 1859 undertaking not to use guns in Bonny, was ended by King George, who brandished a pistol and 'threatened to blow some of their brains out'.[47] The consul however considered that an agreement should be drawn up for the preservation of the peace in Bonny and this was done on 20 January 1869 in an agreement which repeated and elaborated the conditions agreed to in 1865 in regard to the neutral party, and forbade fighting with firearms or guns of any description or the ambushing and seizure of canoes both 'in the country' and 'in Eboe'.[48]

Jaja was now ready to move. A fire had destroyed three-quarters of the town and provided an additional reason for leaving. The quarrel between Oko Epelle and Jaja came to a head. Oko Epelle claimed to be an independent house on the grounds that his master the founder of the house was a freeman who had attached himself voluntarily to the Anna Pepple main house, because he wanted to trade and could not speak English. Although in the 1865 agreement he had undertaken to renounce all claims over it, Jaja now claimed the Epelle house as part of the Anna Pepple group. The Manilla chiefs naturally supported Oko Epelle's claims and Jaja allowed the situation to develop until on Sunday, 12 September 1869 the Anna Pepple group sent a challenge to the Manilla Pepple group to fight. The Manilla Pepple group replied that they could not fight on Sunday 'we serve God today but we be ready for other service tomorrow at noon'. The bombardment began at noon on the 13th

---

[45] He signed as George Rex first in 1867.
[46] The European records do not refer to this.
[47] F.O. 84/1277.
[48] Appendix B. 5.

in the usual way, each group firing at the other across the open space in the centre of Bonny town. It continued until the 14th when in the words of the consul 'Anna Pepple's men ran away. Very few men were killed, King George's palace suffered most as it stood between the hostile cannon. Not a stick was left. The King had prudently retired to Juju Town on Sunday.' Oko Jumbo, the real head of the Manilla Pepple house, declared that he was ready for a settlement between them saying, 'we be tired of war, it cost too much, before our niggers worked for us now we have to support them in idleness'. It was proposed to fine Anna Pepple a 'moderate sum' and to 'concluded a treaty on the basis that both set free all the small houses recently absorbed as a powerful body of small independent houses is deemed a political necessity.'[49]

But Anna Pepple never came back, the artillery duel was a blind to cover the withdrawal of his group to the Andoni country, where he established himself as king of the new state of Opobo and was joined there by way of the E-Kom-Toro river, by the Brass traders de Cardi and McEachen.

Bonny was also actively involved in the war with Kalabari described in the next chapter. The Andoni remained neutral; they accepted Jaja in their territory and supported him in this establishment of the new town and port of Opobo, but continued to remain on friendly terms with Bonny. The war whether against Kalabari or Jaja was indecisive and casualties were negligible, both sides took up entrenched and stockaded positions, avoided pitched battles and confined themselves to raids upon outlying settlements of their enemies and ambushing and interfering with their enemies' trading canoes. But to these states who lived by trade, it was very costly both in money and in time, and they could not afford to continue it for long. By 1871 Kalabari and Bonny were ready to avail themselves of the consul's unceasing efforts to arrange first a truce and then a treaty. The war with Jaja went on longer. The British community at Bonny were naturally strongly behind the Bonny chiefs and pressed for British intervention on the grounds that a continuation of the war would ruin the oil trade. All that was needed to end it, they felt, was a consular embargo on trade with Jaja. The acting consul agreed with them. The consul, Livingstone, did not and as long as Jaja could go on trading he could afford to wait. In 1872 Livingstone wrote 'The Bonny Opobo difficulty may now be considered in fact practically settled. Jaja has all the Eboe and Qua markets and our

[49] F.O. 84/1308

five great English firms in the Opobo are doing an immense trade. Oko Jumbo has the Okrika markets and the eight firms in Bonny are doing a comparatively small trade. But the total of oil from the two rivers is probably as great'.[50] The accounts of the warfare were grossly exaggerated and Oko Jumbo had said 'that they never knew anything about them till they read the accounts in the Liverpool papers'. By December both sides agreed to submit to the arbitration of New Calabar and Okrika and on 3 January 1873 they signed a treaty under which six markets on the Imo were assigned exclusively to Bonny, and all members and houses claimed by Jaja as part of the Anna Pepple group and who were still in Bonny were to be 'returned to Opobo'.[51] Most of them, for example Warriso and George Goodhead, had already made their way to Opobo, the most important remaining ones were Kuke (Cookey), and Oko Epelle and their people. Kuke had with George Goodhead sought asylum at Juju town (Finnema). Oko Epelle had been fighting against Jaja and he refused to remove to Opobo. The consul immediately applied an embargo on trade in Bonny until Oko had been made to comply with the treaty. The Secretary of State, shocked at this gross interference with Oko Epelle's personal liberty, ordered its immediate revocation. But by the time his despatch had arrived Oko Epelle had gone to Opobo and made his peace with Jaja and trade had been resumed.

But trade never returned to Bonny, the bulk of the Imo oil trade and most of the Anang (Qua) remained with Opobo which replaced Bonny as the wealthiest and most powerful Eastern Delta state. Jaja was able to enjoy his triumph for a brief decade and then came into conflict with the British Government which had now taken over the country. Jaja, who had pioneered the inland movement of trade from Bonny to Opobo, now found himself trying to stop the British carrying this trade still further inland. He was deported and the Bonny and Opobo monopoly of the Imo and Qua trade was broken though Opobo continued as the main port for the Imo river oil trade for another thirty years.[52]

[50] F.O. 84/1356.
[51] Appendix B 8.
[52] The final transfer of this trade to Aba and to the Eastern Railway did not come until 1927 and was one of the principal local causes of the 'Women's Riots' of 1929, in which thirty-one Opobo market women lost their lives in an attack upon the Opobo Government Treasury.

In 1864	In :
	Black Du [Duke A Jack Ree
Standfast Jack B	Standfast Young Ja
Will Barboy B Will Braid B	[Will Bra
Jim Braid B	[Marian [Davis B [Jim Brai
George Will B	George V
Manuel A Horsefall Manuel B	Bob Man Horsefall Manue Charlie H
Dick Barboy B	
Don Pedro B	[Bealnut Young D Granville

IX

The History of Kalabari

I. PREHISTORY

EARLIER oral traditions[1] trace the movement to Elem Kalabari in the Eastern Delta of an Ijo community called Owame, residing near the Ibo village community of Amafo on the right (west) bank of the New Calabar river. Here they formed one of a number of small independent Ijo communities of heterogeneous origin, some of whom claim to have moved into the delta previously to Kalabari, others to have always been there. Contemporary traditions refer to the founder of this community as Kalabari, whom they derive from the Mein group of Ijo tribes of the Central Delta. His son Ende, they say, led this migration from Amafo and he was joined at Elem Kalabari by another group of migrants from the East ('from Efik') under Opu-koro-ye, who brought with them Owame Akaso the tutelary deity of the community. This community, which became known as Kalabari, was composed of a number of wards of independent origin, the most important of which were those of Ende (Endeme) and of Opu-koro-ye (Korome).

Contemporary tradition also refers to an Ibo doctor Kamalu, who succeeded to the leadership of Endeme, and to a period when the neighbouring village of Bile was temporarily dominant under its King Agbaniye Ejike.

2. PROTOHISTORY

The 'time of Owerri Daba'

Neither the early nor the contemporary tradition makes any reference to the period when Kalabari was the principal slave-trading state on the Rio Real and legends of the origin of this trade are placed either in the prehistoric dawn period of Owame, where it is connected with Opu-koro-ye,[2] or in the 'recent' and historic period of Amakiri.

---

[1] E.g. those collected by Talbot in 2.
[2] E.g. in the Jack Rich house tradition.

References however to another period, 'the time of King Owerri Daba', survive in the Korome ward (Kalabari) traditions and in Bonny legends and this king is associated with the introduction of the slave trade to Kalabari and to Bonny and of the cult of the Long Juju of Arochuku to the delta, and is regarded as the founder of the Kalabari houses of Duke Monmouth and Duke Africa and of the house now known as John Africa in Bonny. These traditions suggest a period when Korome was the dominant ward in Kalabari and when the section which traced its descent to Owerri Daba supplied its kings. They also indicate a period of civil strife which resulted in the fission and dispersal of this section, part remaining in Kalabari and part removing to Bonny. We can assume that this happened before 1699, since James Barbot records having given presents to two Duke Monmouths—one at Bonny and the other at Kalabari. Of the other Kalabari chiefs whom he names—King Robert, the Duke of York and Captain Jan Alkmaers—we can say nothing except that King Robert was probably one of the kings of that Endeme dynasty which traced its descent from Kamalu and which, according to tradition, was ruling before the time of Amakiri.

The 'time of King Amakiri'

No eighteenth century record makes any reference to the founder of the Amakiri dynasty and for a chronicle of his reign we have to rely entirely on oral tradition. It is clear however that he must have been adult at least by the mid-eighteenth century to have accumulated the wealth that enabled him to lead his people to victory in the period of general warfare which Bonny, Kalabari, and Okrika traditions all refer to. He must also have been alive late enough in that century to have begotten Karibo (Amakiri III) who died in 1863. If we accept the traditions about Ogoloye Fubra he must also have survived well into the reign of Opobo, that is, into the nineteenth century. There is not so much difficulty here, however, as with the founder of the Pepple dynasty. In the first place we do not have to try and take Amakiri back to the time of James Barbot and in the second place Kalabari traditions all stress the fact that Amakiri died at an advanced old age. A very long reign is also supported by structural consideration as well as by tradition. Reference to Table 4 will show the number of houses which derive directly from Amakiri. The establishment of the Odum (Barboy) and Ombo (Harry) canoe house groups would have been more than sufficient for a normal reign and would equate with the number of houses founded by King Pepple of Bonny, but there are in addition the Briggs, the West India, and the Birinomoni groups and these were obviously, as their traditions maintain, established at a later date than the two senior groups.

The oral traditions of the foundation and subsequent fortunes of the Kalabari canoe houses are much fuller than those of Bonny and afford us a very clear picture of the structural development of Kalabari during the early nineteenth century. They have been examined in Appendix A. Most of them were founded in the reign of King Amakiri and their traditions taken together with the Amakiri legendary cycle suggest a division of his reign into three successive periods, the first when the Kalabari state was fighting for its existence, the second when Amakiri was consolidating his position and the Kalabari social structure as we know it today was established, and the third when Amakiri was in his dotage and when the political division that characterized the Kalabari political system in the nineteenth century was developed.

It is not possible to attribute any definite dates to these periods and many of the particular episodes preserved in the separate traditions of the various houses may have occurred either in the second or third period.

a. *The early period*

Traditions would like us to believe that the seven independent sections or wards of Kalabari, after a disastrous fire and other calamities, decided to summon Amakiri to become their leader and this may well be true. Fires, as the historical records of the nineteenth century show, were a fairly regular occurrence in the overcrowded and inflammable settlements of New Calabar and Bonny and with the quantities of gunpowder stored there they could be very devastating. It was a period of warfare, the most outstanding episode of which was a very successful raid by Okrika, which found Elem Kalabari unguarded and with most of her men absent in the up-river markets. Another episode of this period was a battle at Opu Ido in the Andoni country in which the Kalabari, presumably fighting with the Andoni, defeated Bonny. Kalabari traditions claim that in this battle Amakoro the son of Amakiri killed Okoni, a chief of Bonny, and that Igbulu the King of Bonny's eldest son was drowned and his head brought back and used in a Kalabari Peri dance. Bonny traditions record the death of Igbulu, fighting against Andoni. The present Kalabari village of Ido claims that after this battle

K

to avoid King Pepple's revenge for Igbulu's death, the people of Opu Ido dispersed, some going to Okrika and others, who were their founders, joining Amakiri and being shown a place to settle by him.

b. *The middle period*

This was a period of consolidation during which according to tradition King Amakiri repeopled the town by the purchase of slaves from the hinterland thereby increasing its wards from seven to fourteen. The Amakiri legends also depict the king as bringing all the outlying communities in the Kalabari territory under his sway, either by contributing to the restoration of their ritual and other buildings, or by protecting them from the attack of their enemies or by offering them asylum when they were fleeing from the wrath of the King of Bonny, and the legends all stress the pacific and protective policy of King Amakiri in contrast to the violently destructive behaviour of King Agbaniye Ekije of Bile. A comparative study of the traditions of these satellite and dependent villages and of the Bonny tradition shows, however, that there is no means of determining when and how most of these communities became attached to the Kalabari state. The control over distant villages exercised by this state obviously depended upon the amount of power and wealth it possessed at any given time. What is clear however, is that with the introduction of the canoe house system and the continual foundation of new canoe houses, these villages became increasingly drawn into the Kalabari political system, as an ever increasing number of their menfolk became attached to these canoe houses and involved in the rivalries between the different canoe house groups.

It is also quite obvious that whereas some communities like Ido were probably offered asylum by Kalabari 'in the time of King Amakiri' others like Tombia and Abalama had removed from the Bonny area to the neighbourhood of Elem Kalabari very much earlier. Similarly the traditions preserved by some of these communities, notably Kula, maintain that they were reduced by force of arms.

The picture of the expansion of Elem Kalabari from seven to fourteen wards is revealed as myth rather than historic fact, as soon as the traditions of existing Kalabari houses are examined. It was indeed a period of expansion but this expansion was primarily that of the Endeme ward, and it was also at the expense of other wards. It was during this period, for instance, that the Korome ward disintegrated and ceased to be a politically effective unit. Seliye

Fubra, the head of its most powerful segment, had lost the favour of the gods by refusing the kingship, and in the Okrika raid the Korome suffered more than any other ward. Later its strength was still further reduced when, after an affray between its members and those of Amakiri's house, the house was punished by being ordered to transfer Asukein, one of its leaders, and his people to Amakiri's house. By now the Endeme ward had segmented into two divisions, one headed by Awo, son of Amakiri's stepfather Kalagbea and therefore a descendant of the previous Kamalu line of kings, the other by Ombo, the son of Amakiri's slave and derived directly from Amakiri's own household. Awo died prematurely and was succeeded by his son Odum and tradition makes Odum and Ombo the principal chiefs and henchmen of Amakiri, Odum being placed in charge of his barracoons and Ombo of his cask houses, Odum's English name of Barboy is said to be a corruption of Barracoon Boy. But Ombo's English name was Harry and it is unlikely that Amakiri survived long enough to see the establishment of either barracoons or cask houses. Barboy could more easily be associated with another function, for which this house with its close association with Ifoko village was famed, that of pilotage of vessels over the bar.

This expansion resulted not only from the introduction of slave members from the Ibo hinterland but also from the absorption of the personnel of other houses, sometimes as a result of conflicts settled by judicial action, as in the case of Asukein, but mainly by more peaceful methods. There is a tradition of the Briggs house which traces its origin to Duenala (Black Jim) who so embarrassed his house of Akialame as a result of his gambling losses that they sold him to Amakiri to help meet his debts. He became a faithful henchman of his master and his success in getting people from Akialame and other wards to sell or otherwise transfer themselves to Amakiri's group earned him the nickname of 'Amakiri's retriever', and the reward of being established as chief of his own canoe house. These and other traditions record much the same techniques of absorption of the personnel of declining houses as we find being used in Bonny and Kalabari in the later nineteenth century.

c. *The period of Amakiri's old age*
This was a time when King Amakiri was too old to rule firmly and to control the actions of his sons and other powerful chiefs. The princes Owuso and Amakoro and chiefs like Asukein, Ogoloye Fubra, Okwu, and Amakiri Oboko (Big Fowl) were fighting among

themselves and raiding any village that had incurred their wrath or their cupidity. Internally the rivalry between the Amakiri and Barboy divisions came to a head in a dispute which tradition represents as a quarrel between Prince Owuso and Odum, and the latter was obliged to withdraw to Onya village. Asukein, the head of the Duenala house, took to piracy, that is, he ambushed and looted the canoes of his rivals. Ogoloye Fubra supported him and had to seek asylum in Bonny. Okwu of the Sofa house 'fought with the town' until Amakiri made peace between him and the other chiefs. No village in the Kalabari territory was safe unless it had established close relationship with a powerful Kalabari house which placed it under its protection. Amakiri Oboko (Amakiri's cock) had earned his name, which became anglicized as Big Fowl, because he was for ever crowing to wake his king up and to urge him to go to war. He eventually met his death in a raid on Ilelema village,[3] while Ogoloye Fubra, Orikadibia, Elebike, and some say even Prince Owuso, raided Bonny.

This was also the period when the West India and Birinomoni canoe house group came into being. Their founders were warriors and traders who had made their names and their fortunes in Amakiri's later years. For instance Nwananaku (Hand, Annie) was the captain of King Amakiri's war canoe when the king was too old to lead his people into battle and when Awo, the founder of the Barboy house who had been the drummer in Amakiri's original war canoe had long been dead. Duenala (Black Jim) was also dead, Asukein had succeeded him and the canoe house that became the West India group was formed of Orikadibia, Elebike, Osiagu, and Eleru and their followers to live in the same part of Elem Kalabari and control him. By this time Elem Kalabari was so overcrowded that there was no more space left for new houses, and the name given to the house founded by Nwananaku, Amakiri Oboko (Big Fowl), Angaenemenea, and Ejemenike is derived from Biri, quarter, and Omoni, slaves, tradition explaining that by the time this house was founded the only place left for settlement was beside and among the slave barracoons.

d. *The reign of King Amakoro* (*Amakiri II*)

There are no references to Amakiri's immediate successor in the English records and Kalabari tradition has remembered very little about his reign. It tells us that Amakiri's eldest son Prince Owuso died before him and it implies that Amakoro's succession to the throne

---

[3] A village in the Kalabari tribal territory.

was uneventful. The 'authorized version' maintains that his reign was short and peaceful. Other traditions say that he raided and destroyed outlying villages, but these may refer to the time when he was still a prince and achieving his nickname of Tiger. The fact that his succession was peaceful suggests that he had for some time before his accession been acting for his father. The shortness of his reign is supported by the facts that apart from his own house of Tiger Amakiri, which was founded in his father's reign, there are no other houses which trace their origin to him, and that the only canoe house which tradition claims to have been founded in his reign was that of Owukori (Manuel).

3. HISTORY

The reign of King Karibo (Amakiri III)

In contrast with Amakoro's the reign of Karibo is said to have been a long one and other factors support this. Karibo came to the throne as chief of a single canoe house and by the time he died this had expanded into one of the wealthiest and most powerful canoe house groups in Kalabari, and this despite the fact that other powerful canoe house groups, the Barboy and the Ombo, were also expanding. This suggests a reign of more than average length. We have also the evidence of the ivory trading tokens which are associated with chiefs who attained their position during Karibo's reign, and this suggests a date for Karibo's accession well before the dates recorded on the tokens, namely 1834 and 1836. We know that he died in 1863.

The death of King Amakoro brought the rivalry between the Barboy and the Amakiri (Ombo) groups to a head in a struggle over the succession. According to tradition Amakiri had entrusted his two sons Prince Ekine and Prince Karibo to the care of these two groups. Prince Ekine who is said to have been the elder was the Barboy candidate, Prince Karibo the Ombo. Peace was restored and the dispute settled in favour of Prince Karibo by Edi Abali (Harry Braid), a chief of the Ombo group who began his career as a bought slave and had built up his wealth and power while resident in Tombia village (New Town), and who now returned to throw his weight decisively into the scales. Thenceforward he remained the head of the Ombo group in its external affairs, though not the chief of the main house (Big Harry) as the succession was confined to direct descendants of Ombo. Tradition does not relate on which sides the other house groups were ranged, nor does the war between Barboy and Amakiri (Ombo) appear to have been very sustained. The only important casualty that tradition can now remember was Taria (Goodhead) of the Birinomoni group, who lost an eye in the fighting.

King Karibo was an able administrator and trader. The earlier part of his reign, according to tradition, was peaceful and prosperous and it saw the consolidation and expansion not only of the king's house but of other groups of houses as well. In addition to the would-be dominant houses of Barboy (Odum) and Harry (Ombo), lesser groups which had suffered a decline were able to rally and re-establish themselves—West India under Datubo, Duenala under Oruwari (Briggs), Standfast Jack under Oba. King Karibo preferred to live at peace with the Barboy group and although Harry (Ombo) tradition claims that Edi Abali (Harry Braid) was Karibo's principal chief and 'prime minister' it is clear that at least by 1850, when we can refer to historical records, it was the chief of the Barboy group who appears to have been ranked after the king. This name, Will Barboy, appears on most of the early treaties before Harry Braid and usually immediately after 'King Amachree'. We can assume that by this time Kombo Agolea (Barboy Braid), a bought slave of the Barboy house, had succeeded Otaji (Long Will) as chief of the Barboy main house. The fact (related in Appendix A) that he was a brother (*Mbre*) real or classificatory, of Edi Abali (Harry Braid), the chief of the Harry (Ombo) group, may have temporarily eased the rivalry between these two groups.

With the establishment of a British consul at Fernando Po Kalabari reappeared in historical records. Consul Beecroft lost little time in making his authority felt at Elem Kalabari. The traditional anchorage for vessels trading in the New Calabari river with the Kalabari state was opposite Ifoko. The Kalabari king and chiefs had been able to make the supercargoes come further upriver and anchor opposite Elem Kalabari, which the traders believed was inimical to the health of their crews. The king was also making what the supercargoes described as exhorbitant demands for comey. The consul visited Elem Kalabari on 1st October 1850 in H.M.S. *Jackal*, and ordered the European shipping to move downstream to Fouchee (Ifoko). He went ashore and called upon the king and asked him to return the visit the following day on board H.M.S. *Jackal*. When the king failed to do so a messenger was sent ashore to inform him that he 'had insulted the British Flag and also the Queen of England's representative and that if he did not deem it fit to fulfill his duty he would be corrected for not returning the visit'. King Karibo appeared to the messenger to be ready to return the visit but his chiefs would not let him. Lieutenant Beddington was then asked to fire a shot over the town, and after half an hour to fire another shot. After another half hour he was asked to fire a shot 'at the roof of one of the principal houses. The instant the gun was depressed and pointed at this house and its flagstaff up went the Flag of truce. They had been watching all our movements with spy glasses. A boat was sent ashore and shortly afterward the King and his second in command made their appearance'.[4] The name of this chief was not given but the mark which follows King Amachree's on the treaty is that of Will Barboy. This commercial treaty of 1850 was signed without further delay, in the 'King's mansion' at half-past three the following day. Its form was the same as that of the Bonny treaty which was signed by the king and chiefs of Bonny the next day.[5] The only significant differences between these two treaties of 1850 were the inclusion, in the New Calabar treaty, of a clause (Article XIII) defining Fouchee as the trading anchorage and, in the Bonny treaty, of three articles relating to difficulties over the protection of cask houses and to abuses of the trust system which only affected Bonny (Articles IX, XVI and part of VIII). It is to be assumed that there was little serious trouble over the trust system in Kalabari. Beecroft's successors maintained that King Amakiri (Karibo) had forbidden trust in his dominions but it is very doubtful if this was correct. Trust was such an essential part of the trading system of these Oil River states that it is difficult to see how it could have operated without it. All the descriptions of the system of trade on these rivers[6] stress its uniformity in this respect, while explaining other differences, for example in the matter of currencies. We know that at the end of the period trust was being given in Kalabari but only to house heads, and in 1887 Sir Walter Hunt Grubb in his address to the chiefs of the Oil Rivers Protectorate specifically referred to the New Calabar chiefs as being obstinate debtors and named three of them—King Amachree (Abbe), George Amachree, and John Bull.[7] It would be safer therefore to assume that Karibo and his chiefs

[4] F.O. 84/816.
[5] The preamble even refers to 'renewing Articles I, II and III of the former Treaty dated 9 April 1837', this being the Bonny treaty of that date, for no such treaty was ever signed by the Kalabari. For these two treaties see Hertslet Vol. IX, p. 24 and Appendix B 2.
[6] Whether given by Smith, Hutchinson, Burton, Livingstone or de Cardi.
[7] F.O. 84/1828.

had agreed to prohibit the giving of trust except when supported by adequate security, such security being provided by the chief of the house through which the debtor traded. Such a prohibition would operate to the advantage of both European traders and the chiefs of these houses. Consul Beecroft himself was convinced that trust was an evil which should be stopped and inserted a clause into both treaties in which the king 'shall not, nor shall he permit any of his chiefs to demand or enforce any trust from any of the ships upon any pretence whatever'.[8] But this remained a dead article as far as Bonny was concerned and presumably in New Calabar as well.

Beecroft also approached King Karibo about the signing of a treaty to prohibit the slave trade in his dominions, similar to that signed by the kings of Old Calabar and Bonny. King Karibo said he would prefer to receive a commission on every slaver whose presence he betrayed to the British Naval authorities. It would appear from Beecroft's reply that this trade had recommenced in the New Calabar river.[9]

King Karibo and his chiefs may have agreed to sign a commercial treaty but they had no intention of adhering to it. In February 1851 they insisted that the European ships return to the Elem Kalabari anchorage and demanded payment of the old comey to the king and to the 'Juju-King', refusing to break trade for them unless they did so. The supercargoes were not prepared to submit to these demands and trade was stopped on the New Calabar river for nine weeks. On the 7th August the consul was able to visit Elem Kalabari again and the same procedure was followed when the king failed to answer the consul's summons. After two shots had been fired 'at the juju house' one of which went right through it, Jim Amakiri 'the King's son came off with his father's mouth' asking them to fire no more and promising that his father would come off the following morning. On the 8th Captain Stone (one of the supercargoes) went to fetch them and eventually King Karibo arrived 'accompanied by Will Braid, Will Barboy, Emanuel and West India'. The consul pointed out that the king 'had broken all the articles on the commercial treaty except two' and fined him fifty puncheons of oil which later he agreed to reduce to thirty. A new anchorage for the European shipping was negotiated, the King wanted it 'off juju point' the consul

---

[8] Articles X of the Bonny and IX of the New Calabar treaty.

[9] Beecroft refers to a slaver he (Karibo) had allowed to resume this traffic in this river which had been captured by H.M. Brig. *Contest*. F.O. 84/816, and to another which had got away successfully and which he thought was the *Deseada* which was captured on its second visit in July 1857 by H.M.S. *Bloodhound* (84/856).

off Fouchee but agreed to a position between Young Town and Brass Creek. 'The next palaver was the treaty for the suppression of the foreign slave trade. It being fully explained to him. I (the consul) succeeded in getting it signed on the spot'. It was the same in form and content as those signed by Bonny and Old Calabar but the inferiority of New Calabar, at least in consular evaluation, was to be seen in the compensation provided. For Old Calabar this was a present of 2000 dollars (Spanish) annually for five years, for Bonny 'an annual present for five years of goods of British manufacture to the value of 2,000 dollars'. But for New Calabar the value of the goods was 1,000 dollars and the period three years. The same compensation was proposed for Brass (Nembe) in the event of the consul getting its kings to sign such a treaty.[10]

A Spanish slaver, the *Deseada*, had been captured by the H.M.S. *Bloodhound* the previous month. Ten were all that could be found of her complement of slaves, and after having made arrangements for their transfer to Bonny and for the collection of King Amachree's fine the consul returned to Bonny where he proceeded to fine King Pepple and his chiefs for breaches of the Bonny Treaty of Commerce.

The British supercargoes and the Kalabari chiefs viewed the commercial treaty in very different lights. The former hoped to use it to minimize the exactions, 'customs bars', 'shake hands' and other 'dashes', imposed upon them by the Kalabari rulers; the latter, having signed it under duress, had no intention of adhering to it unless it suited them or unless they were forced to do so.

The treaty like the original Bonny treaty of 1837 represented an attempt to codify the trading conventions which had come into being during the early nineteenth century and which by 1850 were already out of date. Apart from the depreciation of the iron bar, the unit of currency in which comey was assessed, those firms which had established themselves in the oil trade of the Rio Real were consolidating their position, and the supercargoes of visiting merchant vessels were being replaced by a limited number of resident agents permanently stationed in hulks on the New Calabar and Bonny rivers. The supercargo of a ship made a formal present called in Bonny 'shake hands' to the king on commencing trade, but resident traders who remained in the river for a much longer period might be expected to pay a proportionately higher 'dash'. This seems to

[10] See treaties dated respectively 6/12/41, 21/11/48, and 8/8/51. Hertslet Vol. VIII, p. 878, Vol. VIII, p. 51, and Vol. IX, p. 26. Provisions banning slave trading were eventually inserted as Article I of the Brass commercial treaty (Appendix B 4).

have been the main cause of a dispute between the European and Kalabari traders which brought the consul back to Elem Kalabari in December 1852. The consul read over the treaty to King Karibo who 'had broken it by not opening the Hulk Andois's trade although comey was paid. He demanded the customs bars 480 of which was paid, the latter is optional, the same at Bonny.'[11] 'Customs bars' in this despatch would appear to refer to 'shake hands', for the 'Custom bars' referred to by Beecroft's successors was a tax paid by African traders to the chief of their house. We know from later Bonny sources that this dispute was settled by the payment of 'a large present' by an agent on his assumption or resumption of his office',[12] and we can assume that it was settled in a similar manner in New Calabar. No further reference to it occurs in the correspondence, and the next trouble in which consular intervention was called for was a dispute over the alteration of the size of the casks in which the oil was collected. The European traders complained that the Kalabari traders had learnt the craft of coopering and altered the size of casks which were given out to them by the Europeans for the collection of oil. These difficulties were eventually settled by an agreement to standardize the size of casks and in January 1855 the acting consul Lynslagher visited Elem Kalabari, and with the king and chiefs and supercargoes drew up and signed additional articles to the Treaty of commerce which fixed the size of the cask (puncheon) of oil at 40 inches. When this proved unsatisfactory further additional articles were made and signed in September which reduced the size to 38 inches, which was the same as that used at Bonny.[13]

Consul Beecroft had died the previous year and his successor Consul Hutchinson reached Fernando Po in 1856. With a new consul in office the Kalabari chiefs attempted to revive the 'ancient custom' of the 'juju king' receiving additional comey. The supercargoes petitioned the consul who wrote to King Karibo in 1857 drawing his attention to the Commercial Treaty and in January of the following year visited Elem Kalabari. There was no need for a display of gun fire. The king and his chiefs and the juju king, whose name was given as Akoko, came aboard promptly; the consul explained 'that Her Majesty's government recognized king Amachree only' and 'after a few minutes in conversation with his chiefs and the juju king, who it would appear agreed in his arguments, he promised me (the consul)

---

[11] F.O. 84/920.
[12] Referred to in Consul Hewitt's despatch of 19 April 1886, F.O. 84/1749
[13] Hertslet, Vol. X, p. 19 and p. 26.

faithfully that it would not occur again'. This was the last occasion on which the consul had to intervene in trade disputes between the European and the African communities on the New Calabar river. Thenceforward the troubles that beset the Kalabari state were political, internally in the rivalry between the Amakiri and Barboy house groups, externally in warfare with her neighbours, Nembe and Okrika, with Bonny supporting the latter. Relations with the European community gave no trouble.

A court of equity had been established and the consul in 1858 gave his approval to various regulations defining the function of its chairman and specifying that each supercargo should hold this office in turn for a month. Although they had to conform to the local African system of trade and maintain separate trading establishments on the two rivers, the relations between the British traders in the Bonny and New Calabar rivers was very close. Many of these traders indeed were established on both rivers[14] and when the hulk system was introduced it became customary for trading firms to maintain their main agency at Bonny with a second agency on the New Calabar river which was subordinate to it.[15]

Kalabari versus Nembe and Okrika

King Karibo Amakiri died in April 1863 and was succeeded by his eldest son Abbe whose English name was Prince Will. Kalabari tradition represents his reign as a period of conflict, with warfare against Nembe, Bonny, and Okrika and civil war between Will Braid of the Barboy group and the rest of Kalabari, and contrasts it with the prosperous and peaceful reign of Karibo. But civil conflict remained latent during Karibo's reign and war with Nembe broke out several years before his death.

The period of warfare, in which all the Eastern Delta communities except Andoni were very soon involved, can best be understood if seen against the economic background. The overseas slave trade had been ended, the expansion of the palm oil trade, which had been very rapid up to 1850 was coming to a halt, for unlike the slave trade difficulties of transport prevented its extension to hinterland markets not accessible by water. With palm oil left as their sole export[16] Kalabari and Bonny set about developing new markets close to the

[14] Cf., for instance, their signatures on the Bonny and New Calabar treaties and on contemporary letters addressed to the consul from the courts of equity for these two rivers.
[15] Hutchinson (1), p. 104.
[16] Until the development of the Palm Kernel trade after 1870.

delta and extending their oil-buying further afield and into their neighbours trading areas. At the same time they found themselves having to deal with communities which sought to control their passage through these waterways to their own advantage—Ohombele for Bonny, Okarki for Kalabari and Umon for Old Calabar.

The Kalabari developed new markets on the Sombreiro river, which was fast-flowing and difficult to navigate above Degema, but their main expansion was at the expense of Nembe, into that part of the delta referred to in the records as Long Brass or Eganny, an area marginal to Kalabari and Nembe. Here the Engenni river, which joined the Sombreiro river at Degema, led westwards and then northwards before it divided—one arm, the Ndoni creek, leading to the Lower Niger and to the markets at the northern apex of the delta, while the other, now called the Orashi river, turned northwards to Oguta lake which tapped the western Isuama Ibo oil markets. Bonny developed the Ibo and Ogoni oil markets on the mainland bordering Okrika and sought to expand at Kalabari expense by encouraging Okrika to lay claim to the 'Obiatubo' markets on the New Calabar river, and by asserting 'ancient' rights to trade in the Sombreiro[17] and Lower Niger markets.

It is clear from statements made to the consul whenever he tried to intervene in these wars that the former system of free trade which operated in the time of the Barbots—that is, in the late seventeenth century—still prevailed to some extent, and that in addition to markets completely within the monopoly of a particular trading state there were others, notably on the Lower Niger at the head of the delta and beyond, which were open to traders from all three states, provided they could get there.[18] Transport differentials would favour Nembe in these markets but they were offset by the higher prices paid for oil on the Rio Real. In addition there were food markets closer at hand, for example in Abua and on the Sombreiro in the Kalabari trading area, in which Bonny had previously been free to trade during the heighday of the slave trade, and food in those days included palm oil. It would seem also that in the early part of the century in the time of King Opobo people who were not members of these trading states were also free to move about the delta and pass through or temporarily reside in the territories of states other than

---

[17] E.g. Ndelli and possibly the unidentified Billituro, which may be another name for the site of Old Bile on the Sombreiro river.

[18] E.g. Laird and Oldfield, writing of the period 1832–3, refer to Bonny traders buying slaves at Idah and using the Ndoni creek 'when they come to trade in Palm Oil and Ivory'. (Laird and Oldfield, Vol. 1, p. 124; 11, p. 143.)

their own—the Okrika men to fish there the Akassa people to sell canoes to Bonny. But with the hardening of the oil trade each state now sought to exclude its rivals from buying oil in markets which it wished to make its own, and at the same time to extend its 'trading empire' at the expense of these rivals and to restrict them and people trading with them from passing through its territory.

The first repercussions were reported in 1854, when Consul Beecroft at the request of the European trading community, intervened to 'settle a long standing dispute of most serious detriment to the genuine interest of trade between Eganny and the New Calabar chiefs, or rather the two factions of the New Calabar town, one side being willing and anxious for an amicable adjustment whilst the other has as stubbornly opposed it unless upon their own terms'. The consul's answer was to get the Kalabari king and chiefs to sign an agreement in which they faithfully promised 'to settle the dispute between the Eganny country and ourselves and cause trade to be opened as formerly within the space of one month or forfeit five puncheons of good palm oil'.[19] Whether they honoured this agreement is not related, since Beecroft died soon after. Kalabari tradition defines the Eganny community as the Okarki and refers to a war between Nembe, Okarki and Kalabari, with the Okarki occupying the high ground which dominated the passage of the Engenni River below their village. King Karibo had died and the two factions were disputing the succession. The Amakiri faction put forward Abbe (Prince Will) and the Barboy Alambo, a descendant of Kamalu, whom they had elected to the head of the Barboy main house on the death of chief Braid. The goddess Owame Akaso intervened in the dispute and decreed that whichever chief should force the passage of the Engenni first should succeed to the throne. So did the 'Long Juju' of Arochuku when the matter was referred to it. Abbe was successful, Alambo held back, and, when they returned to Kalabari, Abbe was made King and the Barboy house deposed Alambo and elected Will Braid (Ibanibo) the son of Braid Barboy (Kombo Agolea) in his stead.

There is no firm date for the beginning of this war with Nembe. No reference is made to it when the consul visited Elem Kalabari in January 1858 but in February 1859 he reported a visit to King Ama-kiri as a result of his preventing 'the Bonny Traders going to the Brass (Nembe) country for oil', and states that the Bonny regents

---

[19] Letter dated 24/1/54, enclosed in consular despatch No. 48 and published in P.P. 1854/5, Vol. LVI, and Hertslet, Vol. X, p. 12.

were willing to let the Kalabari pass through their territory to Qua (Ibibio) and Humballa (Ohombele) in their trading territory, and that King Amakiri agreed to withdraw the prohibition on the passage of Bonny traders through Kalabari territory. During the next few years when Burton was consul the war languished and is not referred to until 'in July 1863 shortly after Amacree's death the feud between his people and the Nimbi of the Brass river revived. It is however certain that the Brass people have been the victors. In one day they 'chopped' it is said three canoes containing thirty of their enemies and have altogether captured or killed a hundred of the New Calabar men who can hardly show a skull in return. There is a chronic enmity between the two rivers which nothing save interest can check'.[20] By the time Livingstone became consul in December 1865 the war had been extended to include Okrika , who were ambushing Kalabari trading canoes on the New Calabar river 'on their way to the fairs', and Bonny was preparing to go to war against Kalabari because of its continued stoppage of the passage of Bonny canoes through Kalabari territory. The consul immediately invoked Article III of the Treaty of 1854 and ordered all trade to be stopped in Bonny till debts due to European firms had been settled. He also tried to mediate, even going so far as to visit Okrika. In the course of these negotiations it was alleged by the various sides,—that Okrika had attacked an 'outlying Kalabari village and killed, cooked and eaten 103 men', that Kalabari had attacked a Brass village 'in the last war' and killed forty-three Brass men, that King William Dappa Pepple of Bonny had offered to mediate between Kalabari and Brass but had actually encouraged the latter and given them 200 kegs of powder, and that as a reprisal the Kalabari had stopped the passage of Bonny canoes through their territory. It also transpired that Bonny wanted to go to the Brass area to buy canoes not oil, and to have access to the northern delta oil markets on the Lower Niger (i.e. in the Ndoni area which Livingstone mistakenly called Andoni), and that they were behind the claims which the Okrika were now putting forward to the Obiatubo markets on the New Calabar river. No reference was made to the Engenni area and it was clear that Kalabari's main trouble was now with Okrika. But if the Okrika were harassing Kalabari trade on the New Calabar river, the Kalabari were seriously interfering with their fishing activities upon which, as King Phibia of Okrika dramatically demonstrated to the consul,

[20] Burton's letter dated 15/4/64 in F.O. 84/1221 and P. P. 1865 Vol. LVI.
[21] Appendix B 3. and Despatch of 2/8/60 in F.O. 84/1265.

they depended for their existence. The Kalabari king and the chiefs were prepared to make peace provided Bonny and Okrika were prepared to swear an oath of peace with them.[22] The consul thought he had managed to bring representatives of the three states together to do so on 28 September 1866 but Okrika with Bonny support finally refused to attend. Commander Verney of the H.M.S. *Oberon*, reported however, that as a result of the consul's efforts 'a tacit understanding was arrived at among the natives not to go on with a war at present' and that hostilities had ceased since 8th September and trade quietly and peacefully resumed.[23] Hostilities dragged on with Okrika for the next three years, but the Kalabari now moved their trading canoes under 'a convoy of war canoes' and on November 22 1869 their king and chiefs told the consul that they had not been troubled so much by the Okrika, that no fighting had occurred with Brass for the past year and that 'there was a juju or sacred village on the border whose head man had been working as a peace maker between the two tribes' and they asked the consul to 'negotiate a peace with Brass'. The consul also reported that in the previous year the Brass chiefs had asked the Brass agents to send presents of powder and muskets from them to Bonny for the latter 'to hire the Okrikas to fight New Calabar'. The agents had refused, the presents could not be sent through the creeks, and Bonny was too distracted by its own civil war to 'listen to any Brass fighting project'.[24]

By 1871 the effects of King Jaja's control of the Imo trade had made itself felt and the Bonny chiefs decided to combine with Okrika in a final effort to crush Kalabari. On June 26 1871 the combined forces of Bonny and Okrika attacked Elem Kalabari, the fighting and bombardment continued the whole day without effect and at nightfall they withdrew to their respective countries. The agents on all three rivers were now thoroughly alarmed and sent three similar letters to the consul reporting that 'the various tribes populating the enormous extent of oil producing country from the Brass to the Opobo river are now all involved in a complicated and universal war'. By the time he arrived at Bonny all the states had come to the conclusion that there was nothing to be gained by continuing the war. A truce was agreed upon and this was followed by 'Perpetual Treaties of Peace' between Kalabari and her three enemies. In the Bonny treaty of 27 October,[25] the parties bound themselves to stop cannibalism

[22] Chop juju with them'.
[23] F.O. 84/1265.
[24] F.O. 84/1308.
[25] Appendix B.6

(Article 4), to allow the Okrika men to fish wherever they had fished before so long as they were on friendly terms with the Kalabari, and Okrika was barred from using the Obiatubo markets which were to belong to Kalabari. Bonny and Okrika were ordered to revoke the juju they had sworn together against Kalabari, Bonny was to be allowed to trade jointly with Kalabari in the Billituro and Ndelli markets on the Sombreiro River and Kalabari was to open the creeks between Bonny and Brass and allow Akassa men safe passage through them. In the Okrika treaty[26] which was signed the following day, the fishing rights of Okrika were further defined as the right to pass through and make fishing settlements in any of the creeks belonging to New Calabar and Brass, the boundaries of the Obiatubo markets were described as beginning at Annia on the one side and ending at Ewaffa on the other, and Deobo markets (near the present Port Harcourt) which adjoined Okrika territory were stated to belong exclusively to Okrika.

The treaty with Bonny was declared to be binding for five years (Article 10). No time limit was mentioned in the treaty with Okrika. A similar treaty was concluded on 21 November between Kalabari and Brass, repeating the first four articles of the Okrika treaty which related to the cessation of hostilities ('a perfect truce shall endure between ourselves and between our successors repetively for ever more'), and agreeing to the consul enforcing the treaty ('the maintenance of the peace now concluded shall be watched over by Her Majesty's consul who will take steps to ensure at all times due observance of all articles of the treaty'). No further articles were added to the Brass treaty, nothing was mentioned about markets, and no boundaries were defined.[27]

The war against Will Braid

The internal history of Kalabari during the nineteenth century closely parallels that of Bonny. Both are concerned with a struggle for political dominance between two groups of houses, derived from the founder of the ruling dynasty. In Bonny they were the Anna Pepple and Manilla Pepple factions, in Kalabari the Barboy and the Amakiri. But the latter struggle took a different course and had a different ending. The struggle first came to a head on the death of King Amakoro (Amakiri II) and produced two evenly matched factions, with the Barboy group of houses opposed to a combination of the Harry (Ombo), Birinomoni and West India groups under the

26 Appendix B 7.
27 These three treaties are not published in Hertslet. Copies are in F.O. 84/1343.

leadership of the first named. Neither tradition nor historical records recall the alignments of the other Kalabari houses on this occasion. King Karibo (Amakiri III) was strong enough to maintain a balance between the two factions and when at the end of his reign their rivalry again came into the open, Consul Burton gives a clear statement of the alignment of all the important houses in Kalabari. This alignment, which has been given in Table 4, shows that the Amakiri faction was now greatly increased in power by the addition of the powerful canoe house group founded by King Karibo while the Barboy faction had suffered by the internal dissentions of the Manuel (Owukori) group, which had resulted in a split into the house or houses following Manuel's son, Bob Manuel, and those following Horsefall (Omekwe). Henceforward these chiefs and their houses could be relied upon to be on opposite sides in any Kalabari dispute. In 1863 Horsefall Manuel supported the Barboy and Bob Manuel the Amakiri; thereafter the positions were reversed. In addition to the capital of Elem Kalabari, neighbouring villages were also involved, Ifoko supporting the Barboy, Abalama village the Amakiri, and Tombia (New Town) being split between them.

During King Abbe's (Amakiri IV) reign the protagonists in this struggle were George Amakiri (Idilolomari) and Will Braid (Ibanibo). George, like Oko Jumbo in Bonny, was able to make the subordinate house of which he was the head, the wealthiest house in the community—tradition maintains that although it remained a single house it mustered four war canoes—while King Abbe (Amakiri IV) was unable to emulate his father and enlarge his own house (Prince Will) or the Karibo main house, to which he succeeded, to comparable strength. Will Braid was also able to continue his father's work of expanding the Barboy main house, but this resulted in a division of the Barboy group into two segments, the Braid group of houses which included the Barboy main house, and those other Barboy houses (George Will, Manuel, Don Pedro, Dick Barboy) established before Braid became the chief of the main house. This division also became extended to the other Kalabari houses attached to the Barboy faction, the Standfast Jack and Briggs houses, which considered themselves of pre-Amakiri origin, associating with the other Barboy houses, the new houses of Iboroma in Ifoko, and Yellow (Iyala) in Tombia continuing their association with the main house.

The wars with Nembe and Okrika kept the Kalabari united during the early part of King Abbe's (Amakiri IV's) reign, but as these ended the internal struggle came into the open. Consular records tell

L

us nothing about it; Kalabari tradition has a lot to say but is coloured to some extent by the reaction against the later dominance of the George Amakiri house. Will Braid's father Kombo Agolea was, like George Amakiri, a bought slave, but his mother was a daughter of Odum and through her he could claim to be of Kamalu descent. Tradition makes much of Will Braid's enlisting the support of the traditional elements in Kalabari society by keeping alive the remembrance of his rival's servile origin and blocking his attempts to engage in rituals reserved to those of Kalabari descent, the performance of which would have supported a claim to superior status. Such behaviour, if indeed it actually did occur, would have been very dangerous to adopt in the Kalabari of the mid-nineteenth century, when most of the ablest chiefs were of slave or stranger origin. George Amakiri did not operate alone; he remained the head of a coalition of chiefs the ablest of whom were the parvenu chiefs, Horsefall Manuel and John Bull (Erekosima), whom the consul named as being 'exceedingly bitter against him (Will Braid)'.[28] John Bull was the founder of a subordinate house in the Harry (Ombo) group and he came to replace Harry Braid as the leader of this group. Horsefall Manuel, having broken with the Barboy group, proceeded to build up an association of his two houses (Horsefall Manuel and Charles Horsefall) with the West India group and with the Jack Rich house and became accepted as the head of this combination. By 1871 these two had established their position as chiefs second only to George Amakiri and Will Braid.[29]

Tradition suggests that King Abbe (Amakiri IV) tried to maintain a balance between Will Braid and George Amakiri, which is likely enough, but also makes the more improbable statement that George Amakiri turned against Will Braid when the latter refused to support him in intrigues against King Abbe. Consular records are silent on these matters but they confirm George Amakiri's efforts, successful as far as the Consul was concerned, to acquire superior status and they accord him the royal title of prince. Efforts to break the power of Will Braid were first confined to attacks upon his supporters. Thus Chief Iyala (Yellow) found himself accused of sorcery and obliged to submit to the 'Long Juju' of Arochuku to clear his name. More successful was the fomenting of dissension between the Braid and the Manuel and George Will houses.

By 1873 George Amakiri had become recognized as the dominant

[28] 84/1593.
[29] In the three treaties of Peace the names of the Kalabari signatories are King Amachree, George Amakiri, Will Braid, John Bull, Horsefall Manuel, followed by Harry Braid, Bob Manuel and West India.

chief in Kalabari. When Bonny and Opobo were at last prepared to accept the consul's suggestions of making peace and submitting to the arbitration of Kalabari and Okrika it was 'Prince George Amakiri' who was described by the consul as 'by far the ablest man in the country' and recommended for a present from Her Majesty which was superior to that recommended for King Abbe (Amakiri IV).[30] King Abbe was to receive a blue frock coat with epaulettes, Prince George a similar coat and also a silver-mounted staff with his name on it. Among the names of chiefs who signed the treaty as arbitrators were those of Bob Manuel and George Will; that of Will Braid is conspicuously absent. The climax came in 1879. The records are silent about the details and only state that Consul Hopkins was enquiring into 'a serious dispute between two rival factions, the Will Barboy and the Amakiri house' in August and that he died in September before he could write his report. On 10 October the acting vice-consul wrote to the Commander of the African Station requesting 'at once a man of war to put an end to the war between Bonny and New Calabar', and on 21 November he reported the war settled 'on the basis of the two treaties enclosed' (the treaties are no longer enclosed in the file. Fortunately they have been reproduced in Hertslet's Treaties).[31] Kalabari tradition tells us that Will Braid, finding that he could not prevail over the coalition of George Amakiri, John Bull, and Horsefall Manuel, decided to fight the town; the other Barboy houses refused to do this and Will Braid therefore decided to follow the example of Jaja Anna Pepple and removed all his supporters to a fortified site at Ewofa in the Okpo-mbu-tolu area, which commanded the passage up the New Calabar river. He could count on the support of Bonny and Okrika and on the neutrality of Opobo[32] and he hoped for consular favour. But nobody except Will Braid and his small following wanted another state in the Eastern Delta, and the presence of H.M.S. *Dido* was sufficient to make the Bonny chiefs anxious to make peace, the more readily as the Kalabari chiefs were prepared to concede to them exclusive trading rights in the Sombreiro river (the 'Ndelli markets'). Will Braid had no alternative but to sign a perpetual Treaty of Peace with

---

[30] See Despatch of 16/1/73 in F.O. 84/1377.

[31] Hertslet Vol. XIV, pp. 1194-5 and Appendix B 9.

[32] King Jaja told the consul that he was at first friendly towards Will Braid who went to seek his advice. He went into Will Braid's resources 'and told him it was absurd to think of seceding from New Calabar as his means were inadequate'. After Will Braid's visit an embassy was sent from Opobo to New Calabar. It is not known what transpired but from that time Jaja 'turned quite against Will Braid' (F.O. 84/1593).

the king and chiefs of New Calabar in which they bound themselves to allow Will Braid to return to Kalabari, to trade freely in their area, and to retain the property and the status which he had formerly held there, while Will Braid bound himself to evacuate Ewofa and to trade exclusively in the Kalabari trading empire. The king and chiefs of Bonny, Opobo, and Okrika were to act as arbitrators between Kalabari and Will Braid and to see that the provisions of the treaty were carried out.[33] The Perpetual Treaty of Peace between Kalabari and Bonny, which was signed the same day, was similar in form and content to that signed in 1871[34] except that there was no time limit; a clause was added that Billa (Bile) were 'free to go wherever they pleased' and 'the Bonny people were given the exclusive right of trading in the Andelli markets', while 'the New Calabars' were to have 'the exclusive right of trading at all the other so-called Brass markets'.

Will Braid may have signed a treaty with Kalabari but he had no intention of complying with its terms and the war continued. The Kalabari, that is, the Amakiri group of houses and the Barboy houses which had remained with them, constructed fortified positions opposite Ewofa to contain Will Braid's forts, and at Degema to command the passage of the upper Sombreiro and Engenni rivers. Kalabari tradition describes the organization of the war under a triumvirate of the senior ranking chiefs—George Amakiri, whose trading organization provided the wealth, John Bull and Horsefall Manuel, who conducted the military operations. Hewitt, the new consul, set about trying to enforce the treaties and called a meeting of the signatories in July 1882, at which he issued a decretal order that Will Braid should remove from Ewofa to Bakana, and defined the Ndelli markets as Ndelli, Ekpafya, and Merikpe. Will Braid still refused to move, the Kalabari forts continued to fire on Bonny canoes in the Sombreiro, and Bonny used her fleet to protect her own canoe traffic and to blockade the Kalabari trading port of Ifoko. The consul called a further meeting in November the following year. He ordered the Kalabari to dismantle their forts at Degema 'and other places in the Endelle creek', and Bonny to withdraw her war canoes from the New Calabar river. He found Bonny the more to blame[35] and he fined New Calabar 60 and Bonny 200 puncheons of oil and ordered trade to be stopped in these rivers till the fines were

[33] Appendix B 9.
[34] Appendix B 6.
[35] 'The trade of New Calabar has been entirely stopped by Bonny since March 9th'. F.O. 84/1617.

paid. This appears to have brought the war with Bonny to an end and no further reference is made to it. Lacking support from Bonny, Will Braid had no alternative but to return to the Kalabari state. He was heavily in debt to the Bonny chiefs, and he could not trade direct.[36]

By 1884 Will Braid had removed most of his people to Bakana and there he remained resisting all consular efforts to get him to move closer to the other Kalabari villages. Meanwhile the Kalabari had moved from Elem Kalabari away from close proximity to Bonny and resettled on the northern margin of the delta, the Barboy houses and their supporters at Abonnema, the houses of the Amakiri faction first at Degema and then at Buguma on the waterway which connected the Sombreiro with the New Calabar River. The agents who traded with them followed, living first in hulks on the Sombreiro River and then ashore at Abonnema and Degema; so did the satellite villages of Tombia, Ifoko, Abalama, Ido and Tema, which settled near Buguma and Bakana leaving the New Calabar estuary deserted except for Ke. The Kalabari state had assumed its modern form, its king reduced to a nonentity, its government an oligarchy of chiefs, the heads of houses who had brought their war canoes from Elem Kalabari, and with a stable social structure based on the Amakiri vs Barboy, and Barboy vs Will Braid political divisions.[37]

[36] An attempt to trade through an 'interloper' was blocked by the Bonny Court of Equity which impounded his oil on the grounds that it had not paid comey either to Kalabari or to Bonny. F.O. 84/1634.

[37] The Amakiri Group were settled at Buguma Village; those of the Barboy group opposed to Will Braid were settled at Abonnema village, those supporting him at Bakana.

Part Four

POLITICAL DYNAMICS

X

The Structure and Development Cycle of the Canoe House

TRADITION maintains that the canoe house like the ward which it replaced was the result of the expansion of the household of its founder. But whereas the ward was usually a group that had been founded in the remote past, most of the important canoe houses were founded in the late eighteenth and early nineteenth centuries. The details of their households and the ways in which they expanded are remembered and preserved in recent tradition. It is therefore possible to study the process of the development from household to canoe house to an extent not possible in the case of the older wards.

In considering the expansion of the canoe house the normal patterns of lineage or house expansion and segmentation could be ignored. One did not have to wait for the founder's household to expand through the natural increase of his patrilineal and other descendants. A potential founder of a canoe house could use his wealth to buy more dependants, the work of these dependants in turn produced more wealth to buy still more people. It was a cumulative process, wealth begat people, and people begat wealth. The limiting factors were mainly the competition of other leaders and other houses all engaged in the same process. The wealth was used to buy slaves, to marry *eya* wives into the household and in ways calculated to attract other unattached households to the founder's group until it had become large enough to be capable of manning a war canoe. Then, provided it was in the interests of the main house to do so, the would-be founder of the new canoe house was presented by his chief to the king and chiefs of the state and, if they were satisfied he had filled his canoe, he and they performed the rituals that created him a chief and founder of his own canoe house.

The traditional house or ward was thought of as something static and unchanging. There was no institutionalized procedure for its expansion. When it became over-large, unless there were other factors promoting its unity, it tended to segment as a result of internal conflicts and rivalries as a means of lessening or resolving such conflicts. If they remained unresolved, it split into two wards. By contrast the canoe house was dynamic. It was supposed and expected to expand and, if it failed to do so, it declined and eventually went into liquidation. This expansion of a canoe house was institutionalized in such a way that instead of being a process which might disrupt the group, it was one which the head of the canoe house, his most able lieutenants, and their supporters were able to plan together. The establishment of a lieutenant as chief of his own canoe enhanced the authority of the main house from which it derived. The incentive on the part of lesser leaders to support such a lieutenant in filling his canoe was the hope of being established by him in due course as chief of yet another canoe house derived from this lieutenant's house.

The members of a canoe house were distributed between a number of units which can be called households, this term being used to describe a domestic and political unit composed of a man, his wife or wives, his children, servants, slaves, and other dependants permanently or temporarily attached to him. Households varied very much in size and composition. At the one extreme were those of poorer individuals which might consist of a single family or part of a single family. At the other were the greatly enlarged households of chiefs and wealthy men. These, which can be distinguished as greater households, subdivided into the sub-households of each wife, sister, or other married female dependant of the household head.

A household again was a dynamic entity, it had a cycle of growth and decay. The original household of a man, his wife or wives and his unmarried children or dependants developed into a group of households composed of the original household together with those households of his married sons, daughters, sisters and other dependants, which could be said to belong to him through rights of descent or of ownership and which had not been transferred to other groups. If it did not expand in this way it contracted and disintegrated, the surviving members becoming incorporated into other more successful households. Such an expanded household will be referred to as a household group and such a group will be distinguished where necessary as simple or composite, a simple household group being composed of a group of households derived from a single original household, a composite group being a group of households derived from more than one such source. A canoe house in its initial stage was made up of one or more of these composite household groups.

A canoe house also had its cycle of growth,—an initial stage, a stage of growth, and a stage of expansion. In the first, which was usually prior to its receiving official recognition, the canoe house came into being as a new canoe house. This was when its component households were consolidated, normally into a single, greatly enlarged, composite household group, the core or nucleus of which was the greater household of its founder, that is, the man who was recognized as the chief of this house. This stage was followed by one of regrouping within the canoe house once it was established as a new house. The structure of the house became more fluid, the original composite household group broke up, and its component households regrouped themselves into a number of composite household groups and these groups constituted in effect separate segments of the canoe house. Some of them has a single greater household as their nucleus, others might contain a number of such households. In the third stage the canoe house became large enough for one or more of these segments to hive off and become recognized as another canoe house. The parent house became an *opuwari*, a main house, the new canoe house a subordinate house, a *kalawari*, and a satellite of this main house.

A canoe house that failed to conform to this cycle of expansion usually followed a reverse one of contraction and elimination. It failed to accumulate the capital needed for expansion and lost first any wealth it might have, and then its members themselves, who were gradually sold off to other houses to pay its debts. When it was finally unable to meet its liabilities it went into liquidation, the surviving members becoming incorporated into the canoe house which bought them, that is, which assumed responsibility for these debts. If these survivors were at all numerous they often retained their coherence as a group. They became one of the segments of the house that had bought them and formed a distinct group with its own special interests and loyalties, which differed to some extent from those of other segments within the canoe house. Such a group will be referred to as a submerged house. In Kalabari most of the canoe houses which could claim to be *duowari* contracted and were absorbed in this manner during the eighteenth and early nineteenth century. Some of these submerged houses later managed to recover and become established again as canoe houses under another founder.[1] In Bonny many *duowari* were able to survive as canoe houses during

[1] For example the Orikadibia house of the West India group. Appendix A II (c).

the nineteenth century, but only by becoming attached as satellite houses to the canoe house group which had paid their debts.

I. THE CANOE HOUSE IN ITS INITIAL STAGE

A canoe house in this initial stage was composed of a greatly enlarged composite household group. Its founder's own greater household formed the nucleus of this group and to it were attached a number of other greater or lesser households and household groups. They were attached to him primarily by ties of self interest but these were usually reinforced by more definite kinship and contractual relationships. The composition of both this nucleus and its attachments is examined below.

The nucleus

At this initial stage the greater household of the founder of a canoe house differed mainly in size from the greater households of the leaders associated with him. It sub-divided into the sub-households of a number of wives, some of them married to the founder as slaves (by marriage 'within the house'), some of them married under the *egwa* system and some under the *eya* system; others again were widows of deceased patrilineal relatives who had been inherited by him. The personnel of the greater household was distributed by its head between the sub-households of his wives, each wife being responsible for the feeding and housing, not only of her own children but also of the slaves, servants, and visitors allocated to her by her husband. Some of these wives were more important than others, either by reason of the priority of their marriage to the household head or because of their administrative efficiency or because of their birth, and they will be distinguished as greater wives. Most of the personnel allocated by the head were incorporated into the sub-households of these greater wives, either temporarily or permanently. A greater wife would also find herself responsible for some of the lesser wives of her husband, women who by reason of their youth, or infirmity, or for other reasons were unable effectively to support themselves. Some of these greater wives again brought with them on their marriage slaves and other dependants of their own, who had been given to them by their fathers or brothers at the time of their marriage.

This distribution of the personnel of a great man's household among the sub-households of his principal wives determined to some extent the lines of future cleavage within his household in the course of its growth from a domestic to a political unit and indeed this is how local tradition regards it. Many houses of Bonny and Kalabari like to derive themselves from such sub-divisions of King Pepple's or King Amakiri's household and many more seek to justify their later political alignments on the grounds that their founder had once been attached to the sub-household of one of these greater wives. But although of political importance such a division of personnel was governed in the first place mainly by domestic and economic considerations. Each of these greater wives was the manager of a residential and catering co-operative. In the Ijo idiom she was the 'mother' who was responsible for organizing and providing the members of her sub-household with food and shelter. The adult women of her group worked together under her direction in the female domestic tasks of the household. The men contributed their labour and their money for the purchase of food and other needs. As the sub-household grew in age and size it sub-divided into smaller units, most of its married women catering and cooking for their own husbands, children and any other dependants allocated to them; but there were always occasions involving feasts and the entertainment of visitors in the preparation of which all the womenfolk of a sub-household had to co-operate and to which most of the men had to contribute, while, in the case of major entertainments, all the greater wives of a chief or king and their sub-households had to co-operate together and divide the work between them.

The members of such a sub-household were of two kinds, permanent and temporary. The permanent were those who belonged specifically to the wife and, besides her children, they included any slaves given to her or bought by her, as opposed to those she was merely required to look after. As a sign that they belonged to her she ritually shaved their heads in the same manner as she shaved the heads of her children and, in the Opobo idiom, these permanent members were distinguished as her 'razor house'.

The others were her 'kitchen house'. She was responsible for their feeding and accommodation as long as they were living under the protection of her husband. They included strangers and servants, as well as her own or her husband's cognatic relatives and affines. They also included friends and trading associates and also the children, slaves, or other dependants of these friends. Like the trading communities of the hinterland, the Bonny and Kalabari people held that a son learned better from a master than from a father and both real and adopted sons were often sent to live with trading relatives or friends for training as apprentices.[2] Such temporary members were free to leave their 'kitchen house', at their own or their relatives' or master's pleasure. Some of them who had no better place to go to might remain there permanently, 'marrying within the house' of their master.[3] Others again might be merely business connections of the head of the household who whenever they visited his town would lodge in this sub-household. But those who had stayed for any length of time with her sub-household, particularly if they had grown up in it as children, tended to develop strong ties of affection between themselves and with their 'mother'. Because they were under no jural obligations towards her and towards each other such 'kitchen house' members, particularly those who had returned to their own 'razor houses', derived considerable satisfaction from helping each other and from visiting their 'kitchen house mother'. They endeavoured to attend and assist at feasts organized by her household and when she died, they made a special point of being present at her own funeral feast. By contrast the members of a 'razor house', though they formed a united group as against other 'razor houses' and were held together by much stronger and more permanent bonds, were to a considerable extent rivals or potential rivals and competing against each other. This formed a paradox which found expression in the Opobo aphorism: 'A kitchen house is stronger than a razor house'.

Leadership within a 'senior' wife's sub-household devolved, as he grew old enough to exercise it, upon the ablest of her 'sons'.[4] His 'mother's' sub-household became his household as he proceeded to expand it with the assistance of his 'father'—the head of his mother's household. When there were two or three able 'sons' each proceeded to expand his own personal household and to secure the attachment to it of any personnel which his father might be distributing. But the common interest of the brothers lay in keeping together as a group until they had established their 'mother's' household as a canoe house under the chieftainship of the 'brother' best qualified to head it. Once this was achieved he and they could go on to found their separate canoe house chieftainships. In this final process the original mother's sub-household disintegrated, its personnel being

---

[2] Some were even apprenticed to English supercargoes, for example, George Amakiri.
[3] For example, in the case of Soku Taria the father of Ombo, the founder of the Ombo (Harry) group of houses in Kalabari.
[4] This term including both natural and 'adopted' sons.

distributed between the households of the new chief and his 'brothers'.

The attachments

Turning from the greater household of the founder and examining the other households attached to it we find that they fall into three different categories depending on whether they originally belonged to the same house as the founder or to different houses or to different communities. The first category was composed of the households of persons who were either closely or distantly 'related' to the founder this term including slaves and their descendants as well as true kin. There were, for example, households of widows of the founder's father or of widows inherited by that father and who had never been specifically inherited by the founder himself. Or, to take another example, there were households which traced their descent ultimately to the same ancestry as the founder and his father, but by collateral or distant lines.

The second category consisted of the households of persons who originally belonged to other houses and who carried with them into the house that had 'redeemed' them some of their former loyalties, which differentiated them and set them apart from the households of persons in the first category.

The third category differed from the two preceding ones in that such households belonged to houses in two different communities. These were the households of persons who were freeborn members of a satellite community and who to advance their fortunes had moved to the state capital and attached themselves to the household of either the founder of the canoe house or of one of the gentlemen who had helped the founder to 'fill his canoe'.

The households of people in all these three categories tended to form groups among themselves, either on a basis of common descent or of common membership of their former house or of their natal village. Some of these groupings were ephemeral, were deficient in leadership and disappeared, some were more tenacious,[5] and some were able to preserve their unity and to expand their wealth and their personnel until they were strong enough to become established or re-established as a canoe house.

Households of people in the third category played a greater part in the formation of canoe houses in Kalabari than in Bonny. Bonny

[5] There still exists in Bakana in the Braid group of houses, a small group of households whose members consider themselves the direct lineal descendants of King Kamalu.

had few satellite villages and these were so close to the main settlement that they soon became virtually a part of a single community. The more distant Bonny settlements were overflow or 'plantation' settlements established by the larger Bonny houses for their own members. The Kalabari satellite villages, on the other hand, were at some distance from Elem Kalabari and remained separate local communities. But many of their houses became closely associated with particular Kalabari canoe houses. This association developed out of the association of individual members from the satellite villages who found it to their advantage to live in the Kalabari house as servants of either its head or of some other prominent leader in this house. They thereby established a relationship between the servant's natal household and that of his master. Should the master reach a position where he could aspire to recognition as a canoe chief, he could count on his servants being able to bring forward their relatives living in the satellite village to help fill his canoe. The association could also be developed the other way round. An ambitious gentleman from a Kalabari house might find that he could advance his fortunes more rapidly by residing in a satellite village and by swelling his household group there through the attachment to it of local households.

<h2 align="center">2. THE SECOND STAGE</h2>

We have described the structure of a canoe house when it came into being as made up of a nucleus consisting of the founder's greater household, to which was attached a number of other households and household groups. Once established, however, this structure broke down and re-formed, some of the individual households retaining their original groupings, others changing their orientation and forming new combinations. In considering this process we can once again discard the patterns of lineage or house expansion observed in other Ijo or hinterland communities. The original design of such fission may have been laid down by the founder in his distribution of the personnel of his greater household between a limited number of 'greater' wives, but the factors finally determining the lines of cleavage and re-grouping were the qualities of leadership that developed within the sub-households of these wives and in the households of other leaders that had attached themselves to his greater household. All of these actual and potential leaders looked to the founder and his successor in office as head of their house and all were united behind him in opposition to other houses, but the need to assert and emphasize this solidarity was not now so great. They had achieved recognition as a canoe house and were now free to regroup themselves within this house in ways which would best accord with its future development and their own particular interests. It was in the common interest of all members that their house should continue its expansion but there was no definite predetermined pattern for this and whether the expansion succeeded or failed depended to a very considerable extent upon individual choice and individual initiative.

The internal structure of the house thus became much more fluid. The greater household of the founder segmented into a number of separate greater households, one of them remaining the household of the founder and each of the others coming under the leadership of one of the more able of his actual or 'adopted' sons and becoming a potential nucleus of a new canoe house. Similarly, in the case of the households originally attached to the founder's greater household they too had their own leaders, some of them as capable and determined as any of the founder's sons and the heads of greater households of equal potentiality. Not all these leaders, whether drawn from the founder's household or from its attachments, were of equal capacity. Some were more formidable than others and were able to expand their greater households at a faster rate.

Thus, in its second stage, the canoe house consisted of a limited number of greater households and a considerable number of lesser households. Some of these latter formed part of a household group and were attached to one or other of these greater households; some were less firmly associated and in a position to transfer their attachment to whichever greater household made it worth their while. The structure can be presented as made up of a number of competing greater households, each the potential nucleus of a new canoe house, combining with and against one another in various ways and for varying periods, while at the same time striving to attach to their particular combinations as many of the lesser households and household groups as possible.

On the death of the founder the leader of one of these combinations was chosen by the members of the canoe house as his successor. What remained of the founder's greater household disappeared, its property and personnel being distributed between the greater households of his 'sons'. If the leader chosen to succeed had already established his own canoe house before this, he might find himself called to take over the chieftaincy of the main house, leaving his own

M

satellite house in charge of another chief chosen by and from among the members of this house.

The distribution of power

European accounts and local tradition both agree that the canoe house was self-governing in its internal affairs. They disagree on the form this government took. To the Europeans the power of the chief was absolute and autocratic. According to local tradition the government of the house was in the hands of the chief in council with other important men of the house, and these included not only those we have termed leaders but also men valued for other social qualities, ritual, judicial, and forensic.

What is very apparent is that the house developed a high degree of political and economic leadership among its members and that it enabled this leadership to be exercised in a manner that was beneficial to the house and that did not detract from its solidarity. It was to the immediate advantage of the members of the house to align themselves behind its best leaders and to withdraw their support from those who proved inadequate. It was again to the advantage of the leaders to compete economically among themselves and with leaders of other houses, with the object of increasing their own and their followers' wealth. Yet this competition did not lead to the disruption of the house by rival leaders, for above them was the chief who had the wealth and power to maintain a balance between them, and should any one of them show signs of becoming more powerful than his fellows the system enabled the chief to advance this process by assisting this leader to add to his wealth and to his following until he was strong enough to be allowed to separate off and establish his own satellite house.

Power in this system depended on wealth, but only if used to secure the support of others, and those without wealth could withdraw their support from those who had it if this wealth was not used to their ultimate advantage. Thus power in a canoe house can be represented as distributed and balanced between the ordinary members, the leaders, and the chief, and it is proposed to take these in turn and examine their positions in the system.

(a) Ordinary members

All persons, men and women, slaves and freeborn, had their own private incomes, but this did not mean that wealth was at all evenly distributed—rather the reverse. It came to be very largely controlled by the few most able to acquire it and to increase it. Having acquired wealth, however, these few had then to use it in maintaining, as members of their households and household groups, the many who were without it.

The ordinary member of a canoe house was by no means defence-less under this system, he might be poor but he was also a member of a household whose members were bound to support him should he be involved in a dispute with a person of another house-hold. He was also, unless a bought slave, related by birth to other households and he could rely on their intervention to mitigate the consequences should he fall foul of his household head. The except-ion to this was the newly bought slave. He was allocated by his master to the sub-household of one of his wives and could hope for her intervention should he get into trouble with his master. The value of such intervention would depend on the position the wife occupied in the greater household. But until the slave had become accepted by the other members of his master's household, a bought slave was entirely dependent upon his master. Not only was he without supporters should his master turn against him but, should he normally be in receipt of his master's favours, he could also count on the hostility of the other members of his master's household who were competing for these favours. It is noticeable, when one examines the European accounts of brutal and arbitrary cruelty executed by chiefs upon their house members, that the victims are normally persons in this category of slave. This defencelessness however was only one side of the medal. Because he was so dependent upon his master and devoid of relatives and pseudo-relatives who could make competing claims upon his services and wealth, a slave's interests could coincide more closely with those of his master than could those of other members of the master's household. For this reason a slave able to advance his master's interest might find himself the recipient of his master's favours and find his rise to wealth and power facilitated by this initial position of complete dependence. It was not only his master's favours that could aid a slave's rise to power, there was also his 'mother's'. An astute 'greater' wife, who enjoyed the confidence of her husband, could play a very influential part in advancing the fortunes of able members of her 'razor house'.

(b) Leaders

The ultimate objective of every leader, whether a 'son' of the founder of the canoe house or the head of another household in it, was to 'fill his canoe'. He could not hope to do this unaided; he needed the support of the founder or his successor in office, of other leaders and of other households. To gain this support, a potential leader had first to give proof of his quality by developing the trading capacity of his household. The expansion of its resources in men, trading canoes, trade goods, goodwill, and other assets, marked him as a successful trader and administrator and attracted the support of those other lesser households and individuals not firmly attached to other leaders. Once recognized as a leader he could hope to achieve his objective either directly or at one remove, depending on his wealth and the size of his household and following. In the former case his importance and value to the house would have to be such that he could receive the assistance of its chief and the support of some of his fellow leaders to fill his own canoe. In the latter case he could attach himself and his following to an important leader of this sort on the assumption that he would occupy a superior position in this leader's own canoe house once it had come into being. But attachment to a single important leader, though the normal, was not the only way to advance towards a canoe house chieftainship. It was also possible, at least in the latter part of King Amakiri's reign, for two or three leaders of equal status to combine together and be recognized as co-founders of a canoe house. The West India and the Birihomoni groups both claim to have originated in this manner.

(c) *The chief*

Contemporary European accounts like to describe the chief of a canoe house as absolute, but they produce little evidence of this apart from instances of the brutal treatment of their slaves. The members of a canoe house accorded to their head a considerable measure of power and authority: very much more than that exercised by the head of an Efik ward. But with this increased power went a very considerable increase of responsibility. The chief was the manager of a trading and fighting corporation engaged in fierce economic competition with other similar corporations. This increase in power was necessary if his management was to be effective. The members of his house were interested primarily in this effective management rather than in abstract principles of justice. The more efficient his management, the greater his authority became and the more his house was prepared to tolerate occasional arbitrary applications of it. The more inefficient his management, the more he could expect his authority to be challenged until ultimately he would find himself deposed and replaced by a more efficient head. He was, like every other person in his house, ultimately dependent on the ordinary members of the group mobilized either for or against him by their various leaders. He exercised control over considerable wealth but he could not use it for his own as opposed to the house's advantage. While he was in office little or no distinction was made between his personal wealth and the house funds; both were expected to be used for the common good of the house which was held to be identical with the chief's own interests. Should he be deposed, a division could be made between his own and the house property but, by the time matters had come to this pass, the debts of the house were usually sufficient to have swallowed up any personal capital he might lay claim to. The chieftaincy of the canoe house, particularly of the main house, was thus no sinecure and tradition makes frequent reference to leaders and chiefs of subordinate houses who refused election to this office as they were convinced that it would merely ruin them.[6] The degree of actual power exercised by a chief was never constant, it depended primarily on his own personal qualities and on those of the leaders in his house. But until he reached the stage where his deposition was imminent it was necessary that, at least in the external relations of the house, the chief should appear as its ruler. Whether he or one of his leaders was actually responsible for a decision, it was clearly to the chief's advantage that it should appear to the people of his house to have the support of their leaders, and to the leaders and to people both inside and outside the house that the decision should appear to come from the chief himself.

The primary objective of the chief of a canoe house was to promote the continued expansion of his house. This could best be achieved by administering the funds and other resources of the house so that its various leaders, actual and potential, were assisted in expanding their households. It could also be used to promote and support combinations among these leaders that might ultimately result in a separation of the most successful of them as new canoe house chiefs. At the same time, the chief had to ensure both that his own household was not too depleted in wealth and man-power by this division of its members between himself and the various leaders of his greater household, and that the main canoe house was not left too impoverished by the establishment of subordinate canoe houses.

[6] In the case of both the Manilla Pepple and Anna Pepple main houses, for example.

The succession

On the death of the founder or later head of the canoe house or group of canoe houses his successor was chosen by the members of the house or group of houses. Tradition now maintains that the founder of a house should, if possible, be succeeded by one of his sons. His superior qualities, it was felt, could be transmitted to his natural sons but not any further and when these sons were dead anyone was eligible for election thereafter to the chieftainship. This however did not necessarily mean that a founder was succeeded by his sons. The proof of the superior qualities they might have inherited lay primarily in the size of the household and following they had been able to build up. There was no question of the founder being able to establish a dynasty where the succession passed as a right to his sons and grandsons, though this could happen where a founder was blessed with a number of able descendants (as for instance in the case of the Ombo house in Kalabari). In the situation of intense political and economic competition which prevailed in Bonny and Kalabari only a house that lacked effective leaders and that cherished no political ambitions could afford the luxury of a hereditary chieftainship. Those who wished to remain in the struggle had to have the best leadership they could find. This is very clearly brought out as soon as details about the actual succession in the Bonny canoe houses are enumerated. Succession in almost all the *duowari* houses passed from founder to son and then to brothers or son's sons (nine out of eleven cases). In the other houses, which for this purpose can be taken as those established during and after the reign of Captain Pepple, the succession in well over half passed from founder to slave (sixteen cases to a slave, seven to a son or other close male relative, five no details or not clear).[7] If one takes the politically important houses, the founders of all but one of them (Captain Hart) were succeeded by slaves.

In Kalabari, there were, by the nineteenth century, practically no houses of ancient foundation left and almost all the houses derived from the original household of King Amakiri. Details of these houses show that there is no obvious difference between houses of ancient or of recent foundation. In fourteen out of forty-two houses the founder was succeeded by a slave, in seven by a series of sons and

---

[7] These slaves are invariably referred to as 'adopted sons' and in a number of cases it is clear that the slave had been acting for some time as the manager of his master's trading and financial interests.

and then by grandsons, in twelve by a son and then by a grandson, in three by a son and then by a slave, and in six the details were not clear.

The founder of a house or his successor in office was, of course, in a position of advantage if he wished to influence the succession. He could, for example, establish one of the more promising of his sons as a canoe house chief by attaching to him one of his more able leaders to help the son fill his canoe. He could be sure that even though the leadership of the son might be immature, this able leader would promote the further expansion of the new house and would guide and work with its chief and build up his wealth and position. The more successful this leader was in this the more chance there was that on the death of the father this son would be elected to succeed him in the main house, leaving the leader as chief of the satellite house founded by the son. In default of sons a chief with daughters could marry them to the more able leaders in his house in the hopes that one of them would succeed him and would then provide for the succession to pass to the chief's grandson (his daughter's son by this leader).

The choice of a successor, however, rested with the members of the house, not with the chief or with his household and descendants. Bearing this in mind it is interesting to observe to what extent the members of Kalabari houses preferred to elect where possible sons or other descendants of the founder and of later chiefs. In some instances, notably in the succession to George Amakiri's house, they elected a leader to act as chief of the house during the minority of the founder's sons.

3. THE THIRD STAGE—THE CANOE HOUSE GROUP

A canoe house, though it constituted a separate fighting and trading corporation, could not survive as an independent political unit. During its first and second stages, therefore, it formed part of a larger unit—a group of canoe houses. Informants see this group as the final stage in the development of a canoe house, when the original canoe house has expanded into a main house with a number of satellite houses derived from it, and this indeed is what one finds in the present structure of Nembe. This divided into two separate sub-communities, Ogbolomabiri and Bassambiri, each of which consisted of a small number of simple canoe house groups of this type, each of which originated in a single canoe house which expanded during the nineteenth century into a simple canoe house group. But in Bonny and Kalabari the composition of many canoe house groups was much more complex than this. Expansion and contraction of some canoe house groups was much more rapid and the combinations of the surviving houses much more heterogeneous. There were combinations like the Dappa-ye-Amakiri group of Opobo which consisted of a number of originally separate *duowari* houses, which held together on a basis of 'kinship' as their founders were sons or 'adopted sons' of the two Bonny Kings Opu Dappa and Amakiri. There were combinations like the Briggs and Standfast Jack group of Kalabari, who were united by the fact that they lived in what had formerly been the Igodome ward of Elem Kalabari. There were units like the West India and the Birinomoni groups, which began as single canoe houses founded by a number of leaders each of whom succeeded in founding his own separate house. In the case of the West India it later became reduced to two canoe houses, and then combined with a remnant of the Korome ward, the Jack Rich canoe house, and with the Horsefall Manuel house which had broken away from the Manuel house in the Barboy group.

The expansion of a canoe house from a single unit into a group of houses was not easily achieved, and apart from the phenomenal expansion of the Amakiri house in the eighteenth and early nineteenth centuries of which we have only traditional accounts, and of the Manilla and Anna Pepple houses in the nineteenth century whose expansion took a rather different form, it did not occur very frequently. The mid-nineteenth century, when we can check traditional accounts against historical records, was mainly a period of trade recession and we can therefore expect to find houses engaged in consolidating their resources rather than in expanding, only the most efficiently administered houses being able to continue their expansion and then mainly at the expense of other houses. Even, however, in the earlier nineteenth century and at the end of the eighteenth century, which was one of boom conditions, Kalabari tradition clearly shows that a canoe house could remain static for a considerable time while its principal leaders and their followers gradually consolidated their position and established themselves as distinct segments of the canoe house, hoping for a favourable time for expansion into a number of satellite houses. It was the same in the nineteenth century and if we turn to the traditions of houses established after 1884 we find that many of them refer to segments of this kind and to the leaders who originally formed them. Such a satellite house, even though it might take the name of its actual founder, could be regarded as deriving from the segment formed by this original leader. It was one of the ways in which the chief of a canoe house group could obtain a following for a son whose canoe he wished to fill, and the support of the members of his canoe group for the establishment of another house. It also enabled the members of such a newly created house to establish a longer 'pedigree' by taking their origin back to one of the heroes of the golden age of King Amakiri, who although not recognized as the founder of his own canoe house had yet made an enduring impression on Kalabari tradition. Such a pedigree bridged the gap between their house and other houses in the group which had been established earlier, and enhanced their claim to equality of status with them.[8]

Expansion into one or more additional canoe houses might be to the advantage of the main house as it lessened tensions within it and provided more chiefs to represent the group in political and in other social functions. On the other hand, the consolidation of the resources of the main house as a single trading unit might, particularly in times of political and economic stress, be a sounder policy. The proliferation of the Don Pedro house (Barboy group) into three houses was an expression of the weakness of its leadership and meant the disappearance of this unit as a political force in Kalabari politics. Its three houses disintegrated as a canoe house group and the component houses only managed to survive through attachment to other house groups (two joining Manuel and one Will Braid). By contrast, the Jumbo and Banigo houses in Bonny remained single units, though probably the largest houses in Bonny, and the George Amakiri house still signed as a single house on official records. Bonny tradition makes it clear that it was the Jumbo and Banigo houses that provided the bulk of the wealth of the Manilla Pepple group in their struggle with Anna Pepple; Kalabari tradition says the same about the George house in the coalition against Will Braid.

The expansion of a canoe house into a group of houses, did not necessarily mean a break away or a separation from the group to

[8] Thus in the case of the Birinomoni group, the house of Frank Goodhead traces its origin to Angaenemenea's 'adopted son' Oku. Angaenemenea was one of four leaders who combined to form the original canoe house of this group. Two of them went on to found their own houses (Big Fowl, and Arney). Angaenemenea had two 'adopted sons' Taria and Oku. Taria succeeded to the headship of the Angaenemenea group and was able to fill his canoe and found the Goodhead house, from which at a much later date the Frank Goodhead house was founded. But by tracing its 'descent' to Oku this house can claim to be equivalent in status to the main Goodhead house which was founded by his 'brother'.

which it originally belonged. Whether this larger group held together as a single unit or broke up into a number of smaller canoe house groups was largely determined by other internal and external political factors. The dynamics of this process of further expansion of canoe house groups is discussed in a later chapter. Here we can conclude by saying that there appears to have been an optimum size for a canoe house group. A group unable to attain this size by simple natural expansion disappeared as an independent political unit, its remaining houses becoming attached to other more successful groups. If it increased beyond this size, it either broke up into a number of canoe house groups or else it became involved in a struggle for political dominance. The inevitable outcome of this struggle, however, was an ultimate breakdown into a number of canoe house groups of approximately the same size. The Anna Pepple group and its satellites once it was established in Opobo became restructured as fourteen canoe house groups, some derived from the original group and the rest composed of combinations of *duowari* and other 'neutral party' houses. The same occurred in Bonny with the Manilla Pepple group.

XI

Development and Decline of the Monarchy

I. THE DEVELOPMENT OF THE MONARCHY

INTELLIGENCE records, government officers' reports, and other similar material imply that these Oil River States constituted the principal exception[1] to the general rule that the Eastern Region of Nigeria was an area of chiefless societies. But this is an over-simplification. Almost every community had a recognized and traditional administrative office, that of head of the community. The authority vested in it was primarily ritual and ceremonial rather than political and its holder was one of a number of ward or village section heads among the Ibibio, of village heads among the Ibo, whose ward (or village) had either a traditional right to this office, or was powerful enough to secure this office for its head.

The name now given to such community heads among the Eastern and Central Ijo is *amayanabo*, thanks to the government enquiries which preceded the establishment of the Native authority system of local government. But this name, like the Ibo equivalent of *eze* or *eze ala*, carries with it a connotation of political authority which did not originally apply to such heads.

The Kalabari, Bonny and Okrika people maintain that *amayanabo* should be used to designate only the office of 'king', that is, the chieftaincy of a community which was vested in a single dynasty. They contrast this office of king with the former office of village head, called in Okrikan *amadabo*, which it replaced. This, they say, was of much less power and could be held by the head of any ward in the community. Such a village head's administrative functions are said to have been limited mainly to 'presiding' at village council meetings and at other ceremonies and in representing the community in its external relations with other communities. Even in these functions his duties were restricted, the village usually having also a 'spokesman' who announced the decisions of the council and who did most of the talking and negotiating at meetings with outside groups. The village head's authority lay in ritual and ceremonial rather than in political

[1] There are a few others derived from Benin and Idah.

177

matters. It was also possible throughout the region for an exceptionally able political leader to acquire sufficient power to become the recognized and *de facto* political head or chief of a ward or a village and less frequently of a whole community. This was frequent enough among the Northern Ibo for the position to become institutionalized under the title of *eze*, a term usually translated as king. Such a self-made chief might very well succeed to the traditional headship of a ward or village or of a community if he could satisfy the hereditary and other qualifications required for these offices. What they were unable to do in the hinterland was to establish this position of king and the political authority they had been able to associate with it, so that it became an office which passed to their descendants.

In the Eastern Delta states things were different, thanks to the wealth brought by the overseas slave trade and to the organizational demands of this trade. In these states the qualifications required for succession to headship of a ward were not restrictive or exclusive. Any member was eligible provided he could trace his descent to the founder of the ward. It was therefore easy for an able and politically ambitious man, if he were also a good business man, to accumulate sufficient wealth and with it a sufficient following to secure his election to the headship of his ward. It was also to the advantage of the ward in its competition with other wards to have at its head an able and powerful leader, and to support him in his efforts to secure election to the headship of the community. The political authority of a ward chief in these Oil River States thus tended to be greater than that of the corresponding ward or village heads of most hinterland communities.

At the same time the needs of the European traders produced an even more striking development in the power and authority of the head of the community. They expected to find, and to a very considerable extent they either found or developed in each of the Oil River States with which they traded, a supreme administrative head who had the authority to negotiate with them the conditions under which they conducted their trade, and the power to see that these conditions were adhered to by the members of this community. This person they called the king and to enable him to carry out these duties effectively they provided him with revenue in the form of comey (trading dues). It is clear that the heads of the other wards saw to it that they had a share in these duties and rewards, but it is also clear that the king was in a stronger position than they were in controlling their distribution. He was also able to use his position as the head of the community to obtain other 'spoils of office' from the Europeans supercargoes in the form of additional and superior gifts and trading advances and concessions.

The office of king thus developed into one of considerable political authority. It involved the control of very considerable wealth by West African standards, and it enabled a man who was already wealthy and powerful when he attained the position of king to enhance his wealth and power still further. As the trade with Europeans increased so did the power and authority which could be exercised by the holder of this office, and the more valuable a prize did it become for the chiefs of competing wards.

Once a ward and its chief had obtained the kingship however, the office tended to remain with it and with that chief's descendants. But this did not mean that there was a 'Royal ward' the chieftaincy of which went with the kingship. During the time its chief was king a ward expanded and segmented into a number of sub-wards founded by the king's sons; on the king's death the princely chief of one of these succeeded to the throne while the other segments became separate and independent wards. When this second king died he was succeeded as king either by one of his brothers who was the chief of one of these independent wards, or, should his reign have been a long and a successful one, by one of his sons who was the chief of one of the sub-wards into which his, the second king's, ward had expanded. We can observe this process in action if we refer to the genealogy of King Asimini of Bonny in Tables 2 and 3.

Alternatively, if the expansion of a king's ward resulted in undue competition and conflict between would-be chiefs of its sub-wards, political fission replaced lineage segmentation. The cohesion of the ward was lost and the field was open for the chief of another ward to claim the kingship. This is what seems to have happened in Kalabari when the Korome Ward or group of wards, which had been dominant in the time of King Owerri Daba, split and the kingship passed to the Kamalu dynasty of the Endeme ward.

These processes of expansion, segmentation, and fission are examined in the next chapter. The two points to be noted here are firstly that a successful political leader, although he could acquire the kingship and pass this office to his descendants, could not transfer to his successors the command of the corporate group whose power had won him the kingship, each of his successors had to build up his own power structure: secondly, that the longer the dynasty continued, the greater became the number of wards founded by kings and their descendants whose chiefs were eligible to succeed to the kingship.

Now the Kalabari tradition maintains that 'true kingship' did not begin until the 'time of Amakiri', and Bonny tradition supports it to the extent of implying that although it was Asimini who established hereditary kingship it was a new kind of monarchy that Captain Pepple introduced to the Eastern Delta, one in which the king was so powerful that he could claim to own everybody. If we accept these traditions we can distinguish three successive types of community head. There was firstly the earlier type of village head whose authority was ritual rather than administrative or political. This was replaced by the *amayanabo* (king) type whose power derived from being the chief of the most powerful ward in the community. This in turn gave way to the Pepple or Amakiri type of *amayanabo* whose power was so great that the King could be said to own the community.

2. THE PEPPLE AND AMAKIRI MONARCHIES

(a) *The king's wealth*

What were the sources of this superior power? Neither the African nor the European traditions tell us much about it. It is obvious, however, that one of the principal sources of this power was the control of the wealth which the king received as money from the European trading vessels. We do not know exactly how he disposed of this revenue but we can assume that a strong king would be able to exercise a greater control over its distribution than a weak one and that in the hands of an able king it would constitute a very powerful political weapon. There were also, particularly in the eighteenth and early nineteenth century, the standardized 'gifts' made to the king by vessels on their arrival and departure, and there were later in the nineteenth century similar gifts made by agents on assumption and resumption of office. In addition to this there were other trading concessions which the king could expect to receive from supercargoes desirous of obtaining and retaining his 'goodwill'.

(b) *The king's house*

We can also note that comey was reckoned in iron bars and that this currency depreciated from about 2/6 a bar at the beginning to 6d. by the middle of the century. This might help to explain the weakness of King William Dappa Pepple of Bonny in comparison with his predecessor King Opobo, were it not for the fact that King

William's contemporary, King Karibo Amakiri of Kalabari appeared to be unaffected by this loss of revenue and was regarded alike by Europeans and Africans as a strong king.

The feature in which King Karibo differed from King William Dappa and resembled the latter's father King Opobo was in the possession of a strong canoe house. King William Dappa had a single canoe house which was destroyed in 1855. King Karibo was able to expand his into a group of houses which under the leadership of his 'adopted son' George Amakiri became one of the most powerful groups in Kalabari. There is also sufficient historical evidence to show that both King Opobo and King Karibo were astute traders, they were men who were able to make money and thus increase their own and their houses' wealth. King William Dappa only lost money in his attempts at trading.

We can conclude from this that one of the main sources of a king's political authority derived from his control of wealth, this wealth being used to build up a power structure, directly through the enlargement of the king's own house group, indirectly by securing the goodwill and support of the heads of other groups. The wealth he was able to use for this purpose came from three sources, the state revenue (comey), the spoils of his office ('dashes' and trading concessions) and house funds, namely, the trading profits made by him as head of his house and the work bars, customs bars, and other contributions made by house members.

(c) *Ritual and conservative factors*

But the control of wealth and of a powerful house were not the only sources of the king's authority. There were others which may be described as ritual. The king was not a ritual head in the sense in which this term is applied to the Oba of Benin, whose person was the embodiment of former Obas and was identified with the well-being of his community. Nor was he a ritual head like the *Okpara Uku* of an Ibo village group, who represented the authority of the founder of the community, who held the founders' *ofo*, the symbol of this authority, and who ministered to the ancestral shrine of the founder and his patrilineal descendants. Yet his office was not an entirely secular and administrative one. To his person and office there adhered something of the mystical power, the *mana*, of the founder of the dynasty and the more successful the king was in building up his political authority the more he and his supporters were able to enhance this mystical and ritual aspect of his kingship.

Associated with this type of ritual authority was another factor which can be called conservative or traditional. The office of king was endowed with something which no chief, however powerful, possessed; the king alone was head of the state and as such the superior of any other person in it. This traditional authority might not have much effect upon those actively involved in the struggle for political dominance but it could and did affect those who were neutral and whose reaction to any threat to the kingship was to rally to its support against those who were seeking to challenge the established order.

We need not overestimate the importance of these ritual and traditional aspects of the king's authority. The people of Bonny and Kalabari were hard-bitten business men, who were more likely to be affected by practical political and economic consideration rather than by other more emotional attitudes. But on the other hand, these aspects should not be underestimated. They were attributes which a successful monarch like Opobo was able to develop and enhance during the course of his reign, but even when the holder of the office was commercially unsuccessful they were still of value, for, unlike the more tangible economic attributes, these were attached to the office itself. It was this traditional authority which was very largely responsible for keeping King William Dappa Pepple so long in office lacking any powerful house of his own, and forfeiting as he very soon did the support of the powerful Manilla Pepple group which had brought him to the throne.

But, as King William Dappa Pepple's example showed, such traditional authority was no ultimate substitute for the power derived from the backing of a powerful canoe house group.

(d) *The succession and the king-makers*

All these factors, economic, ritual, and conservative, and the support of a powerful house could also be said to characterize the type of kingship that preceded King Pepple and King Amakiri. The only real difference lay in the scale, in the size of the power structure which these kings and their immediate successors were able to organize as a result of the increase of wealth produced by the expansion of the slave trade which took place during the eighteenth century. This power structure did not descend intact to their successors any more than it had done with their predecessors. Each new king was still faced with the problem of having to re-create it or to build up a new one of his own, but during the nineteenth century a new factor appeared to complicate this build-up of kingly power.

During the eighteenth century the qualifications required for succession to the chieftaincy of a house were changed, while those relating to the kingship remained unaltered. Previously to this the founder of a new house, or ward or of a new kingly dynasty had to be a descendant of the founder or founders of the community. The founder of a new house in each case was expected to be succeeded by his sons in turn and then by any of his grandsons or other descendants who could trace their descent from him through links that were either male (under *eya* marriage) or female (under *egwa* marriage). But King Pepple, according to Bonny tradition, changed these rules. Houses became canoe houses and their chiefs could be of stranger and of slave origin. Such persons could even become the founders of their own canoe houses. These changes were also introduced in Nembe and Kalabari.

The result was the development of two kinds of chiefs, princely chiefs, that is chiefs who could hope to succeed to the kingship, and commoner chiefs, usually referred to in the consular records as 'slave chiefs', whose political objectives was to build up sufficient power to control the succession. They could not become kings but they could become king-makers and it was these king-makers who provided the crucial distinction between these nineteenth century monarchies and those that preceded them.

According to tradition the founder of a dynasty was succeeded by his sons in turn. In fact succession to his office remained a prize that was competed for by house chiefs, but the choice was limited to those chiefs who were also princes. The founder of the dynasty had expanded his canoe house into a canoe house group and among the subordinate houses in the group were some which had been founded by his actual sons and others which had been founded by 'adopted sons'. The latter were ineligible for the throne and it was the size and power of his house which was the principal factor which determined which son succeeded, while sons who had not founded a house were ignored. When the founder and first king died, one of these princely chiefs became the second king, and the other subordinate houses in the canoe house group founded by his father tended to break away and become independent houses. When the second king died the princely chief of one of these independent houses succeeded as the third king, while the house of the second king continued its existence as an independent house, separate from and usually opposed to the house of the third king. On this king's death another brother and chief succeeded, and when this first generation of princely chiefs was exhausted the succession was open to the chief of any house founded by the first and subsequent kings or by any of their successors, provided, and in these Delta states it was an important proviso, that they were of royal descent. For, unlike those African states where the main problem of the succession was how to choose a successor from among the large number of able sons left by the deceased king, the Eastern Delta states were faced with the opposite difficulty. The infertility of their kings, princes, and chiefs was such that despite the multiplicity of their wives, they seldom left behind them a sufficiency of heirs for the requirements of the succession.

We can observe how these rules of succession operated and how they were affected by these qualifying factors if we refer to the case of Nembe. Superficially it would appear that in both Bonny and Kalabari the system of succession changed during the century from one of brother succeeding brother, to one of eldest son succeeding father. In fact the change was fortuitous and due only to the dearth of other possible heirs. In Nembe, where there was not such a deficiency, we can, if we turn to Table 2, see the system functioning more normally.

In Ogbolomabiri three sons of King Mingi succeeded in turn, each the founder of a house which continued its separate existence after the kingship had left it. The fourth king, Kulo, was succeeded by his son, Amain and on Amain's death a successor was found in a collateral line, that of Okorotie (the house of Mingi's father's father's brother) through a female link (Okorotie's son's daughter). On the death of this sixth king (Kien) a successor, namely Ockiya, was found in the Mingi lineage, again through a female link.

Similarly in Bassambiri four sons of Obodo succeeded in turn and founded their respective houses, then in default of a suitable successor the sixth king was found once again in the Okorotie lineage in the person of Mein (Okorotie's son's son), and the succeeding kings were drawn from the houses founded respectively by Mein's two sons and two daughters. Here the pattern is clear enough. A strong king is succeeded by those of his sons who are fit to rule and when these are dead the chiefs who determine the succession choose the most suitable princely chief.

(e) *King versus king-makers*

Nembe was a poorer state and it was not so easy for able leaders to accumulate wealth and power as considerably and as rapidly as in

Bonny and Kalabari. The founders of various kingly dynasties were blessed with more offspring and commoner chiefs were able to stake a claim to the succession through marriage to a king's or prince's daughter, which meant that if this princess bore him a son this son would be eligible to succeed to the kingship.

This was not the case in Bonny and Kalabari, where the number of eligible princes continued to decline while the power structure built up by some of the kings continued after their death to develop under commoner chiefs until it came to dominate and control not only the succession but the kingly office itself. In Bonny King Pepple left only two eligible heirs, the princes Fubra (Manilla) and Opobo (Anna). His two elder sons had been killed in battle and only one of these Ibolu, had founded a house. But Ibolu left no descendants and on his death the house came under the chieftaincy of Kweni (Indian Queen), a refugee from Kalabari who had become a member of this house. Prince Fubra (Manilla Pepple) succeeded to the kingship and after him Prince Opobo (Anna Pepple). King Fubra (Manilla Pepple) was childless and when he died the chieftaincy of his house passed to his 'adopted son' and trusted lieutenant, Ibani, who was able to continue the expansion of the house initiated by his master. King Opobo begat at least three sons namely Datu (Dappo), William Dappa, and Fubra Akworo. The last, for reasons which Bonny tradition does not explain, was never considered for the kingship. William Dappa is said to have been the son of a wife of King Fubra who was inherited by King Opobo. He could therefore be considered a jural son of King Fubra, but there was no question of his succeeding to King Fubra's house; that was under the chieftaincy of Ibani Manilla Pepple. Prince Datu had pre-deceased his father and during the minority of Kala Fubra, Datu's infant son, his house was under the chieftaincy of Datu's principal slave, Maduka, while the chieftaincy of King Opobo's main house passed on his death to Opobo's principal slave whose name also was Maduka. Traditions and other records do not say whether Prince William Dappa had succeeded in founding his own house before his father's death, but it is clear that there was no obvious or suitable successor to King Opobo. Bereibibo (the son of King Pepple's daughter and a chief of the *duowari* House of Bristol who could trace his descent to Alagbaria the founder of Bonny) was elected king but this compromise failed. Bereibibo was deposed and eventually Prince William Dappa, the candidate supported by the Manilla Pepple group of houses, was made king after British intervention. King William Dappa was unable to build up a powerful house or to maintain a balance of power between the structures controlled by the rival king-makers, Erinashabo and Iloli who had succeeded respectively to the chieftaincies of the canoe house groups of Manilla Pepple and Anna Pepple. They united against him and he was deposed. The only heir available for the succession was Prince Fubra, the Anna Pepple candidate, and when he died King William Dappa in default of any other candidate was re-elected king and was succeeded by his son Prince George Pepple.

In Kalabari a cleavage had already occurred before his death in King Amakiri's power structure, the one group headed by the chief of the Barboy group of houses who could trace his descent to the founder of the previous dynasty, the other headed by the chief of the Harry group of houses founded by King Amakiri's principal slave Ombo (Harry).

There were four princely chiefs who were eligible for the succession and Prince Amakoro, the eldest of these, was powerful enough to succeed without question. But when he died a struggle broke out over the succession between the Barboy group who supported one son, Prince Ekine, and the Harry group who supported another, Prince Karibo. The latter group was successful and Karibo became king and expanded his house into the Karibo group of houses, while at the same time maintaining a balance between the two power groups headed respectively by the Barboy chief Barboy Braid (Kombo Agolea), and the Ombo chief Harry Braid both of whom were of slave origin.

When King Karibo died the only suitable successor was his eldest son Prince Abbe (Prince Will), who had the support of the Harry group. King Karibo's brothers had all died without issue and the Barboy group had no candidate of the Amakiri lineage whom they could support. Instead they elected as chief of the Barboy main house a descendant of King Kamalu and claimed the kingship in his name. King Karibo, however, had built up a powerful canoe house group and it was a combination of this with the Harry group that prevailed. But the leadership of King Karibo's power structure devolved not upon his son Prince Will, but upon his 'adopted son' George Amakiri.

In both states the king was now without power and this had become concentrated in the hands of two rival king-makers. There was no dearth of able subordinate chiefs who could replace a king-maker when he died or failed in his leadership. In Bonny Oko Jumbo became the king-maker in the Manilla Pepple group, and Jaja in the

Anna Pepple. But the heirs to the monarchy both in Bonny and Kalabari had become reduced to a single minimal lineage completely attached to one of the power groups, leaving the other group without any legitimate candidate whom they could put forward for the kingship. Jaja Anna Pepple's solution was to legitimate himself by withdrawing from Bonny and founding his own state of Opobo with himself as its king. Will Braid, the Barboy king-maker in Kalabari, tried to do the same but could not carry the other Barboy houses with him.

(f) *The end of the monarchy*

Kalabari and Bonny were left with a powerless king and a dominant king-maker, but the value of the kingly office still remained and the stage was set for the establishment of another dynasty by the king-maker or by one of his successors. But at this point external factors intervened and brought the kingship to an end.

European traders had originally brought the Oil River monarchies into existence by producing a need for a powerful administrative head and by providing the means whereby such a head could maintain and enhance his power. Now the British Protectorate brought them to an end by vesting this function in their own local officers and by abolishing the means whereby a king or a king-maker could build up his power—namely comey, the monopoly of trade with the interior, warfare, and slavery.

The value of the office of kingship disappeared; it was no longer a prize that was worth competing for by the chiefs of houses who formed the members of the local councils of Bonny, Degema, Opobo, and Brass. It was no longer even recognized by the government as a superior rank. Presidents were appointed for courts and for native councils and these offices were not held by the king but rotated among the chiefs nominated to sit on these tribunals. What remained of comey became a subsidy and it was distributed between various chiefs at the whim of the Colonial government and its local representative.[2]

[2] Newns 1949.

XII

Structural Change

I N the political systems of the Ibo hinterland, which in an earlier chapter were compared with those of the Eastern Delta states, the power structure built up by political leaders were of short duration and did not normally result in any change in the social structure of the community. The majority of the people in these hinterland communities were only indirectly involved in these political struggles, and although a village might, in the context of intra-village rivalry, be split into two rival factions, these factional loyalties were not strong enough to lead to any change in the segmentary structure of the village. Its members remained united as a corporate kin or quasi-kin group in balanced opposition to other similar villages, and were held together by common interests in land, religious cults, and other institutions which were not involved in these political rivalries, and which were strong enough collectively to resist the disintegrating effects of factional rivalry within the village or within the village group.

In the Eastern Delta states and to a lesser extent in Old Calabar this was not the case; there was much greater scope for leadership at the higher levels of the structure, the rewards for successful leadership were very great and, particularly in the Eastern Delta, this leadership could be identified much more completely with the political objectives of the primary segments of the community—its wards or canoe house groups. Struggles between political leaders had a much more disruptive effect upon the social structure and tended to result in either a partial or in a complete restructuring of the community.

The dynamics of these processes of structural change are examined in this chapter. Such changes were ultimately the result of uneven expansion and distribution of population which had come about in a number of different ways. They can be subsumed under three processes which can be termed population drift, lineage accretion and segmentation, and political accretion and fission. The first term refers to the gradual movement of people, either singly or in small groups from territorial units whose resources are stationary or declining to others where there are more of these resources available. The second is applied to processes which, whatever their real causes, are considered by one's informants to have been the result of a natural increase of the descendants of the founder of a lineage, and the segmentation is represented as following lines of cleavage laid down in the household of the original founder. It is not suggested here that such segmentation is in fact based on such simple lineage ramification or that the reasons for it are not political, they may well be so; but this type of segmentation is seen as a natural and a peaceful process which maintains rather than destroys the social order. It is this which distinguishes it from the third process, political fission and accretion, which results in the destruction of the original seg-mentary structure and its replacement by another which is based either upon a single political association built up by a single leader and his followers and their supporters,—political accretion, or upon the associations built up by two rival leaders,—political fission. Such processes could be limited to a part of the original structure— limited accretion or fission, or involve the whole community— overall accretion or fission.

I. POPULATION DRIFT AND LINEAGE SEGMENTATION IN THE EFIK STATE

The economic environment of Old Calabar differed from that of the Eastern Delta states. Its people were settled on arable land, not in barren mangrove swamp. They were not therefore entirely dependent on trading and fishing for their basic foodstuffs, but had an alternative choice of becoming farmers. Thus, while the wealthier members of the community and their households engaged in trade and politics and others continued as fishermen, the poorer members and a large proportion of the slaves turned to agriculture, and on the cessation of the slave trade at the beginning of the nineteenth century moved inland and supported themselves in agricultural settlements and small villages on land which they had cleared from virgin forest and which thus became the property of the particular wards and towns to which the settlers belonged. There was no longer any necessity for these people to become involved in the political rivalries of their ward chiefs, and indeed once they had become established in these 'plantations' they intervened in Duke Town or Creek Town politics only when they felt their interests were endangered. This was only when the reigning king died or when it was believed that his life was threatened. With the dispersal of population during the nineteenth century into the hinterland the structure of the Efik community attained a relatively stable form.

The emphasis placed on descent in the Efik social organization produced a division into nobles, commoners and slaves. The former alone could trace their descent though male or female links to one or other of the founders of the Efik community and they alone were eligible for political or ritual office. The Efik system, unlike that of the Eastern Delta, permitted the marriage of cousins of any sort and as a result these noble families formed a closely intermarried group of kinsfolk differentiated by reason of their pedigrees from other Efik, divided against each other by the rival political interests of the particular wards to which they belonged. Commoners and slaves, though barred from political office, could engage in trade and some of the latter were able to become extremely wealthy. But they were not permitted to become members of the highest grades of the ruling Ekpe society and the society discriminated strongly against slaves, particularly recently-bought slaves who were not members of the society and therefore outside its protection. These were principal recipients of the floggings and killings by the 'Egbo runners' and other agents of the society.

The fact that nobles alone could aspire to political office did not mean that only they were engaged in Efik politics. Wealthy slaves and commoners were also involved, their names appear on Treaties and some of them were the most influential members in their wards. But they could never become chief of a ward or even of one of its subdivisions, and they could only operate as the principal advisers and supporters of such chiefs.

Because of the great value attached to descent in Old Calabar, genealogies were of considerable importance and formed a charter not only for each ward but for the whole political structure, which was represented as the ramification of one or of two family trees to which the head of every political segment had to be able to trace his descent. This genealogy can for political purposes be abbreviated in the diagram on page 191. This diagram combines two conflicting genealogies.[1]

[1] One, which is that given by the group of wards which were originally dominant and which derive directly from Atai Ema and Eyo Ema, traces the descent of all Efik wards to their apical ancestor Ema, making Effiom Ekpo the son of Ema and making the founders of the Eyo Nsa ward the sons of Eyo Ema. The other, which is that of the group of wards that subsequently became dominant, makes their founder, Effiom Ekpo, a brother or paternal cousin of Ema and the founders of the Eyo Nsa ward the sons of Odo, one of his daughters.

TABLE 5   EFIK STRUCTURAL GENEALOGY

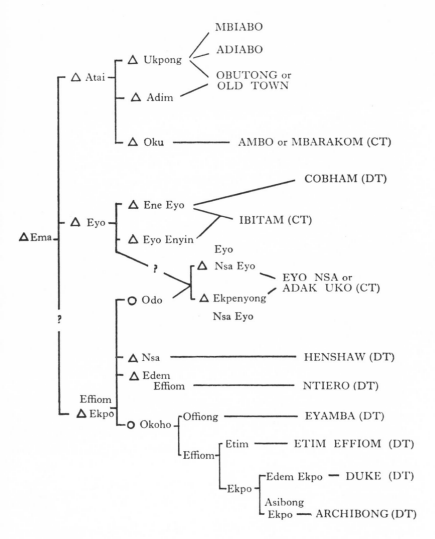

Notes: Wards and Towns in Capitals. Founders in lower case.
(DT) = DUKE TOWN.   (CT) = CREEK TOWN.
The genealogy has been turned on its side.

These genealogies illustrate a simple pattern of partial accretion and lineage segmentation, in which a political structure expands unevenly, and in which one segment (ward), which from its history we can assume to have been the dominant one, increases more rapidly than the others and then either segments into two wards or is split by fission to achieve much the same result.

This increase was not the result of normal lineage expansion, nor was it achieved primarily by the purchase of slaves or of the personnel of other wards as in the Eastern Delta states. It was mainly the result of the process we have called population drift. We can see the process at work if we examine the development of the Henshaw (Nsa) ward. Its structural genealogy is given on page 193.

The Nsa ward was one of the four primary segments of the Effiom Ekpo group which founded Duke Town (Atakpa) under the leadership of Effiom Okoho. Nsa later segmented into the five ward sections shown in the diagram. One of these, Nkoro Nsa, rapidly disappeared, its personnel being absorbed into the Etim Effiom and Duke wards. Of the remaining four sections, one, Ewa Nsa, expanded, while the others declined some of their members and leaders becoming incorporated into the Duke ward, and others into the Ewa Nsa section of the Henshaw ward.

Today the Henshaw ward segments into four recognized ward sections and one potential ward section, namely Effiom Ewa. Three of these derive from Ewa Nsa section and so does the potential ward section. The original ward section of Effiom Nsa is extinct, the descendants of its original members now constitute two ward subsections in the Duke ward and part of the present Ewa Ekeng section of the Henshaw. Another original section, Ekpo Nsa, is also extinct, its descendants constituting part of the present Ekeng Iwatt section. A third original section, Efaña Nsa, split into two, Efaña Offiong and Efaña Efaña ; the first named remained in Henshaw while the last named removed to the Duke ward where it became known as Duke Henshaw. It returned to the Henshaw ward in the present century and the two segments were reunited as the Efaña Offiong or Duke Henshaw ward section. The fourth ward section, Andem Nkoi, is said to derive from a man from the related Enyong Tribe, who attached himself to the Ewa Nsa group and married Ewa Nsa's daughter. The potential ward section, Effiom Ewa, also derives from Ewa Nsa. Like the Efaña section it split into two parts one of which removed to the Duke ward. The Henshaw ward council is not prepared to recognize Effiom Ewa as a ward section until it prevails upon its relatives in the Duke ward to return to the Henshaw ward.

TABLE 6. STRUCTURAL GENEALOGY OF THE HENSHAW WARD

(Original sections)   (Present Sections)   (Remarks)

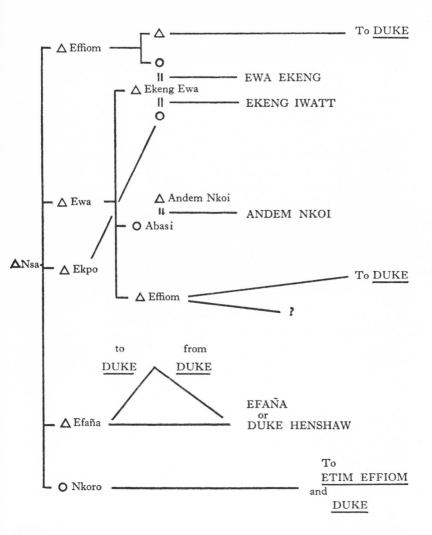

Notes: Ward sections in Capitals. Founders in lower case. Wards underlined and in Capitals.

It is clear from this example that we are not concerned with natural increase of population but with one of population drift, which is represented in Efik tradition as the movement of a noble son or daughter and of his or her followers. This movement operated at two structural levels: at the higher level the drift was from other wards to the dominant ward; at the lower level and within the Henshaw ward the drift was from other ward sections to the dominant Ewa Nsa section. Such a drift in the case of the accession of a considerable number of people was represented in the ward's genealogical charter as the marriage of a daughter of the chief of the losing section to the chief of the receiving section.

We can observe the process of lineage accretion and segmentation at the ward level in Duke Town if we turn to the Efik genealogy and examine the continuous division into dual segments of the dominant ward of the Effiom Ekpo group. One of these new segments continued its existence as a new ward, the other, which we can assume to have been the one that retained or acquired the kingship, continued its expansion only to divided once again into two wards. This process of expansion and segmentation of the dominant ward continued until the death of the Great Duke Ephraim (Effiom Edem Ekpo) in the early part of the nineteenth century, when it finally ended. The Great Duke left no descendants, there were no outstanding political leaders in Old Calabar who could replace him, and the drift of population changed its direction. The movement from weaker wards to the dominant ward declined and the majority of the poorer people, while remaning members of their respective wards, moved away from Duke Town into the hinterland.

This process of lineage accretion and segmentation in the Okoho Effiom Ekpo group seems to have proceeded without much political tension. Efik tradition depicts it as lineage segmentation not as political fission and the wards which resulted from it, while considering themselves of equivalent political status to other Efik wards, also preserved a feeling of closer political unity as opposed to the other less closely related wards of Henshaw and Ntiero. The office of king, for example, remained within the Okoho group and rotated between the chiefs of its four wards.

2. LIMITED POLITICAL FISSION

For an example of partial fission we can turn to the Ema group and take the case of the Eyo Ema segment. Atai Ema was originally the dominant segment in Creek Town but the political fission in it, which resulted in the establishment of the rival town of Obutong, left the other Ema segment Eyo Ema temporarily dominant in Creek Town. Tradition claims that during this period of dominance Eyo Ema consisted of four segments, namely the original segments of Ene Eyo and Eyo Enyin Eyo and two others which were 'brought out' at this time, namely Ekpenyong Nsa Eyo and Eyo Nsa Eyo. These last two segments, which form the Eyo Nsa (Adak Uko or Eyo Honesty) ward, and are now dominant in Creek Town, dispute this and claim relationship not with Eyo Ema but with the Effiom Ekpo group. What is clear is that at least by the time of the establishment of Duke Town by the Effiom Ekpo group, there existed in the dominant Eyo Ema group of Creek Town a dual division into the Ene Eyo and Eyo Enyin segments on the one side and the Eyo Nsa and Ekpenyong Nsa segments on the other. Eyo Enyin disintegrated as a political unit and Ene Eyo secured the kingship of Creek Town and expanded into nine segments each claiming a son or daughter of Ene Eyo as its founder and with the Akabom Ene Eyo segment dominant. The Eyo Nsa—Ekpenyong Nsa division however expanded at an even faster rate through its association with the Effiom Okoho wards of Duke Town and eventually wrested the kingship of Creek Town from the Ene Eyo division. Its failure to retain it led to its fission into two parts, one of which removed to Duke Town where it became the Cobham ward. Of the nine segments of Ene Eyo the dominant segment of Akabom Ene (Cobham), which gave its name to the new Duke Town ward, was split into two parts, as were two other segments. In each case one of these parts remained in Creek Town and the other removed to Duke Town. The remaining six segments did not split but moved as complete segments to Duke Town. The three parts which remained in Creek Town became the three ward sections of the Ibitam ward.

This fission of the Ene Eyo group which occurred sufficiently recently for tradition to retain its structural details, enables us to amplify and elucidate similar occurrences whose details have now become obscure or forgotten, for instance the earlier fission of the Atai Ema group, or the fission of the Korome ward, now almost forgotten in Kalabari tradition but referred to in Bonny tradition and supported by James Barbot's journal. We can see this as a fission which divided the Korome ward (Duke Monmouth) into two parts, one of which removed like the Cobham group to an adjacent and rival community. The fact that both the Bonny and Kalabari nineteenth century houses which derived from Duke Monmouth were called Africa suggests that, as in the case of the Eyo Ema fission, it was not a simple matter of rivalry between two major segments in the ward, but rivalry within a single dominant segment for the leadership or headship of the whole ward and with it of whole community. Such rivalry ended in each case by splitting the dominant section of the ward, Akabom Ene in the case of Eyo Ema, Duke Africa in the case of Korome and Ukpong Atai in the case of Atai Ema.

3. OVERALL POLITICAL ACCRETION AND LINEAGE SEGMENTATION

Such a pattern of fission, following not the lines of previous segmentation but being based on the political affiliations of political leaders and their followers, is more clearly brought out when we come to examine Eastern Delta material relating to overall accretion and fission, where we can see political leadership in action unhampered by the limitations of descent which affected it in Old Calabar, and stimulated by the incentives offered to commoners and slaves to become chiefs of their own canoe houses.

The best example of overall accretion is the political machine built up by Amakiri and described at length in Appendix A. This was based originally on the Endeme ward, and it succeeded not only in breaking up and absorbing the other Kalabari wards but also in completely destroying the previous internal structure of this ward itself. All the houses into which it segmented were new foundations established by members of King Amakiri's expanded household The sole remains of the other wards were politically powerless remnants that survived only in association with some of these new houses—Igodome as Standfast Jack in association with Oruwari (Briggs); Korome split into three houses each associated with a different and eventually rival new house—Jack Rich with West India—Black Duke with George Will—Duke Africa with Will Braid.

A similar process can be seen in Bonny in the expansion of King Pepple's political machine. Here the process of accretion was not carried so far and a number of houses of older establishment were able to avoid disintegration and absorption, but by the nineteenth century all the powerful houses (opuwari), were derived from King Pepple's original house.

The examples of the build-up of the Amakiri and Perukule power structure also illustrate the process of lineage segmentation which invariably accompanies expansion in political systems of this type. A leader as he expands his political machine is faced with the problem of keeping it together, particularly when, as in the Eastern Delta or Old Calabar, this expansion is mainly in his own house or ward. Rivalries among his followers and their lesser leaders, can be resolved or at least reduced by a division into segments which, while it accepts the implication of these rivalries, at the same time limits the authority of these rivals as heads or leaders of their own segment and clearly defines their position in the structure. The logical development of this process occurs in the canoe house. Here segmentation is encouraged but only as a process carried out by the house chief and lesser leaders in combination, and as a reward for those subordinate leaders who have been most successful in advancing the main house's fortunes and their own. Segmentation of this kind, however, leads not only to greater administrative efficiency within the canoe house group but also to an intensification of political rivalry at the higher political level. The head of the canoe house group and his lieutenants, with political tensions inside the group largely resolved, are freed to devote their joint energies more exclusively to political and economic competition with other house groups. In Old Calabar by contrast, lineage segmentation appears more as a means of relieving political tension and not necessarily as a reward for efficient leadership. Only those of noble birth could be recognized as head of a segment, but if a sufficient number of persons could be grouped together and attached to a son or other close descendant of a ward or ward section head, they could claim and would be accorded recognition as a new ward, or ward section, or ward sub-section according to their size. Such lineage segmentation at the ward level amounted virtually to a peaceful form of fission as the new ward became politically independent of its parent. In the canoe house group this was not the case. A newly segmented canoe house remained politically a part of the canoe house group and actively involved in this group's struggle for political dominance.

4. LIMITED POLITICAL ACCRETION AND LINEAGE SEGMENTATION IN THE EASTERN DELTA STATES

But this was not so in the Eastern Delta before the eighteenth century and the time of King Pepple. The success of the Amakiri expansion has effaced the Kalabari traditions of earlier dynasties but the Bonny traditions are clearer and are summarized in the structural genealogy in Table 3.

Here we can see a more gradual process of expansion in which, as in Old Calabar, accretion and lineage segmentation proceed side by side, so that although the majority of wards or houses in the community could be said to derive from a single original ward, the process was a very gradual one in which, as in the Duke Town example, rapid expansion was confined to the segments which became successively dominant. According to Bonny tradition, the community consisted originally of four wards, derived respectively from Alagbaria, Opu Amakubu, Okpara Ndoli, and Asimini. Alagbaria's descendants survive today as the minor house of Bristol, the second and third named wards have disappeared, all the other houses except John Africa and Brown of Finnema derive from Asimini. They can be ranked in five successive groups. The first originated as segments of the expanded house of Edimini ba Kamba. This had two divisions or branches, one of these being the royal house of King Kamalu, the other, whose genitor was Biriye, developed separately in the adjacent village of Peterside. The royal segment under King Kamalu expanded to produce the second group of houses, whose survivors are known today as Dublin Green and Tolofari, and one of these former houses, the house of King Opu Dappa, expanded to produce the third group of houses known today as Duke Norfolk, Black Fubra, Halliday, and Finebone. Meanwhile the second branch of Edimini ba Kamba had segmented to produce the fourth group of houses (Ndiepiri, Ubani (or Grand Bonny), Shoo Peterside, Wilcox and Perukule or Captain Pepple), and when no segment of the Opu Dappa group was powerful enough to retain the kingship it passed to a segment of this branch, namely the house of Perukule which segmented into the fifth group which provided the *opuwari* houses of the nineteenth century, namely Allison, Captain Hart, Fine Country, Jack Wilson Pepple, Ukonu, Manilla Pepple and Anna Pepple.

If one turns to Nembe the same process of expansion of a single group or ward may be observed. There were according to tradition three original groups, namely Ogboloama, Olodiama and Onyoama or, if one considers the Isselema as a separate group, possibly four original groups. Of these only Ogboloama survives. Political rivalry between two leaders (grandsons of a King Peresuo) split it into the two moieties of Ogbolomabiri and Bassambiri each under its own king. This was followed by continuous accretion and lineage segmentation (illustrated in Table 2), so that of the present, eighteen canoe houses of Ogbolomabiri nine derive from King Mingi, the successful leader who was left in possessions of Ogbolomabiri eight derive from his third son Kulo (A4) and one from Opu the son of King Peresuo's brother. While of the thirteen houses of Bassambiri, six derive from the unsuccessful leader Obodo, who withdrew with his followers from Ogboloama to found this sub-community, six from Mein, who was another descendant of Opu and who became its sixth King, and one was founded by Epelle a stranger from the Ibo town of Onitsha on the Niger.

5. OVERALL POLITICAL FISSION

Bonny tradition represents the expansion of the Asimini ward as successive processes of accretion and lineage segmentation. Kalabari tradition remembers almost nothing of the period immediately preceding Amakiri, and the fission that regrouped the people of Nembe into the dual divisions of Ogbolomabiri and Bassambiri was equally effective in obliterating all recollection of the ward structure that had immediately preceded it. To see the process of total fission in operation we have to turn once more to Bonny and Kalabari, this time in the nineteenth century.

In the Kalabari example we can see a cleavage already appearing in the Endeme ward during the later period of King Amakiri's reign. Present-day tradition presents this as developing from a natural division of the ward into a senior group, who were descendants of the original members of the ward and of the Kamalu line of kings, and a newer group composed of persons introduced into it by King Amakiri. But traditions relating to individual houses and legends telling of the 'golden age' of King Amakiri alike refer to rivalries between leaders and would-be leaders who originated in King Amakiri's own house, a house which by this time had segmented into a number of houses each founded by one of these leaders. In the build-up of followers to 'fill the canoe', founder and followers alike would appeal to and be affected by sentiments of previous kinship and similar group loyalties. Thus one would expect to find descendants of the Kamalu line associating with and being included in the house founded by their most successful relative Awo and by his son Odum. Later combinations of leaders would also seek to justify and to reinforce their association by appeals to earlier kinship and domestic groupings. What is however quite clear when these traditions are

o

taken together is that King Amakiri's political machine divided into
a number of segments (canoe houses) founded by his leading sons,
servants and slaves, and that these houses contained in addition to
slaves and strangers most of the former population of Kalabari which
was distributed between them irrespective of their former kinship
and political alignments. In the next reign, if not before, these
segments had become aligned into two rival political associations
which were headed respectively by the two most successful of these
leaders, Odum (Barboy) and Ombo (Harry). The houses of each of
these leaders had already expanded into a group of canoe houses and
these groups were now competing against each other for control of
the kingship.

It was the same in Bonny. Two of the seven houses into which
the house of King Pepple had segmented, namely Manilla Pepple
and Anna Pepple, had become so large that on the death of King
Opobo they were able to split the Pepple political machine into two
rival groups which eventually divided Bonny between them.

The course of these struggles has been described in Chapters VIII
and IX; what is relevant here is their eventual outcome. In both
cases we have a pattern of total or overall accretion followed by one
of total fission and in both cases the final result is the establishment
of new and separate sub-communities based on the political machines
of the rival leaders. The new Kalabari structure is given below.

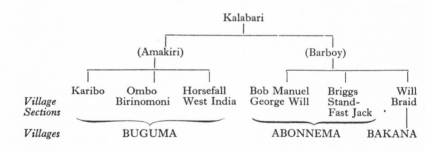

6. REAPPEARANCE OF SEGMENTARY SYSTEMS

When we examine these new communities at the end of the
nineteenth century we find that the earlier structural pattern of
balanced politically equivalent segments had reappeared. Opobo
had divided into fourteen canoe house groups and Bonny into
twelve, while in Kalabari as in Nembe a superior structure had been

created with the pattern of balanced segments carried to a higher level and applying to the sub-communities. Thenceforward Kalabari consisted of six major segments grouped into two divisions and distributed in three villages in a manner which perpetuated the final distribution of power in the state.

7. BINARY DIVISION

The political history of all the Eastern Delta states provides very clear examples of the binary division which characterizes political rivalry of this sort when carried to extremes. In these Eastern Nigerian communities the potentiality of fission is latent at every level of the structure and the essence of political leadership lies in preventing such a division in one's own power structure while promoting it in those of one's rivals. It may appear strange that political rivalry should always become concentrated into two and not more parties. The explanation would appear to lie[2] in a simple theory of games. Political leaders supreme in their own village (or ward) or canoe house group and competing for dominance at the higher or community level, and who can be called greater leaders, are competing against each other for the support of lesser leaders and their followers, these lesser leaders being men competing against each other for dominance at a lower political level within their various segments. The choice of these lesser leaders is not entirely free but is constrained firstly by loyalties and ties fixed by the social structure, and secondly by the existing rivalries and disputes in which they are already involved. These latter may be of long standing and may be of more concern to the lesser leader's supporters than to the lesser leader himself.

Subject then to these constraints a lesser leader will support which-ever greater leader he considers most able to maximize his (the lesser leader's) political gains. There may be initially more than two potential greater leaders but if political rivalry becomes intensified they will soon be reduced to two, as lesser leaders desert those who fall short of their expectations, and as such deserted leaders seek to retain the remnant of their following either by attaching themselves to one of these successful greater leaders, or by leaving the system and the community and attaching themselves to another leader in another community. This reduction of redundant greater leaders does not continue beyond two unless one leader becomes so

[2] As Barth (1959) has pointed out.

pre-eminent that lesser leaders have no valid choice but to support him. In such a case this leader is left supreme; political rivalry in his community is relegated to a lower level while the leaders within the political machine of this dominant leader reorient themselves and feel their way towards the positions they are going to take when this dominant leader dies or becomes senile or loses his control over his machine.

With no such pre-eminent leader available the choice lies between two relatively equal leaders. Where a lesser leader is himself involved in political disputes this is no real choice, since he is almost bound to have to range himself on the opposite side to that taken by by his particular rivals. Thus political rivalry becomes intensified in the community with the protagonists of all its major disputes becoming concentrated into two opposed factions. While rival parties are building up their power the community may be said to divide into three—the two rival groups and the rest, for example the 'neutral party' of the consular reports on Bonny. But this 'third party' is not a coherent unity and the only choices open to any of the groups which compose it and to its leader or leaders is either to move as a single unit to join one or other of the rival parties or to be split between them.

Table 3 seeks to show this in the case of Bonny in the mid-nineteenth century. The two dominant groups were the Manilla and Anna Pepple groups. Of the houses derived from King Pepple, the commoner houses of Allison, Captain Hart, Fine Country and Jack Wilson Pepple supported Manilla, while the princely house derived from Ibolu supported Anna Pepple. Of the *duowari* houses founded before the time of King Pepple, two houses (Halliday and Dublin Green) supported Manilla Pepple the others supported Anna Pepple. The satellite villages of Peterside and Finnema were split in the same way between these two rival groups.

Similarly in the case of Kalabari we have the Barboy and the Amakiri groups, dividing the community during the nineteenth century as can be seen in Table 4. The Kalabari material also provides excellent examples of the way in which weaker groups and groups which lost the struggle for dominance broke down or were broken down according to this binary pattern. By 1860 the Barboy house had a latent division between the main house now under the leadership of Will Braid and the houses founded by Barboy's sons, namely George Will and Manuel. The first crack in the Barboy structure came with a division in the Manuel house, now expanded into a group of houses, between Bob Manuel and Horsefall Manuel. Thenceforward one of these divisions was always found opposed to the Barboy group and associated with the Harry (Ombo). After the death of King Karibo, the leader of his group of houses in coalition with the Harry (Ombo) group was able to exploit the division between the Braids and the other senior Barboy houses, with the result that when Will Braid led his people away to Ewofa the other senior Barboy houses broke away and refused to join him and ended by supporting the Karibo-Ombo-Horsefall group against him. The other communities and houses which had supported the Barboy group were split between them. The canoe house group of Don Pedro split into two, one part under Bealnut joining Will Braid, the other under Granville remaining with Bob Manuel. The Korome group of houses had already divided between Ombo and Barboy, and the Duke Monmouth houses, which supported the Barboy group, now split again with Black Duke supporting Bob Manuel, and Duke Africa Will Braid. Similarly the village of Ifoko, which had already divided into the houses of Iboroma and of Jack Pilot, divided once again. Iboroma remained united in support of Will Braid, but Jack Pilot was split between the Will Braid and the George Will—Bob Manuel divisions.

This competition between leaders and the power structures they were seeking to construct existed and operated within a social organization that itself imposed certain oppositions and rivalries upon the groups of which it was composed, and which also provided various restraints and checks to maintain some measure of structural stability. As the social structure varied in different areas, so did these fundamental oppositions and loyalties, and the checks and restraints which they imposed on political leaders in their struggles for power. We can therefore expect to find political rivalry taking a rather different form and developing differently in communities where these structural and political factors were different, as for example in the Efik state. Here there were much stronger checks and restraints on the development of political leadership. Binary division was almost completely confined to the level of the ward, and we have a pattern very similar to that of Bonny before the time of King Pepple. In this, one ward remained dominant, but its continuous expansion was checked by binary segmentation or fission within it as soon as it had expanded to a certain size. Apart from the example of the Eyo Ema ward, such binary division occurred at too early a date for tradition to remember how it came about. The effect

however is clear. The expansion of the dominant ward was temporarily halted and the balance between the wards was temporarily
restored by the creation of a new ward from the excess of population
in the dominant ward.

8. CONCLUSIONS

It is not only inaccurate but misleading to attempt to describe the
political systems and the social structure of these Oil River states as
they existed before the establishment of British Colonial rule in the
form of a static model, whether based on a synchronic study of one
phase of their development or on a general characterization that
would perforce ignore and misrepresent the structural changes that
occurred. It is equally unsatisfactory to regard them as systems in a
state of oscillation between political systems of the group A and
group B type. They appear to conform more closely to systems
which pass through successive stages of accretion, segmentation,
and fission. Whether power is concentrated in the hands of an
'absolute monarch' or one who rules by maintaining a 'balance of
power'; whether power is in the hands of a leader of a particular ward
who controls a puppet king or the kingship is open to the head of any
ward that may be temporarily dominant depends on which stage
has been reached when the system is examined.

The political systems of communities in the Eastern Region of
Nigeria can be said to belong to the same general type, one in which
power is distributed between the primary segments of the community,
that is the villages in the case of the Ibo, the village sections, wards,
or canoe house groups in the case of the Ibibio and the Oil River
states. In some of these systems, for example in those of the Northern
Ibo, these segments are so structured that a balance of power is
maintained between them and these can be distinguished as stable
systems in which this balance of power remains relatively unaffected
by the temporary political activities of political leaders. Others,
notably those of the people we have been concerned with in this
study, can be distinguished as unstable systems, in which the distribution of power in the system was upset by the intrusion of external
factors. These factors made it possible for one of these segments
and its leader to become unduly powerful so that the former structure of the segment or, in extreme cases, of the whole community
was destroyed.

We can in the case of these states, identify the principal disturbing
factors as the sudden access of wealth provided by the overseas

slave trade, the recognition by the European traders of their village heads as kings and the association of this office of king with the control and distribution of very large trading dues.

When we compare the Efik state of the seventeenth century and eighteenth century with those of Kalabari and Bonny in the nineteenth century, we can distinguish degrees of instability depending on the degree of competition between the primary segments and on the quality of the political leadership which they were prepared to encourage. In the Efik system, which was characterized by limited accretion and lineage segmentation or by limited fission, the traditional offices of village and of ward heads were confined to lineal descendants of the founding ancestors of these wards. This pattern also seems to have been characteristic of Bonny and of Kalabari before the mid-eighteenth century and the time of King Pepple and King Amakiri. In both cases we can observe a development cycle which affected the dominant ward, that is, the ward which had been able to obtain possession of the kingship. In this the ward passed through successive stages of expansion, followed by lineage segmentation or on occasion political fission, both of which were succeeded by a final stage of disintegration, leaving power once more distributed between a number of independent wards, one of which became dominant and repeated the cycle.

We can also attribute the greater degree of instability which characterized the Eastern Delta states after this period to the increased wealth brought by the eighteenth century slave trade and to the increased warfare that accompanied it, which resulted in the replacement of the ward by the canoe house whose chieftaincy was open to the ablest members in the house without regard to their origin.

In the case of Nembe this fission produced a better balanced structure and there was only limited accretion and lineage segmentation for the rest of the period. Whether this would have continued, and whether this would have been the actual outcome of the conflict in Bonny and Kalabari, we cannot say, for at this point the British Protectorate was established, the disturbing factors were removed, and a different political system imposed on these Oil River states.

APPENDIX A

The Origin and Development of the Principal Kalabari Houses

The social structure of Kalabari has been examined in detail in the second part of this book, we are concerned here with the traditional history of the main social divisions whose leaders determined the political development of the Kalabari state during the nineteenth century. Almost all of these groups were founded or developed during the reign of Amakiri, and their traditions of origin and of their early struggles provide a clear picture of the social organization of the Kalabari as it developed during the late eighteenth century and early nineteenth century.

We can only guess at the social structure of Elem Kalabari before this time. According to tradition there were seven wards, but the number seven is of ritual significance in Kalabari mythology[1] and we are probably on safer ground if we rely on Mr. Grazilhier's description which suggested four major or dominant wards in Kalabari at the end of the seventeenth century. Besides Endeme and Korome three other houses or wards are mentioned in the Amakiri traditions. These are Igodome which became in the nineteenth century the Standfast Jack house; Akialame whose members were absorbed by the Amakiri groups and which seems to have come to a political end during Amakiri's reign; and Amabiame whose chief was the ill fated Ogoloye Fubra who met Capt. Crow in 1807. There were probably other lesser houses the surviving remnants of former wards which like those of the 'neutral party' of nineteenth century Bonny had managed to preserve some measure of their former independence, but were politically ineffective. The only names that occur in the traditions are Akwame which was associated with the cult of Okpolodo, and Bukome.

What is clear from these traditions is that by the end of Amakiri's reign the division of Elem Kalabari into a limited number of residentially separate wards had disappeared. Those wards that had survived the catastrophies of the early period of Amakiri's reign had either disintegrated like Korome into the three single houses of Seleye (Jack Rich), Black Duke and Duke Africa, or declined like Igodome into the single house of Standfast Jack, or had dispersed like Akialame their surviving members being incorporated into other houses. Meanwhile Endeme, grossly over-expanded with the personnel it had absorbed from the other sections or obtained from the Ibo hinterland, had disintegrated into a massive number of canoe houses, some of them separate and some expanded or aggregated into groups, and the two largest and most powerful

[1] For example Soku was founded by seven men who came out of the ground. Ke by seven men who came down from the sky.

of these groups were those derived from Awo (Barboy) and from Amakiri's own household. The traditional boast that Amakiri doubled the number of wards in Elem Kalabari is not completely devoid of foundation, but it is clear from the traditions of individual houses that these fourteen 'wards' or quarters were merely residential areas of Elem Kalabari which retained the name of a kin group which had originally lived there. The names no longer referred to corporate kin groups though Amakiri seems to have attempted to restore something of their corporate character by making some of his newly created chiefs with their canoe house members reside in particular sections and act as chiefs of these sections. Thus he is said to have had placed his son Prince Fubra in the Akialame quarter, Odum in the Alame quarter which became known as Awopolo, and Ombo in Ituruame. But this attempt seems to have broken down through the expansion of population and pressure on the very limited area of dry land available so that the actual political and social unit came to consist of a canoe house or group of houses whose members resided wherever they could find accommodation, not only inside the town, but outside it in neighbouring or distant settlements (plantations) belonging to the house and even within other communities associated with the Kalabari state. Most houses of long establishment had a particular area of Elem Kalabari which was occupied mainly by the dwellings of their members, those more recently founded were more dispersed. From 1850 onward we have a number of documents which detail the names of the politically important houses, at three different periods of Kalabari history. These are, firstly the later part of King Karibo's reign when there are a series of treaties from 1850–1855 signed by the heads of all these houses, secondly consul Burton's letter which gives the political alignment of houses after Karibo's death in 1863, and finally the letter of 1882 given in the Appendix B which was written just before the abandonment of Elem Kalabari and the removal to Abonnema and Buguma and which lists all but the Bakana (Will Braid) groups of houses and one Abonnema house.[2] These names have been arranged in three successive columns in Table 4. The succeeding pages are intended to trace the origin and development of these houses as given in their oral traditions from the time of Amakiri to 1850, and their details have been summarized in the first column of this Table.

I. *The Barboy group*

The interrelationship of the various houses in this group are indicated in Table 4. Awo the founder of the Barboy house had three wives who bore him sons whom tradition now remembers; they were Ikoro of Amabiame, his first wife, who bore him Odum (Will ¡Barboy), Abiatoaa a slave woman, who bore him Otaji (Long Will), and Adida the eldest daughter of Amakiri and the full sister of Prince Amakoro, who bore him

---

[2] Namely Member Briggs, whose chief was too ill to sign.

Owukori (Manuel). Tradition records that when Amakiri gave Adida to Awo in marriage he gave her Abiatoaa as her servant, and much to Amakiri's anger she became pregnant before Adida and bore a son whom Amakiri called Otaji, the name of a bitter herb. Then Adida also conceived and bore Awo a son and Amakiri was reconciled and called the boy Owukori, ('strife ended').

Awo died young and Odum succeeded as head of his house. By this time Obaji (Jack Barboy) and Amabibi (Don Pedro), both slave members of Awo's house, had established their canoe house chieftaincies.

Later a quarrel broke out between Prince Owuso, Amakiri's eldest son, and Odum. Odum had dressed his hair with pearl beads in a fashion that Prince Owuso had reserved to himself. Owuso beat him and shaved off his hair. Amakiri intervened and restored to Odum his severed hair which Owuso was proposing to burn, but Odum found it advisable to remove from Elem Kalabari and lived at Onya until Owuso's death when Amakiri brought him back again. Odum returned bringing with him his severed locks which he gave to his family to help them remember the wrongs done him by the house of Amakiri. This is the Amakiri version. The Barboy version is that Odum did not inherit much of his father's wealth. When Awo died Amakiri attached Otaji and his mother and their household to Ombo, and Owukori and his mother to Prince Fubra. After Prince Owuso's attack on him Odum fled to Onya where he made his fortune by his own efforts and became so wealthy that the goddess Owame Akaso warned the Kalabari that he must be reconciled with the Kalabari if the town was not to perish, and warned them also that he was preparing with 2,200 men to attack the place. Jack Barboy (Obaji) was sent to see Odum and he persuaded him to return in peace. Before his flight, Odum had been accused of thirty-two offences. On his return he was tried and found not guilty of them all and Amakiri received him back and made peace between him and his enemies.

Odum (Will Barboy) like Awo his father, died young and on his death the chieftaincy of the house passed to his brother Otaji (Long Will). On Otaji's death the chieftaincy of the Barboy house passed to Kombo Agolea (Braid), Odum's most important slave, while the chieftaincy of Otaji's own house passed to Otaji's slave and 'adopted son' Otaji (George Will). Another version claims that Otajinta not Otaji was the founder of the George Will house. Kombo Agolea (Barboy Braid) who thus became head of the Barboy group and Edi Abali (Harry Braid) who became the leader of the Ombo group were the two most powerful chiefs in Kalabari in the second quarter of the nineteenth century. Tradition maintains that they were brothers (classificatory or actual) from the Ibo community of Obum.[3] One was sold to the Odum group the other to the Ombo and

---

[3] Obum could possibly be either the Isuama Ibo community of Umuobom or the Nri-Awka Ibo community of Mbom which, local Ibo traditions say, was sacked and destroyed by Ada Ibo warriors brought against it by the Aro.

they grew up to become the leaders of these two rival groups. Their relationship was remembered in their Kalabari nickname Mbre (Brother) which became anglicized as Braid. Kombo Agolea married Agbani, daughter of Awo's sister and by her begat Igbanibo (Will Braid). The early association of Owukori Manuel was with the Amakiri group and with that part of it derived from the former Akialame ward. Amakiri had married Ogun of Akialame who was the mother of Prince Fubra. On Amakiri's death Prince Fubra inherited two other Akialame wives of Amakiri's, namely Kalaroba Mangiaro and Saraba Awo, who was the mother of Adida (Owukori's mother) and of Prince Amakoro (Tiger Amakiri). Owukori (Manuel) grew up in Prince Fubra's household and when Prince Fubra died he became the chief of the house. But the members of the house fearing he would convert it into his own house which would mean that it became linked with the Barboy group deposed Owukori and elected Ogono-Ibiduka. Prince Amakoro who was now reigning as King Amakiri II was vexed at this and created a new canoe house chieftaincy for Owukori, his sister's son, adding to Adida's and Kalaroba Mangiaro's following other members from Amakiri's house.

The establishment of the Manuel house by King Amakoro resulted in the decline and disappearance of the Prince Fubra house, its surviving members becoming incorporated in the Manuel house (and in the Horsefall section of it) and taking with them the ancestral shrine of their founder.[4]

After Owukori (Manuel) the most important men in this new house were Omekwe (Horsefall) and his nephew Wokoma (Charles Horsefall);[5] Omekwe and Wokoma were the son and grandson of Bekeangama a female slave in Kalaroba Mangiaro's household. Bekeangama had just been married (under the *egwa* system of marriage) to Ngo a man of the Korome section. But when the dispute already referred to between the Seleye and the Amakiri houses[6] resulted in fighting between these houses Kalaroba took Bekeangama back from Ngo together with their son Wariboko and married her to Amiofori a member of Amakiri's house. By him she had Omekwe (Horsefall). Wariboko when he grew up was married to Oruame a daughter of Owukori (Manuel) by whom he begat Wokoma (Charles Horsefall).

Wariboko died before Owukori (Manuel) could establish a canoe house chieftaincy for him, and a chieftaincy was established for Omekwe (Horsefall) instead. The Horsefall house maintain that Omekwe established his canoe house chieftaincy by his own efforts, the Bob Manuel house say that Owukori (Manuel) established it for him. In any case when Owukori died in Karibo's (Amakiri III's) reign, Omekwe (Horsefall) was

---

[4] It still survives in the Horsefall meeting house.
[5] Theirs were not the only houses with this name, there was also the Harry Horsefall (Ikpo) house in the Ombo (Harry) group.
[6] On p. 137.

the most powerful leader in what had now become the Owukori group of houses and he demanded that he should be accepted as chief of the main house. But Kombo Agolea the head of the Barboy group said that Owukori (Manuel) had left a son Ekine (Bob Manuel) and that his son should be recognized as head of the Manuel house. This produced a split in the group as Omekwe (Horsefall) taking Wokoma (Charles Horsefall) with him demanded a division of personnel and property between the Manuels and the Horsefalls. Thenceforward the Horsefalls and the Manuels were always to be found on opposite sides in any major Kalabari dispute.

In addition to these houses founded by Awo's principal sons there were two other houses founded by two 'adopted sons' namely Obaji (Jack Barboy) and Amabibi (Don Pedro).

In addition to these various houses all based on Elem Kalabari and mainly resident there, members of the Barboy group were also resident in the neighbouring communities of Tombia (Young Town) and Ifoko (Fouchee). The latter which supplied the pilots for the European shipping anchoring in the Kalabari 'roads' consisted in the second quarter of the nineteenth century of two political divisions or houses, namely Owolo (Jim Fouchee) and Iboroma (Tom Fouchee). Owolo otherwise known as Jack Pilot or Jim Fouchee claim to derive from Daba (Jackson) who was recognized as its *amayanabo* by Amakiri. The Jim Fouchee house was closely affiliated to the George Will house. The Iboroma house claim to have been founded by Iboroma, whose mother was of the Korome ward and, because her children died at birth or were miscarried was exiled to Ifoko. There she contracted an *egwa* marriage with Mbimbi of the Ombo group and bore Iboroma who made his fortune and established his canoe house while living at Ifoko. When Ikpo (Ombo's grandson) became head of the Ombo (Harry) main house he tried to attach Iboroma to the Ombo group, but Iboroma was not prepared to accept this affiliation. Kombo Agolea persuaded Iboroma not to resist by force and the matter was settled judicially by the Kalabari chiefs in Iboroma's favour. Iboroma placed himself under the protection of the Long Juju of Arochuku and, as this was far off, attached himself to the Barboy main house.

Tombia (New Town) consisted in the early nineteenth century of four wards, Agarame, Orusarame, Ajeme and Otokiri or Owiye. Agarame divided into two parts, one of which was the house of Iyala (Yellow). Iyala's father was priest of Simingi the tutelary deity of Tombia, on his father's death his mother became the wife (by *egwa* marriage) of Otaji who was then head of the Barboy mainhouse. Iyala because of his late father's wealth and position as head of the senior section of Tombia became very rich and established his own canoe house. His personal English name was India John, a name which he took from an Indian seaman of this name. The Indian was serving on an English trading vessel and the ship's company challenged Iyala to a boxing match with him, wagering several casks of oil on the match. Iyala accepted the wager, knocked the

Indian out and took their wager and with it the Indian's name. In addition
to the Iyala house the canoe house and ward of Owiye (Fine Face) was
affiliated to the Barboy group at about this time, that is, 'when Otaji (Long
Will) was head of the main house.'

Thus by the mid-nineteenth century the house founded by Awo had
developed into the Barboy mainhouse under first Otaji (Long Will) and
then Kombo Agolea (Braid), and the subordinate houses of Obaji, Don
Pedro, George Will and Manuel, as well as Kombo Agolea's personal
house under his son Will Braid (Young Braid). Obaji's house under his
son Dick Barboy (Dikio Obaji) was in the process of decline, the others were
all in the process of expansion and were developing or had developed
subordinate houses of their own. In addition to this the whole of the
neigbouring village of Ifoko and two houses in the larger village of Tombia
were affiliated to this group and, in Kalabari political affairs, formed part of it.

(II) *Houses derived from Amakiri*

The houses derived from Amakiri were of two kinds, firstly there were
the four small houses of the Princes, which Amakiri had established for
his sons Fubra, Amakoro, Ekine, and Karibo; these were houses which
were considered independent of the main house and their heads in later
political disputes tended to be on opposite sides. Secondly there were the
ramifications of Amakiri's own house which came by the end of his reign
to consist of three groups of houses and a number of individual houses.
Some of the latter have disappeared and are no longer remembered; some
have survived as distinct houses but have become attached to other groups,
for example Lawson to the Karibo group, Douglas to the Manuel, Sofa
which was revived as Toye Paka (Pepple Amakiri) to the Karibo group;
while one, the Duenala house, developed into the Briggs group and
became associated with the Iju house (Standfast Jack). The formation
and expansion of these groups in discussed below.

(a) *The Ombo (Harry) group*

This was, after the Barboy group, the largest in Kalabari. It derived
from Ombo, the son of Amakiri's female slave, Ada, whom he married to
Soku Taria a refugee from the village of Soku who had attached himself
to Amakiri. Ombo is said to have been born during the Okrika raid, his
mother managing to escape into the surrounding mangrove swamp. By
the time of King Amakoro (Amakiri II) the group is said to have consisted
of the houses of Ombo's two sons Idonibo (Big Harry) and Ikpo (Harry
Horsefall).[7] Ombo is said to have been succeeded as head of the house by
his brother Debo. Idonibo died before Ombo, and Debo was later succeeded by Obu who was deposed and succeeded by Ikpo who was head
of the house in King Amakoro's time. In addition to the subordinate

[7] It is not clear whether there was not also a house for Ombo's other son Obu and
whether Idonibo's son (Young Harry) was established as a separate canoe house at
this time or later in King Karibo's (Amakiri III) reign.

houses of Ombo's sons there were also houses of Ombo's slaves or servants namely those of Edi Abali (Harry Braid) and of Kama (Warmate). Like the Barboys the Harrys were associated with neighbouring communities and Edi Abali (Harry Braid) had settled in Tombia (Young Town) where he made his fortune and founded his canoe house. Also associated with the Ombo group but not established until the reign of King Karibo was the house of Erekosima or Ikiri (John Bull). Erekosima was the son of Bekinabo, a male slave of Amakiri, and Inoma daughter of Amasa the chief of the village of Tema. Inoma's elder sister was Fan the wife of Ombo and mother of Ikpo, and Erekosima was brought up in Ikpo's household. The Ombo group of houses are said to have lived in the Ituruame quarter which became divided into the two residential divisions Ogonobe and Sukube. East of them was the area of the Barracoons later occupied by the Birinomoni group.

Unlike most other Kalabari chiefs Ombo was blessed with many able sons and these sons in their turn produced able descendants. This seems to have led to a change in the rules governing the succession to the main house which became limited to direct descendants of Ombo. The result of this has been that during the nineteenth century the group came to have two chiefs at its head, the chief of the main house who was a direct descendant of Ombo and who took precedence in internal affairs, and the most powerful chief in the group who represented the group in its external business. After the time of Ikpo external leadership of the group devolved upon Edi Abali (Harry Braid) and in the latter part of the century upon Erekosima (John Bull).

(b) *The Birinomoni group*

The Ombo group was the senior and the largest group of houses derived from Amakiri, the last to be formed was the one which eventually received the name of Birinomoni. The four leaders whose names are associated with it are Nwananaku whose English name was Hand corrupted into Arney or Annie, Amakiri Oboko or Big Fowl, Ejemenike and Angaenemenea. Amakiri either established a joint house for Arney and Big Fowl or else combined together two houses, which they had each founded, into a single group. Ejemenike and Angaenemenea were included in the Big Fowl house and in due course Taria (Goodhead), the adopted son of Angaenemenea, established his own house with the following of these two leaders. These formed the three principal Birinomoni houses in the time of Karibo Amakiri (Amakiri III) and their chiefs appear in the treaty of 1854 as Young Annie (the English name of Itchi who succeeded Nwananaku), Big Fogolo (Big Fowl) and George Goodhead (the name of Nuobuari the 'adopted son' of Taria). This group of houses though regarded as distinct from the Ombo group were very closely associated with it and in major Kalabari disputes they virtually formed a single political unit.

(c) *The West India group*

Tradition does not relate how this group obtained its English name. It was a group which originated in much the same manner as the preceding one, from a combination of four leaders and their followers, namely Orikadibia, Elebike, Eleru and Osiagu. They were placed by Amakiri in the Akwame quarter which lay between the Igodome quarter occupied by the Iju (Standfast Jack) and Duenala (Black Jim) houses, and the Alame quarter occupied by the Barboy group. In the time of King Karibo (Amakiri III) the group consisted of the three houses of Datubo (West India), Dodo (Young West India) and Jongo. Today it has two subdivisions which call themselves Elebike and Orikadibia. These subdivisions each claim to be the senior subdivision and their respective traditions of origin are modified accordingly.

The Elebike subdivision which today forms the numerically larger unit claims that the West India group originated in 'the time of King Amakiri', who placed Elebike, Orikadibia, Eleru, and Osiago and their followers in Akwame to control the activities of Asukein the head of the Duenala house. Elebike and Orikadibia were both established as canoe house chiefs, Osiago and his followers being grouped with Orikadibia. Orikadibia, Elebike and other chiefs including Ogoloye Fubra went to war with Bonny and Orikadibia and Ogoloye Fubra were captured and killed. Orikadibia's son was killed by a shark and the house disintegrated, the survivors becoming incorporated in Elebike's house which redeemed them (paid their house debts). Elebike survived to a ripe old age dying in the reign of King Karibo and was succeeded by his son Datubo. Elebike's trade name was Indian and Datubo's name West Indian, he married a daughter of Osiago who bore him Dodo (Young West India) and Dodo also married into what remained of Orikadibia's group by taking to wife the daughter of Egede who was a prominent trader and member of this submerged house. Thus when a canoe chieftaincy was created for Dodo in Karibo's reign this canoe house contained most of the surviving members of Orikadibia's old house. In due course Datubo died and Dodo was elected to succeed him in the main house (Elebike) while the chieftaincy of Dodo's own house passed to Egede. Dodo's eldest son Tom West India succeeded first Egede in Dodo's own house and then Dodo in the Elebike house, being succeeded in the Dodo's own house by Fubra (David West India) the son of Egede. Egede took the name of West Braid, David and his successors reverted to West India (David West India) and more recently to Orikadibia. Elebike claim that this house or group cannot take the name of Orikadibia as it is contrary to Kalabari usage to revive the house of a chief who has been killed in war. The Elebike subdivision has preserved two ivory trading bracelets which they say belonged originally to Datubo and Dodo respectively. They are inscribed: 'West Indian. A good and honest trader. 1st January 1834. A gift from Captain Jennings. Sch. Mariner.'

'Young West India 1835. An honest trader. 40 puncheons of Palm oil sold to Midgley. Brig Freeland.'

These suggest that we date the Datubo Dodo period of the West India house, and with it the early part of Karibo's reign to the eighteen thirties.

The Orikadibia subdivision claims that it was Orikadibia alone who was placed as a canoe house chief in Akwame. Elebike, Eleru, and Osiagu were placed there with him as members of his house. Orikadibia, whose English name was West India, was not killed fighting against Bonny 'he erred in his relationship with a Bonny friend of his and it happened that he fell into a Bonny ambush while returning from market in a defenceless canoe and was captured'.[8] Elebike succeeded Orikadibia as chief of the Orikadibia house and was in turn succeeded by Datubo. Datubo established a canoe house chieftaincy to the name of his father Elebike and placed Dodo in it as its chief. The descendants of Dodo continued as chiefs of this house while Egede succeeded Datubo as head of the Orikadibia house and his descendants have continued to occupy this position.

The third West India house of Jongo was founded either by Eleru or by his son or successor Jongo, but did not long survive the latter's death. According to West India and Kalabari tradition it was doomed because like Orikadibia it broke a covenant. A covenant made this time by all the Kalabari with Owame Akaso their tutelary deity not to commit homicide within the borders of her town. The house felt compelled to get rid of one of their members who was harming the house, and they did this by making him drunk and then getting him to sit on a chair resting on a mat which covered a deep pit. He did so and fell into the pit and was buried alive in it. Misfortune thereafter dogged the house till it disintegrated, the survivors being redeemed by the other West India houses and becoming incorporated into them.

Like the Birinomoni group the West India group were staunch supporters of the Ombo group in their opposition to the Barboy house. After the death of King Karibo the West India group combined with or was joined by the Omekwe (Horsefall) group and the Jack Rich house.

(d) The Oruwari (Briggs) group

This group which was established under Oruwari (Briggs II) in the reign of King Karibo traced its origin to Duenala (Black Jim) whose history has already been recounted[9] (p. 9); it could also lay claim to a more remote ancestry, as Duenala was originally a free born of the Akialame ward and Oruwari could claim through his mother to be a direct descendant of Akiala the founder of this ward. According to the Briggs tradition, Akiala and Kalagbea were two chiefs of Elem Kalabari.[10] Kalagbea married Akiala's eldest daughter who bore him Awo the founder

[8] Communication from Chief J. David-West.
[9] p. 137.
[10] i.e. of the Akialame and Endeme wards.

of the Barboy group of houses. Akiala had a son Biogbolo whose daughter Ojie was married under the *egwa* system to Beye Amakiri of Ifoko village. Their son was Nnoma (Briggs I) who begat Oruwari (Briggs II). The house was originally founded by Duenala who was succeeded by Asukein who spoiled the house and it disintegrated. It was reconstituted by Oruwari who was recognized as a canoe house chief by King Karibo (Amakiri III). This tradition whether accurate or not explains the independent attitude taken by this group in contrast to the other groups derived from King Amakiri's house. Its members lived in the Igodome area with the Iju (Standfast Jack) house, the independent survivor of the Igodome ward, and in combination with this house it supported the Barboy group as against the Ombo, Birinomoni, West India combination. Within the Barboy group it supported the George Will and Manuel houses as against the Braid group.

The names of chiefs of the Briggs group do not appear on the early Kalabari treaties and the Briggs explanation for this is that as they formed a single group with Iju (Standfast Jack) it was only necessary for the chief of the senior house in the group, namely Standfast Jack, to sign. Consul Burton writing in 1864 refers to the two houses of Young Briggs and Black Jim. The Kalabari name of Young Briggs was Isiowu and he was the 'adopted son' of Oruwari (Briggs II). Black Jim was the English name of Duenala and was the name under which Oruwari traded. The Briggs group still preserve an ivory bracelet inscribed 'Black Jemmy a white man's friend, 1836. From his friend Chas. Caine Oscar'. This indicates that Oruwari was trading under this name at the same time as Datubo and Dodo.

(e) *The Karibo group*

This group developed during the reign of King Karibo (Amakiri III) from the canoe house which he had founded before coming to the throne. It eventually consisted of the houses founded by his three sons, Abbe (Prince Will), Batubo ('Batribe') and Datema, the house founded by his adopted son George Amakiri which became the largest and wealthiest in Kalabari, and the houses of John Amakiri, of Pepple Amakiri, Ogari (Lawson) and Benebo.

John Amakiri was a member of Karibo's house. The Pepple Amakiri house claimed a longer pedigree tracing its foundation to Sofa, a son of Igbesa, a son of King Kamalu. The Sofa house resided in the Agrame quarter of Elem Kalabari in the time of Amakiri. Its chief Okwu an adopted son of Sofa 'fought with the town 'and like Ogoloye Fubra had to seek asylum elsewhere. He was later allowed to return and make his peace. Aganawa a member of the house succeeded Okwu as chief and was succeeded in turn by his son Dubo. Bassa the member who succeeded Dubo 'spoiled the house' and it disintegrated but King Karibo later recreated it for Toye Paka (Pepple) a son of Dubo who had been placed by his father in

P

Karibo's household for him to train. Because the name of Sofa had proved unlucky the house was called Toye Paka (Pepple Amakiri) but it continued to retain and sacrifice to Sofa's ancestral shrine (*duen fobara*).

Ogari (Lawson) was a member of Amakiri's household and the house claims to have been founded in the time of King Amakiri. It was not attached to any of the other Amakiri groups and from the time of King Karibo if not before it associated itself with the Karibo group.

Benebo was a member of the house of Amakiri's son Ekine. Tradition is now uncertain whether Benebo (Benbow) succeeded to the chieftaincy of this house or refounded it in his own name. This house though originally opposed to the Karibo house became under Benebo associated with the Karibo group.

In addition to these houses the house founded by King Amakoro (Tiger Amakiri) which was in opposition to the Karibo group and associated with the Barboy group at the end of King Karibo's reign became attached to the Karibo group during the reign of his successor King Abbe (Prince Will).

Like the Barboy and the Ombo groups the Karibo group was closely associated with neighbouring villages particularly in the case of the Abbe (Prince Will) and George Amakiri houses. Abalama village was virtually a part of the George Amakiri house. Tombia (New Town) was split between the Karibo and Barboy groups. Its senior ward of Agarame divided into two houses, one Igibiri (Davis George) was associated with George Amakiri the other, Iyala (Yellow), with the Barboy house, two other wards, Orusarame and Ajeme under their chiefs Donibo Ekine (Jack Young Town) and Abbe (Abbey Young Town) were associated with the Abbe (Prince Will) house, the fourth under Owiye (Fine Face) was associated with the Barboy group. There was also a further group of people not recognized then as a separate ward and called Abali who formed part of the Edi Abali (Harry Braid) house of the Ombo group.

III. *Independent Houses*

In addition to the houses we have just been describing there remained a number of other houses whose chiefs could trace their 'descent' through freeborn or slave members to the heads of wards founded before the time of Amakiri, and these we have called independent houses. The names of only two groups of these appear in the records namely Iju (Standfast Jack) and the various houses derived from the Korome ward. There were others but most of their original members had become dispersed amongst the more important Amakiri and Barboy houses, and the surviving independent remnants of these former wards were too insignificant for their chiefs to merit inclusion in the list of signatories of the treaties between the Consul and the Kalabari state. There were various reasons for the survival of such small groups provided they could avoid getting into debt or into disputes with more powerful houses, and the most important of these was their association with the more important religious cults and rituals. Amakiri had not interfered with the ritual institutions of the Kalabari, indeed his boast was that he had restored them to their former greatness. The right to minister to these deities and to manage the festivals connected with them remained vested in particular Kalabari wards and belonged to the lineal descendants of their founders. Of these surviving groups the only one referred to in any detail in Kalabari traditions is Amabiame.

(a) *The house of Amabiame*
This ward traced its origin to Amabin, said to be a son of Fraia Akpana, and according to the traditions of this ward it was Amabin and not Kalabari who discovered Obu Amafo when on a fishing expedition and who was joined there by the founders of the other Kalabari wards. His name is said to signify 'I have seen the town'. He is also said to have brought the mythical doctor Amakarasa to the town and the Amabiame house was associated with this cult and with the cleansing rituals associated with it. It was also associated with the cult of Owu Akpana, a water spirit, to whom sharks were said to be sacred and which was connected with an ordeal witnessed by Capt. Crow in 1791, in which the accused had to swim across the shark infested river. In the time of Amakiri the chief of this house was Ogoloye Fubra who became involved with Asukein in 'piracy' and had to flee to Bonny where he met Capt. Crow in 1807.[11] Later he made his peace with King Amakiri and returned to Elem Kalabari bringing with him the secrets of the Bonny deity Ikuba. This induced Prince Owuso and other chiefs to organize a raid on Bonny which was unsuccessful and he and, some say, Orikadibia were captured, killed and eaten. His house lingered on until the reign of King Karibo (Amakiri III) when the town under the leadership of Datubo (West India) decided to get rid of the shark cult by drinking water from the town well in which Datubo had washed a shark which he had caught and killed. Everyone was ordered to drink the water and when it was found that Amabiame had failed to do so, the house was tried and heavily fined. King Karibo redeemed its members by paying the fine and they thus became absorbed into his house and the independence of the house finally came to an end. Others of this ward had already become incorporated into Barboy, and West India houses.[12]

(b) *The house of Iju (Standfast Jack)*
This house is said to be derived from Iju (Jack) son of Kilabo a lineal descendant of Igodo the founder of the Igodome ward. Iju was the head of this section and at home with his men on the occasion of the Okrika raid, and his quarter, the most distant from the waterside, was able to resist the Okrikans and formed a rallying point for fugitives from the rest

[11] Crow, pp. 31 and 141.
[12] I am indebted to Robin Horton for these Amabiame data.

of the town. Iju was succeeded by Tubofia (Standfast) a member of his household who acted as his deputy when he became old and whose trade name is said to be a corruption of 'Stand for Jack', the answer he gave when the supercargoes first asked what his name was. After Tubofia the house disintegrated but was reconstituted by Oba, Kala Dokubo and Oruguta, the two sons and daughter of Onuoha, one of its members. As already mentioned the Iju and Briggs houses whose members were living in the Igodome area and who could both regard themselves as the descendants of the older Kalabari wards of Igodome and Akialame acted together and formed a single political group.

(c) *The surviving houses of the Korome ward*

The traditions of the origin of this ward which have already been related suggest an Andoni origin. They also indicate an early division into two segments which contemporary tradition supports with a genealogical 'charter' which derives them from the two sons of Opu-koro-ye, the ward's founder. One of these sons was Sumbio whose other name was Owerri and he was the father of Daba, the Owerri Daba of Kalabari and Bonny tradition who is associated in Bonny and in some Kalabari traditions with the inauguration of the overseas slave trade, and with establishment of relations with the Long Juju of Arochuku[13] (*suku obiama*).

The name of the other son is said to have been Edesie whose son was Seliye. Seliye married the daughter of King Agbani Ejike of Bile and their son was Fubra, the Seliye Fubra who refused the Kingship which was then offered to Amakiri. Seliye Fubra whose English name was Big or Rich Fubra had no sons and his 'adopted son' who succeeded him was Opuike (Jack Rich).

We have no means of knowing when this division of the Korome ward came about. The European and Bonny records suggest a seventeenth century or earlier date for Owerri Daba himself. They also suggest fission within the Owerri Daba (Duke Monmouth) division which resulted in the removal of part of it to Bonny where it became the Africa house whose head in the time of King Opobo was known as John Africa. This may have been one of the reasons, why it was the other division headed by Seliye Fubra which had become dominant in Kalabari just before the rise of Amakiri.

The Owerri Daba (Duke Monmouth) division was represented in nineteenth century Kalabari by the two houses of Duke Africa and Black Duke. The chiefs of both divisions signed the Treaty of 1850 under the names Big Foobra and Duke Monmouth. In the 1854 treaty four names appear namely Jack Rich, Quaker, Yellow Duke and Duke Mornae, thereafter there are only three, Jack Reece, Yellow Duke, and Duke

---

[13] Its local *ofo* (fetishes) are said to have been lodged with the Jack Rich house in Buguma village and the Black Duke house in Abonnema until they were removed by the Aro after the punitive expedition against Arochuku in 1901.

Monmouth which later becomes Black Duke. Dokubo (Quaker) was a son of Opuike and he held the office of Amasobo or speaker of the Kalabari general council. Tradition says that Dokubo was not a canoe house chief. He was also not associated with the Jack Rich house but preferred to live first with Iju (Standfast Jack) and then with Otaji (Long Will Barboy) and finally with Owukori (Manuel) whose female slave he married. It is clear that there was no political cohesion between the two Korome divisions in the time of King Karibo, and this also seems to have been the case in the earlier period of Amakiri. Tradition refers only to Seliye Fubra and his house which suffered so severely at the hands of the Okrika raiders, and later in conflict with Amakiri's house, and if the Duke Monmouth houses were associated with Seliye Fubra in this conflict tradition has forgotten to record it. The weakness of these Korome houses in the nineteenth century is brought out by the case of the Iboroma house which formed part of the Barboy group and which although it was founded by a Korome member was obliged to seek the protection of this group as the other Korome houses were not able to support it against the Ombo (Harry) group. Their inability to combine together is shown by their political affiliation. The Duke Monmouth division supported the Barboy group the Jack Rich house the West India and Ombo combination, and although the two Duke houses were aligned with the Barboy group, they preferred to support different divisions within this group, the Duke Africa supporting the main house and the Braids, while the Black Duke allied itself with the George Will and the Manuel.

C. *Summary and Conclusions*

Of the mythical seven wards of Kalabari we have only been able to trace five which survived into the nineteenth century, namely Endeme, Korome, Akialame, Amabiame and Igodome. The reign of Amakiri saw the expansion of his ward of Endeme at the expense of the others. It segmented at an early stage into two divisions, the Barboy group which traced its descent to the preceding Kamalu line of Kings and the Amakiri group which derived directly from Amakiri's house. The nineteenth century saw the continued expansion of these two divisions so that by the reign of King Karibo (Amakiri), that is by the middle of the century Kalabari consisted of the six major canoe house groups of Karibo, Barboy, Ombo, Birinomoni, West India, Briggs. These six groups were ranged politically into two rival associations called by Consul Burton the Amakiris and the Barboys. The first named contained the Karibo, Ombo, Birinomini and West India groups, the second the Barboy and the Briggs. The three neighbouring villages of Ifoko, Abalama and Tombia (New Town) were also caught up in this political division. Ifoko being associated with the Barboys, Abalama with the Amakiris and Tombia divided between them.

The remaining houses which still preserved their political independence were only able to do this by associating with one or other of these groups: Iju (Standfast Jack) of Igodome with Briggs, the three Korome houses respectively with West India, Braid and Manuel. The other two original wards of Akialame and Amabiame had disintegrated as political units, and their members had been absorbed by the dominant canoe houses.

APPENDIX B

SELECT TREATIES AND DOCUMENTS RELATING TO THE EASTERN DELTA STATES

1. Agreement with the King of Bonny. 1836.
2. Treaty with the King and Chiefs of Bonny. 1850.
3. Additional articles to the Treaty with Bonny. 1854.
4. Treaty with the Kings and Chiefs of Brass. 1856.
5. Agreement between the King and Chiefs of Bonny. 1869
6. Treaty between New Calabar and Bonny. 1871.
7. Treaty between New Calabar and Okrika. 1871.
8. Treaty between the Kings and Chiefs of Bonny and Opobo. 1873
9. Treaty between New Calabar and Will Braid. 1879.
10. Letter from the King and Chiefs of New Calabar. 1882.
11. Treaty between Great Britain and New Calabar. 1884.

1. *Agreement with the King of Bonny.* 1836.

King Pepple's House,
Grand Bonny,.
25th January 1836.

Article 1. It is hereby agreed, between the undersigned His Britannic Majesty's subjects and the King of Bonny that no English subject shall from this time be detained on shore or maltreated in any way whatsoever by the King or Natives of Bonny under any pretext. By so doing, they will bring themselves under the displeasure of the King of England and be declared enemies of Great Britain and that the Men of War on any complaint will immediately come up the Bonny to protect the English subjects.

2. In case of any misunderstanding between the captains of the English vessels and the King or gentlemen of Bonny that all and every English Captains will go on shore free of molestation and will with the King and gentlemen of Bonny peaceably settle all disputes between the parties.

3. English Captains having any complaint against any of the Natives of Bonny will come on shore and lay his or their complaint before the King, and they hereby promise to give the complainant redress by punishing the offender, and if any English seaman shall illtreat a Bonny man he shall be punished by the captain of the vessel to which he may belong.

4. That for the future all books made between the traders and English captains shall bear the signatures of such responsible officer belonging to the ship with the date and name; by his not doing so the case shall be decided by the Captains of the merchant ships lying in the River who will see that the trader or Native's loss be made good.

5. That after the Captain or Supercargo has paid the regular custom the trade shall be opened, and upon no account shall the trade of any vessel be stopped; excepting the Captain or supercargo act in opposition to any of the annexed agreements, and refuse to pay the fine imposed by the other captains for the infringing of these rules.

6. That every vessel's property shall be properly protected and that no King, Gentlemen, or Natives of Bonny shall roll away the casks of any vessel from the cask house on any pretext whatever.

7. That the King will be responsible for all monies oil or goods that may be owing to the English Captains so that the vessel may not be detained before sailing, and that the Captains of the English ship will see all just debts incurred by any vessel are paid by her to Bonny men with bars or oil before leaving the river.

Signed in Old King Pepple's house
This 25th January 1836 in the presence of
ROBERT TRYON. Lt., H.M.B. *Triniculo.*
ANNA PEPPLE X His mark.
MANILLA PEPPLE X His mark.
WM. H. L. CORRAN   *Vere.*
CHRISTOPHER JACKSON   *Maryhan.*
JOS. FERNIE   *Meg Merrilees.*
HENRY FRODSHAM   *Lousia.*
J. GRANT   MATE Barque *Huskisson.*

2. *Treaty with the King and Chiefs of the River Bonny, October 3, 1850.*

Whereas the 2 Contracting Parties have deemed it expedient, for the effectual protection of British commerce, to proceed immediately to the revision of all former Treaties existing between the 2 countries, for the purpose of ascertaining what stipulations contained therein are proper to be continued or renewed, it is agreed that Articles I, II, and III, herewith subjoined, of former Treaty, dated April 9, 1837, are hereby ratified and confirmed.

ART. I. That the King and Chiefs of Bonny pledge themselves that no British subjects shall from this time be detained on shore or maltreated in any way under any pretence; and if they (the King and Chiefs) do so, they will incur the displeasure of Her Majesty the Queen of England, and be declared enemies of Great Britain; and the men-of-war will, upon any such complaint being made to them, immediately come to Bonny to protect British vessels.

II. That in case of any misunderstanding between the British ship-masters and the King or Chiefs of Bonny, all and every British shipmaster shall be at liberty to go on shore free of molestation, and will, with the King and Gentlemen of Bonny, peaceably settle any dispute between the parties.

III. That British subjects having any complaint against the natives of Bonny, will bring his or her complaint before the King and Chiefs and Masters assembled, and they do hereby promise to redress all such grievances by punishing the offender. And if any British seaman shall maltreat a Bonny man, he shall be punished by the master of the vessel to which such seaman shall belong.

IV. That upon the arrival of any British merchant-vessel in this river for the purpose of trading therein, the supercargoes of such vessels shall, upon the tendering of 5 bars per register tonnage of such ship, to the King or person entitled to receive such comey, be allowed the privilege of trading without further molestation. The comey to consist of a fair assortment of the goods usually brought out for trade, viz., guns, cloth, powder, rum, salt, beads, caps, knives, iron bars, bars of tobacco, earthen-ware, brass rods, or any other goods such ship may have in for trade.

The comey to be tendered upon the ship's arrival, or as soon as convenient, and if not accepted by the King, such ship shall be at liberty to commence trade. This, however, does not exempt such vessels from paying the usual comey, if subsequently demanded.

V. That if at any time the supercargo of any ship (after having paid or tendered the usual comey for the privileges of trading) can prove that the trade of his ship has been stopped, whether directly or indirectly, upon any pretence whatever, the King is to be held responsible for such stoppage, and pay 1 puncheon of saleable palm oil per day per 100 tons register to said ship, as compensation for the loss incurred; the said oil to be paid within 7 days after such stoppage shall have been made, and continue to pay the same so long as the trade of any such ship is stopped.

VI. That the supercargoes are not responsible to any of the Chiefs for the custom bar, but that it must be collected by themselves and at their own cost.

VII. That after the comey has been paid or tendered to the King, every trader shall be allowed to trade in his own name; and neither the King, nor any other trader is entitled to exact any other comey, custom or tax whatever.

VIII. That the King shall from henceforth set apart for the use of the ships frequenting this river for the purpose of trade, that part of the shore facing the anchorage lying between a small creek called John Africa's Creek, and the point called Execution Point, from low and high water mark for 200 yards inshore from the river; and that the King shall prohibit any of his subjects, under any pretence whatever, from frequenting such beach or any of the cask-houses built thereon. And if any natives are found there, unless with a written order from some white trader, they are liable to be arrested and brought before the King, who shall fine them or those to whom they belong. And if the master of any ship can prove that his cask-house has been illegally entered or broken into by any natives and any property stolen therefrom, the King shall make good all such loss himself.

IX. That in the event of the King or any of the Chiefs making any agreement to take any goods from a ship at a certain rate, all such agreements shall be perfectly binding, and in case the goods agreed for are not paid for at the time specified, such goods shall be forfeited, and the oil to be considered due, the same as if the goods had actually been paid; such oil, if not paid during the ship's stay, is to be deducted from the comey of said ship upon a future voyage, or from any other ship in the same employ. This clause is not to prejudice any private agreement made to the contrary, nevertheless.

X. That the King shall not, nor shall he permit any of his Chiefs to demand or enforce any trust from any of the ships upon any pretence whatever.

XI. Whereas several boats have been plundered and lives sacrificed, it is deemed just and right that all aggressions and depredations committed upon British subjects or property between this and New Calabar, within the limits of King Pepple's dominions, shall be satisfactorily adjusted by him.

XII. All just debts having been paid, and the ship ready for sea no excuse shall avail or be admitted for being detained for want of a pilot.

XIII. Upon the death of a supercargo of any vessel trading here, no second tax, payment, or comey, can be demanded under any pretence whatever.

XIV. And further, be it enacted, that any breach of this Treaty shall be punished by the party or parties guilty of the same paying 20 puncheons of saleable palm-oil.

XV. Should any person take any trust from any vessel, and be unable to pay his debt, his house and property to be forfeited and sold by the King, the proceeds of the sale to go to the liquidation of the debt, and that he be no longer allowed to trade. The captain or supercargo of any vessel trading with him after his name has been made known, to be liable to a penalty of 10 puncheons of palm-oil; after the debtor has paid his debt, he shall again be allowed to trade.

XVI. With reference to Article VIII, it is conceded that the King or Chiefs, with their attendants, may walk during the day for the purpose of exercise, but no other, and on no account after sunset. (The King and Chiefs do mean those that have signed this Treaty.)

Dated at Bonny Town, 3 October, 1850.

JOHN BEECROFT, Her Britannic   KING PEPPLE
    Majesty's Consul, Bights of   ANNA PEPPLE
    Benin and Biafra.   MANILLA PEPPLE
NORMAN B. BEDINGFIELD, Lieut.   DUPPO.
    Commander H.M.S. 'Jackal'.
(Signed also by 14 Masters of Vessels, and by 5 other chiefs, namely)
LOVELL for CAPT. HART.   JOHN AFRICA
J. F. ALLISON   J. FISH for BLACK FOOBRA
ARAMBO for OLD JACK BROWN.

3. *Additional Articles to the Commercial Treaty with Bonny, January 23 1854.*

IT having been deemed necessary for the welfare of the country to depose King Pepple and to elect a new King, Prince Dappo was declared King, and the following additions were made to the Commercial Treaty:

ART. I. That the newly-elected King, from this time hence forward after paying his present debts, of which due notice must be given, shall not be allowed to trade, directly or indirectly (by giving trust to Bonny men) but that he shall receive two-thirds of the coomey of every ship coming to trade in the river, for his support; the other third to be placed on one side to go to the exigencies of the country; each party contributing sufficient for the support of Pepple out of their shares, provided he is not possessed of sufficient means of his own. And further, should he, the King be found trading he shall be fined in his own portion of the first coomey that becomes due after the offence. And any person giving such information as shall lead to his conviction of having traded shall be entitled to one puncheon reward; and should he show any resentful feeling, by committing any act of injustice or oppression upon the person giving such information, he shall be fined a still larger amount at the option of the court.

II. That the King or Chiefs shall not be allowed to seize upon confine, or oppress, or cause to be seized upon, confined, or oppressed, any trader, without first consulting, and with the sanction of, the court. And further, that no Chief shall be allowed to seize upon the oil, or boys, or any trader so long as the said party owes debts to the ships. Should such an occurrence take place, the party so offending shall be fined for the first offence 5 puncheons of palm oil, and to be doubled upon a repetition of the offence.

III. That the King or Chiefs shall not be allowed to go to war with any neighbouring country without informing the super cargoes of their reasons and necessity for so doing. And should it be thought necessary for them to do so, it is distinctly understood that all debts owing to the ships must be first paid, saving and excepting they are attacked by any other country, and obliged to defend themselves.

IV. That the headman, officers, and slaves of the deposed King who have been in the habit of trading hitherto, shall still be allowed to trade without hindrance or molestation, and with the same freedom as any other house in the Bonny.

V. That all future meetings are distinctly understood to be held in the Court-house, built for that purpose; and after due notice has been given, any supercargo, king, chief, or trader being called upon and refusing to attend, except from illness or some other satisfactory reason, shall be fined in 1 puncheon of palm oil for every such offence.

VI. That the King and Chiefs upon any decision of the court as to fines, or placing any offending party under arrest, must be responsible to the court that those fines are produced within the time fixed upon; and it is to be understood that all fines are wholly and solely the property of the court, until the present debts upon the house are liquidated, after which time one-half will be used at the discretion of the court, and the other half to the public funds of the country along with the coomeys, etc.

VII. As a number of buoys are about to be placed in the approaches to Bonny, we shall hold the King and Chiefs of Bonny responsible for any acts of wilful damage they may receive. And as an act of encouragement to the pilots, should the master of any vessel enter or leave the river upon his own responsibility, and without requiring their services, they shall be entitled to one-half pilotage. Should they be required and attend, they shall be entitled to the whole pilotage as formerly; but if refusing to attend when called upon, they shall lose all claim upon the vessel, and be subject to such other penalties as the court may decide upon.

VIII. That in the event of any difficulty arising from unforseen circumstances, or such as we have not had brought under our notice before, we may be empowered to draw out such fresh clauses as may be deemed necessary, and which, being approved of and signed by Her Majesty's Consul, may be considered as the laws of the country.

IX. That in the event of any disturbance arising in the Eboo or other place, that injures our trade, and over which we have no control, it shall be the King's duty, assisted by his Chiefs, to immediately send up and take such steps as may be considered requisite for its settlement.

X. That Yaniboo and Ishaca from this time henceforth are to be considered Chief of Bonny, and take their parts accordingly.

XI. That upon the arrival of any ship, the King (not being allowed to trade) requiring certain articles for his own personal use, the supercargo and himself shall be at liberty to arrange the matter, the King allowing the amount to be deducted from his coomey.

KING DAPPO.	ANNIE PEPPLE.	CAPTAIN HART.
MANILLA PEPPLE.	SONJOO ALLISON.	JACK BROWN.
FOOBRA.	WORRASOO.	BONIFACE.
GOGO FOOBRA.	GEORGE GOODHEAD.	TOM TAYLOR.
TOM BROWN.	OGE AFRICA.	CHARLEY AFRICA.
JACK WILSON PEPPLE.	KING HOLLIDAY'S BOY.	ISHAKA.
JACK TELEFAR.	DICK TELEFAR.	

Court House, Grand Bonny, this 23rd day of January, 1854.
JOHN BEECROFT, Her Britannic Majesty's Consul.
CHARLES HENRY YOUNG, Lieutenant, Her Majesty's steam-vessel 'Antelope'.

Additional Article

XII. Any King, Chief, trader, or boy, coming armed to the Court House, or attended by armed followers, or keeping armed followers in the neighbourhood of the court, during any meeting, shall be heavily fined in 50 puncheons of palm oil, in equal proportions from the King and Chiefs, and will also seriously incur the displeasure of Her Majesty's Representatives.

4. Treaty with the Kings and Chiefs of Brass, 1856.

17 November 1856.

A CODE of Commercial Regulations being deemed advisable for further-ing the interests of commerce, as well as for the better security of amicable connection between the British supercargoes trading in the Rio Bento, or Brass river, and the natives of the Brass country, the following Articles have been mutually agreed to by the British supercargoes, on the part of themselves and their successors, with the Kings of the territories adjacent to the Brass river, on the part of themselves, and the people of their districts, sanctioned by Thomas Joseph Hutchinson, Esquire, Her Britannic Majesty's Consul for the Bight of Biafra, and the Island of Fernando Po:

ART. 1. That the Kings and Chiefs of the countries connected in trade with Rio Bento, duly appreciating the benefit of legitimate traffic, hereby guarantee that from this day forward, they shall not engage in, or sanction the exportation of slaves from their country.

II. That the pilotage of vessels entering the river shall be 16 pieces of cloth, or 80 bars of other merchandize; and of vessels leaving the rivers 20 pieces of cloth, or 100 bars of other merchandize; and any vessel detained for want of a pilot, after being ready for sea, all her just debt, and her pilotage paid or tendered, though not taken, shall be entitled, as compensation for delay, to $\frac{1}{2}$ a puncheon of oil per day, from the Chiefs who receive comey, who, on their part, are to reclaim such penalty from the pilot causing this detention.

III. That the comey of vessels entering the river for the purpose of trade be, for vessels of 2 masts, to pay 2 puncheons' worth of goods. Vessels of 3 masts to pay 3 puncheons worth of goods to each King (Kayo of O'Bullamaby and Orishima of Bassamby); that boats or vessels coming here with cargo, and bringing no produce away, are to be excepted; and for each ship taking part produce out of the river as tenderage to complete her cargo elsewhere, the comey be 5 bars for each cask.

IV. That should such comey not have been demanded on or before the 5th day from the arrival of the vessel, the master may hoist his ensign, or fire a gun, as a notification of his being prepared for trade; when all traders, or other Brass men, are to be at liberty to visit the vessel for the purpose of transacting business, equally as if trade had been broken formerly by the Chiefs in person, but without prejudice to the subsequent payment of comey when demanded.

V. That this settlement of comey is not to nullify existing agreements between supercargoes and Chiefs, nor to preclude the making of arrangements to suit particular cases, as in the instance of British merchantile houses who may establish factories in the Brass; such special agreement to be subjected to the approval of Her Britannic Majesty's Consul, and when confirmed to be as binding upon the parties concerned therein, as though embodied as separate Articles in this Treaty.

VI. That the custom bar shall be collected by the Chiefs themselves, and at their own expense and trouble.

VII. That the comey and pilotage being paid, no other tax or payment is to be demanded under any pretence whatever; water is not to be refused in the pilot's town, called Twaw, nor is any demand to be made for the privilege of watering. Ground for the erection of houses, and for the storing of casks and goods, is to be granted free of all charges, and is to be considered whilst in the occupation of any British subjects, as British property, and the occupant for the time being, is authorized by the parties hereto subscribing, to expel trespassers, and to maintain his right of occupancy, and to defend himself and property against any unlawful aggression.

VIII. That it shall, under no circumstances, be compulsory on the master or supercargo of a vessel to give goods on trust, but when trust is taken, that it shall be incumbent on the Kings and Chiefs, and those to whom comey is paid, to see that no losses accrue to British supercargoes from defaulting debtors.

IX. That a limit of time to pay in debt, be given to each trader, to be settled by private contract.

X. That should any trader or gentleman, being indebted to a vessel in the river, fail to pay his debt when it becomes due, a notice of the same is to be given to the Chief of the town where such trader resides, who is hereby required to see justice done to the British supercargo, and if necessary, is to take possession of the trader's oil or other property, and therewith liquidate the debt.

XI. That any Chief of a trading town, neglecting to act in conformity herewith, be held personally responsible for the debt. The Chiefs receiving comey are required, and engage, to see this Article executed.

XII. That long detentions having heretofore occurred in trade, and much angry feeling having been excited in the natives from the destructions by white men, in their ignorance of the superstitions and customs of the country, of a certain species of boa-constrictor that visits the cask-houses, and which is 'jew-jew', or sacred to the Brass men, it is hereby forbidden to all British subjects to harm or destroy any such snake; but they are required upon finding the reptile on their premises, to give notice thereof to the Chief's man in Twaw, who is to come and remove it away.

XIII. That should, unfortunately, any casualty of said reptile's death again occur, the master or supercargo who, by himself or his people, has been guilty of causing the same, shall pay a fine of 1 puncheon of palm oil, and his trade shall suffer no stoppage. Any detention occurring after this amount has been tendered, will render the Chiefs liable to a fine of 1 puncheon of oil per day, as in the ensuing Article.

XIV. That in the event of any vessel's trade being stopped either directly by the Chiefs, or indirectly and secretly by their connivance, without just grounds for such proceeding, the authorities receiving comey will be held responsible for the said stoppage of trade, and a fine or penalty of 1 puncheon of oil per day will be levied from them, as compensation for the vessel so detained during the period of such detention.

XV. That any supercargo or master having cause of complaint against a Chief, or native trader, or Brass subject, shall give notice thereof to the supercargoes and masters at that time in the river, who shall, con-jointly, inform the Chiefs thereof, and require their presence, either on shore, or on board some one of the vessels; and the Chiefs and gentlemen, on their part, consent and agree to assemble when so required, unarmed and without hostile preparation, and then and there discuss the matters brought before them, in friendly conjunction with the white men present. The Brass Chiefs and others are to act in like manner when they feel themselves aggrieved by any British subject; and the supercargoes and others are to meet the Brass men when called upon so to do.

XVI. That the supercargoes and masters, on the one hand, and the Brass Chiefs and gentlemen on the other, being assembled to remove grievances, and discuss matters of complaint existing between them, do, on their several parts, engage to adjudicate thereon in a friendly spirit, and endeavour to finally remove the causes thereof in a manner that shall be satisfactory to the traders who frequent the river, and the native mer-chants. Any settlement so made, to be submitted to Her Majesty's Consul; and, if approved and ratified by him, to become a law of trade, and binding equally with the Articles of this Treaty.

XVII. That in the event of any serious dispute arising between the British and natives, or in the event of any crime or outrage having been committed by either party against the other, the native Chiefs, on their part, and the British traders, on theirs (should it be deemed necessary by the British subjects to solicit the aid of Her Britannic Majesty's Consul), agree to continue amicable relations with each other, and to avoid hostilities (unless life, or the security of property, be threatened or in danger), until Her Britannic Majesty's Consul, or a British naval officer, shall enter the river, when a fair hearing will be given to all parties concerned, a strict investigation take place, and due punishment be inflicted.

XVIII. That upon the death of any supercargo in the river, no second comey can be demanded from his successor, for the ship that is left vacant by such a death; and that all trust given out by any supercargo, previous to such an event, shall be considered a debt to the merchants of whom he is the representative, and to be paid to whomsoever is appointed to succeed him.

XIX. That a copy of this Treaty be furnished to each Chief receiving comey, and a copy of that part referring to the pilotage to the chief pilot; the Chiefs to produce it when receiving comey, and the pilot to show it to the masters upon any vessels entering the river; and that these Articles be held to be the laws existing between British supercargoes and the native for the regulation of trade matters, to be observed, so long as they continue law, by those who were not present at their enactment as by those who were.

XX. That the Chiefs and gentlemen of Brass, satisfied that payment of comey as well as the introduction of legitimate traffic to their country, is sufficient compensation to them for the abandonment of the Slave trade, hereby engage to fulfil the conditions of this Treaty, and to become severally and conjointly responsible for the due payment of all fines to which they, or any Brass subject or subjects, may become liable under its provisions.

XXI. That the Chiefs of the Bento hereby pledge themselves that no British subject shall, from the date of this, be detained on shore, maltreated, or molested in any way or under any pretence whatsoever. If any such maltreatment or molestation shall take place, the Chiefs of the Bento will incur the displeasure of Her Majesty the Queen of England, and be declared enemies of Great Britain.

KAYO, King of O'Bullamaby. ASSAMIA.
ORISHIMA, King of Bassamby. SABOFOOMY.
PRINCE EBEISSAH. INGOSHIGA.
THOMAS P. MITCHEL, Hulk *City of Rochester.*
EDWARD W. McCALL, Barque *Severn.*
E. D. PRAMMAN, Barque *Lottie Sleigh.*
ARTHUR R. WRIGHT, Lieut., H.M.S. *Merlin.*
C. PARKINSON, Master, H.M.S. *Merlin.*

Q

Ratified under my hand and seal, on board Her Majesty's steamsloop
Merlin, lying in the Brass River, this 17th day of November, 1856.

THOS. J. HUTCHINSON, Her Britannic Majesty's Consul for the Bight
of Biafra and the Island of Fernando Po.

5. *Agreement between the King and Chiefs of Bonny for the Preservation of
Peace. Bonny, 20 January* 1869.

It has been deemed necessary and expedient, for the preservation of
peace and unity in this country, to form and construct the following new
laws and regulations:

1. That the neutral party are from date, head of their own respective
houses, and are not, under pretext whatever, allowed to sell or give themselves or houses to either Annie Pepple or Manilla Pepple's houses.

2. That the neutral party are forbidden from date to assist either Annie
Pepple's or Manilla Pepple's houses in fighting or quarrelling, directly or
indirectly, but are to, with the King, mediate and settle any misunderstanding between the two houses, or any other house or houses.

3. That the neutral party are forbidden to give or allow Manilla Pepple
or Annie Pepple's houses to take any of their work-bars.

4. That from date no parties shall be allowed to fight with cannons,
guns or firearms of any description whatsoever in the country or in the
Eboe.

5. In the event of any dispute or misunderstanding taking place, all
parties are forbidden to molest any canoes and men going to and from the
fair, or Eboe.

6. In the event of any dispute arising between any of the neutral party
and Opoobon, or Foubra House Chief or Chiefs, and should that neutral
chief acknowledge himself to be wrong, and intercede and beg accordingly, any such Obobon or Foubra party must listen to the entreaties of
any such neutral Chief or Chiefs.

7. This does not exclude any Chief of the neutral party from paying
debts which they may have owed to the Manilla Pepple or Annie Pepple's
houses previously.

8. Furthermore, it is enacted that any breach or violation of any of the
above regulations shall be punished by the party or parties, house or

houses, chief or chiefs, guilty of the same, paying a fine of 50 puncheons of saleable palm-oil.

9. It is also agreed that these regulations be binding for the period of 10 years from that date, when, at the option of the country, a new one shall be drawn nor not.

Done and dated Bonny, this 20th day of January, in the year of our Lord 1869.   GEO. PEPPLE REX *Bonny*.
                                         OKO JUMBO.

	Their		Their
CAPTAIN HART	X	WOONGA DAPPA	X
JACK BROWN	X	TILLIBO OR DUKE NORFOLK	X
ADDA ALLISON	X	BLACK FONBRA	X
WARRISO	X	FINE BONE	X
DUBLIN GREEN	X	JONGO	X
WILCOX	X	ANTONIO	X
LEMAH SOUJOE	X	DICK TALLIFARI	X
JACK TALLIFARI	X	JOHN AFRICA	X
STRONG FACE	X	OGI AFRICA	X
GEORGE GOODHEAD	X	BONNY FACE	X
KING HALLIDAY	X	OKO APPALAY	X
TOBIN	X	TARRIBO	X
YOUNG TRADER	X		Marks
ANNIE PEPPLE	X		
	Marks		

Hulk *Dayspring*, Bonny River, this 21st Day of January 1869.

Before us: FRANK WILSON, Her Britannic Majesty's Acting Consul, J. P. JONES PARRY, Commander Her Majesty's ship "*Speedwell*", THOS. CAMPBELL, Chairman Court of Equity.

6. *Treaty between New Calabar and Bonny.* 1871.

Perpetual Treaty of Peace concluded under British Mediation between the Chiefs of Bonny and New Calabar.

We the undersigned Kings and Chiefs of Bonny and New Calabar considering that our mutual security and the good of our country require that we should be united in friendship did this day meet together on board Her Majesty's ship *Dido*, in Bonny river, and in the presence of Captain William Chapman of Her Majesty's ship *Dido*, Senior naval officer of the West Coast squadron, Commander George Borlase of Her Majesty's ship *Hart*, Commander the Honble. Archibald St. Clair of Her Majesty's ship *Bittern*, David Hopkins Esquire, Her Britannic Majesty's acting Consul and the gentlemen who have here unto attached their signatures solemnly agree that from this day forth no quarrell, war, or strife shall arise amongst us, and having chosen David Hopkins Esqre Her Majesty's acting Consul as arbitrator for the settlement of the troubles that have so long disturbed the peace of our countries and injured our commerce, we further most solemnly bind ourselves to abide by his decision under the penalties as set forth in this treaty or agreement.

1. The Kings and Chiefs of Bonny will not in any way aid or assist the Okrika men against the New Calabars, they bind themselves under a penalty of one hundred puncheons to observe this article, and the New Calabars also bind themselves in the same penalty not to assist the Okrika should they go to war with Bonny.

2. The Kings and Chiefs of Bonny for themselves and the Kings and Chiefs of New Calabar for themselves agree to let all palavers be bygones and never to bring them up again.

3. The Kings and Chiefs of the Countries mentioned in article two agree that in any further misunderstanding between them they will refer their case to Her Britannic Majesty's Consul for arbitration, and that they will be bound by his decision.

4. The Kings and Chiefs agree to put an end to at once and for ever the disgusting and horrible practice of cannibalism.

5. The Okrika men shall have the right to fish in all the Creeks and waters they have hitherto fished in so long as they are on friendly terms with the New Calabars without molestation.

6. Seeing the deadly enmity that has so long existed between the people of Okrika and New Calabar it is decided for the better and more efficient maintenance of peace and for the lasting welfare of the community that they shall not use the same oil markets, and further that the New Calabar men have by long possession of the Obiartuboo Markets proved their right to them, and it is therefore decided that they shall retain undisturbed possession of them.

7. The Bonny men are permitted to trade conjointly with the New Calabars at Andelli and Billituro and at the end of three months should a real friendship and amity exist between the two contracting nations the questions will be entertained of their attending additional markets.

8. The King and Chiefs of New Calabar shall open the creeks leading to Brass and Bonny and shall not prevent the Akassa men from passing through with their canoes, but shall give them safe convoy.

9. The Bonny Chiefs having sworn juju with Okrikas against New Calabar are ordered to at once remove their jujus.

In the event of any of the articles of this agreement being broken, a fine of one hundred puncheons of Palm oil will be enforced from the agressors.

All trade will be stopped until the fine shall have been paid.

10. That this Treaty and all the stipulations contained therein shall be binding upon the two contracting parties for the space of five years from the date hereof.

Signed on board Her Majesty's ship *Dido*, in the river Bonny, this 27th day of October 1871.

Signatures of Bonny King and Chiefs		Signatures of New Calabar King and Chiefs.	
	His		His
GEORGE PEPPLE Rex		KING AMACHREE	X
OKO JUMBO	X	GEORGE AMACHREE	X
MANILLA PEPPLE or		WILL BRAID	X
WARIBOO	X	JOHN BULL	X
ADD ALLISON	X	HORSEFALL MANUEL	X
CAPT. HART	X	HARRY BRAID	X
JACK BROWN	X	BOB MANUEL	X
DUBLIN GREEN	X	WEST INDIA	X
SQUEZE BANIGO	X		Mark
WILLCOX	X		
FINE COUNTRY	X		
COOKEY			
KING HOLLIDAY	X		
OCCO EPELLE	X		
Mark for JACK WILSON PEPPLE	X		
Mark			

Signed in the presence of:

W. CHAPMAN CAPT. R.N. H.M.S. *Dido*, Senior Naval Officer.
GEORGE BORLASE, Commander H.M.S. *Hart*.
A. ST. CLAIR, Commander H.M.S. *Bittern*.
DAVID HOPKINS, H.B.M.A. Consul.

Witnesses to signatures:
(indecipherable)
WHEELER,
JOHN H. LILLEY.
ALEXANDER TAYLOR.

7. *Treaty between New Calabar and Okrika.* 1871.

Perpetual Treaty of Peace concluded under British mediation between the Chiefs of Okrika and New Calabar.

Knowing the benefits and advantages that must result from a peace amongst ourselves under the mediation of Her Majesty's Government and being fully aware of the evil consequences that have arisen from the prosecution of our feuds, whereby our subjects and dependants have been prevented from carrying on their peaceful occupations in security, and have been exposed to interruptions and molestations when passing through the rivers and creeks on their lawful occasions; accordingly we are determined for ourselves our heirs and successors, to conclude together a lasting and inviolable peace from this time forth in perpetuity and do hereby agree to bind ourselves down to observe the following conditions:

1. That from this date viz. the 28th day of October one thousand eight hundred and seventy-one; there shall be a complete cessation of hostilities between our respective subjects and dependants, and a perfect truce shall endure between ourselves and between our successors respectively for evermore.

2. That in the event of any of our subjects or dependants committing an act of aggression upon the lives or property of those of any of the parties to this agreement, we will immediately punish the assailant and proceed to afford full redress upon the same being brought to our notice.

3. That in the event of an act of aggression being committed by any of those who are subscribers with us to this engagement upon any of our subjects or dependants we will not proceed immediately to retaliate but will inform Her Britannic Majesty's Consul who will take steps for obtaining reparations for the injury inflicted, provided that its occurrence can be satisfactory proved.

4. We further agree that the maintenance of the peace now concluded amongst us will be watched over by Her Majesty's Government and the King and Chiefs of Bonny, who will take steps to ensure at all times the due observance of all the articles of this Treaty.

5. By this treaty is secured to the Okrika men the right to pass through and make fishing settlements in any of the Creeks belonging to New Calabar and Brass.

6. The Calabar men will inform all neighbouring tribes with whom they have entered into agreement against the Okrikas that they have now

made a lasting truce with them and they are to pass in perfect safety through all waters.

7. The Obiartuboo markets belong exclusively to the people of New Calabar their heirs and successors. The Obiartuboo markets commence at Annia on one side and Ewaffa on the other.

8. The Deobo markets belong exclusively to the Okrikas their heirs and successors.

Signed:

New Calabar Signatures		Okrika Signatures	
	His		His
KING AMACHREE	X	KING PHIBIA	X
GEORGE AMACHREE	X	AGBANGALU	X
WILL BRAID	X	ORBUDEEBO OFFORCE	X
JOHN BULL	X	ITCHECHO	X
HORSEFALL MANUEL	X	AHJAROO	X
HARRY BRAID	X		Mark
BOB MANUEL	X		
WEST INDIA	X		
	Mark		

Witness to these signatures
   GEORGE W. PEPPLE Rex, Bonny.
   WARRIBO or MANILLA PEPPLE   his X mark
   CAPT. HART   his X mark
   ADDA ALLISON   his X mark

These signatures of the Okrika's and people of New Calabar were attached to this document in our presence and the signatures of the Bonny men have also been attached as a proof they were a party to this treaty.
   W. CHAPMAN, CAPT. R.N. H.M.S. *Dido*, Senior Naval Officer.
   DAVID HOPKINS, H.B.M.A. Consul.
   (indecipherable)
   JOHN A. LILLEY.
   ADAM W. PRITCHARD.
   TH. E. GLASSON.

8. *Treaty between the Kings and Chiefs of Bonny and Opobo.* 1873.

WE, the undersigned King and Chiefs of Bonny and Opobo, considering that our mutual security and the good of our countries require that we should be united in friendship, did on the 2nd and 3rd January, 1873, meet together on board Her Britannic Majesty's ship *Pioneer*, in the River Opobo, and having referred various matters in dispute to King

Amacree and the Chiefs of New Calabar, and the Chiefs of the Okrika country, as Arbitrators with, Commodore John Edmund Commerell, Esq., V.C., C.B., A.D.C., commanding Her Britannic Majesty's ship *Rattlesnake* and Commodore Commanding-in-chief on the Cape of Good Hope and West Coast of Africa Station, and Charles Livingstone, Esq., Her Britannic Majesty's Consul, as Referees, do hereby bind ourselves to the following conditions, which have been mutually agreed to by the Kings and Chiefs undersigned:

ART. I No more war between Bonny and Opobo from the 3rd day of January, 1873.

II. The Bonny men are not to detain any of Ja Ja's men who wish to return, and Ja Ja is not to detain any of the Bonny men who wish to return.

III. The Bonny men are to have the following six markets for their exclusive use:

> Arguatay.
> Obunku.
> Arata (four markets).

IV. The roads of these markets are to be open in two months from this date, viz., the 3rd January, 1873.
Any guns or forts which are on the creeks to these markets are to be taken away.

V. All armed men belonging to Bonny and Ja Ja are to be withdrawn in two months from the 3rd January, 1873; and Andoney men are to go to any markets they like, and are not to be molested or hurt.

VI. Neither Ja Ja nor the Bonny men are to punish the Ebo men for the side they have taken in the war.

VII. The Arbitrators decided that the Oko Epella and Kuke belong to the house of Ja Ja, and that they should return to Opobo. Ja Ja binds himself in a fine not to exceed 1,000 puncheons not to injure them in any way.

VIII. In case either party infringe any of the Articles of the Treaty, the matter shall be referred to Her Britannic Majesty's Consul, who will impose a fine not exceeding 1,000 puncheons on the offending party, and all trade will be stopped until the fine is paid.

IX. If the Opobo men attack the Bonny men, or the Bonny men attack the Opobo men, the opposite party is not to retaliate, but refer the matter to Her Britannic Majesty's Consul, who will investigate the case, and fine the aggressors.

X. Any houses may be made by either party for trade, but no great guns are to be put in them.

Signed on board Her Britannic Majesty's ship *Pioneer* in the River Opobo, on the 3rd day of January, 1873.

King and Chiefs of Bonny.		King and Chiefs of Opobo.
GEORGE, King of Bonny.	Their	KING JA JA.
His		D. C. WILLIAMS, Secretary
X WARRABOO.	X	OGODOPPO.
Mark.		SAM. G. TOBY.
OKO JUMBO.	X	BLACK JOHN.
ADDA ALLISON.	X	
JACK BROWN.	marks.	
CAPTAIN HART.		

Arbitrators:

King and Chiefs of New Calabar,		King and Chief of Okrika,
Their		
X KING AMACREE.		X ABANDA.
X GEO. AMACREE.		X TODGIBBO.
X JNO. BULL.		X SAWMARY.
X HORSFUL MANUEL.		X WAGO.
X ARRY BRAID.		X EURAKA NOLO.
X BOB MANUEL.		marks.
X WEST INDIA.		
X GEO. WILL.		

Referees:

J. E. COMMERELL, Commodore, Commanding-in-chief Her Majesty's Naval Forces on the Cape of Good Hope and West Coast of Africa Station.

CHAS. LIVINGSTONE, Her Britannic Majesty's Consul for the Bights of Biafra and Benin.

9. *Treaty between New Calabar and Will Braid.* 1879.

Perpetual Treaty of Peace between Will Braid, the Head of the Barboy House, and the King and Chiefs of New Calabar. November 19, 1879.

ART. I. Perpetual peace shall exist between Will Braid, the Head of the Barboy House, and King Amachree, and the Chiefs of New Calabar.

II. Will Braid or his successors and people may at any time return to New Calabar Town.

III. Will Braid and his people shall, at all times, have free access to all the New Calabar markets, and shall trade exclusively in New Calabar.

IV. Will Braid shall leave his present position at Ewaffa, and shall choose any place subject to the approval of the arbitrators.

V. All property in Ewaffa and the other markets held by Will Braid, and proved to be the property of the New Calabar people, shall be returned with as little delay as possible.

VI. Nil.

VII. All property held by the people of New Calabar, claimed and proved by Will Braid to be his, shall be returned to him with as little delay as possible.

VIII. Will Braid shall receive back such of the people as belong to him or his house, but not Chiefs he claims by right of descent.

IX. Any dispute or difference arising between Will Braid and the King and Chiefs of New Calabar shall be referred to the arbitration of the Kings and Chiefs of Bonny, Opobo, and Okrika, whose award, subject to ratification by Her Majesty's Consul, shall be final.

X. The King and Chiefs of New Calabar engage not to interfere with or molest Will Braid whilst under the protection of Bonny, Opobo, and Okrika, and Will Braid and his people engage on their part not to interfere with or molest any subject of New Calabar.

XI. On his return to New Calabar, Will Braid shall retain the rank and privileges he enjoyed prior to his cessation.

XII. If either Will Braid or the people of New Calabar should punish or oppress the Ebo tribe for the part they have taken during this quarrel, it is to be considered a breach of this Treaty.

XIII. Four weeks shall be given to either party to open the markets and destroy these fortifications under a fine of 100 puncheons.
Five months will be allowed to Will Braid to settle finally.

XIV. The arbitrators on this occasion bind themselves to see this Treaty carried into effect on every point, and that they shall regard, as a common enemy, either party that may break any of the clauses of this Treaty.

XV. A fine of 400 puncheons of palm oil shall be inflicted for the breach of any Article of the Treaty, to be divided, 100 to Bonny, 100 to Opobo, 100 to Okrika, and 100 to Her Majesty the Queen, the latter to be paid first, and the Bonny, Opobo, and Okrika peoples shall assist the Consul in levying this fine.

	Their		Their
KING AMACHREE.	X	FINE BONE.	X
GEORGE AMACHREE.	X	YOUNG BRIGGS.	X
JOHN BULL.	X	WILL BRAID.	X
HORSEFALL MANUEL.	X	MANILLA PEPPLE.	X
BOB MANUEL.	X	OKO JUMBO.	X
COOKIE.	X	ADDA ALLISON.	X
PRINCE JA JA.	X	YELLOW.	X
WOGO WAPPA.	X		Marks
	Marks		

Given on board Her Majesty's Ship *Dido*, this 19th day of November, 1879, in presence of:

COMPTON DOMVILE.
C. G. MICHAELSON.
THOS. H. ATKINSON.
S. F. EASTON, *Her Majesty's Acting Consul.*
R. D. BOLER.
W. H. ROBINSON.
R. B. KNIGHT.
JOSEPH HY. ELLIS.
FRED. D. MITCHELL.
THOS. WELSH.

10. *Letter from the King and Chiefs of New Calabar. 1882.*

New Calabar,
West Africa.
18th Agust, 1882.

To the Merchants Trading,
New Calabar River.
Gentlemen/

We the undersigned King and Chiefs of this river beg the Agents, and Sub-Agents representing your respective firms. There are only a few who have the power to act on their own responsibility, the remainder having to consult Agents in Bonny whom they may be placed before they they can give any reply, by this we are entirely subservient to the Bonny Agents.

We wish to inform you that this river is distinctly separate both in trade and natives to Bonny, and we require our Agents to the same.

We now resolve that if you insist on keeping sub-Agents in New Calabar, we shall take the greater part of our trade to the Firms who have free Agents, this to come into force three months after this date. Thus giving you time to alter the position of the Sub-Agents that are here now.

We now hope to have a good trade and trust you will comply with our request so that we can rely on our trade and not be subject to the control of Bonny and in many cases have to take Cargo that they do not require there or have to wait whilst the Bonny people are supplied first.

We the undersigned are,

Gentlemen,

Your obedient servants,

		His	X	Mark
	KING AMACHREE			
1.	GEORGE AMACHREE	,,	,,	,,
2.	JOHN BULL	,,	,,	,,
3.	HORSFALL MANUEL	,,	,,	,,
4.	HARRY BRAIDE	,,	,,	,,
5.	BOB MANUEL	,,	,,	,,
6.	YOUNG BRIGGS	,,	,,	,,
7.	GEORGE WILL	,,	,,	,,
8.	TOM BIG HARRY	,,	,,	,,
9.	STANDFAST JACK	,,	,,	,,
10.	HARRY HORSFALL	,,	,,	,,
11.	GEORGE GOODHEAD	,,	,,	,,
12.	JOHN WEST	,,	,,	,,
13.	TOM WEST	,,	,,	,,
14.	GRANVILLE DON PEDRO	,,	,,	,,
15.	DOUGLAS MANUEL	,,	,,	,,
16.	YOUNG GEORGE GOODHEAD	,,	,,	,,
17.	PRINCE BATUBO	,,	,,	,,
18.	BLACK DUKE	,,	,,	,,
19.	YOUNG ANNIE	,,	,,	,,
20.	BIG FOWL	,,	,,	,,
21.	JACKRECE	,,	,,	,,
22.	JOHN AMACHREE	,,	,,	,,
23.	PEPPLE AMACHREE	,,	,,	,,
24.	CHARLIE HORSEFALL	,,	,,	,,

25.	YOUNG HARRY	His	X	Mark
26.	TIGER AMACHREE	,,	,,	,,
27.	WEST BRAIDE	,,	,,	,,
28.	BESTMAN BRIGGS	,,	,,	,,
29.	YOUNG JACK	,,	,,	,,
30.	TOM LAWSON	,,	,,	,,
31.	WARMATE	,,	,,	,,
32.	YOUNG DON PEDRO	,,	,,	,,
33.	PRINCE DICK	,,	,,	,,
34.	BENIBO GEORGE	,,	,,	,,
35.	DOUGLAS YOUNG ANNIE	,,	,,	,,
36.	DAVIES GEORGE	,,	,,	,,
37.	FINEFACE	,,	,,	,,
38.	ABBEY YOUNG TOWN	,,	,,	,,
39.	JACK YOUNG TOWN	,,	,,	,,
40.	JAMES FOUCHEE	,,	,,	,,
41.	BENIBO TOM TOM	,,	,,	,,
42.	BIG TOM TOM	,,	,,	,,

Certified true Copy from the original true Copy.

(*Note.* The original letter has been lost. The above has been taken from copies sent to me by the chiefs respectively of Tombia and of Abalama villages. In a copy which I saw in Bugama village the signatories were not numbered. They were in the same order except that an additional name, Datama, occurred between Young Jack (29) and Tom Lawson (30). Numbers 36–39 were chiefs of Tombia, No. 40 of Ifoko and Nos. 41 and 42 of Abalama villages.)

11. *Treaty between Great Britain and New Calabar.* 1884.

Her Majesty the Queen of the United Kingdom of Great Britain and Ireland, Empress of India etc., and the Kings and Chiefs of New Calabar, being desirous of maintaining and strengthening the relations of peace and friendship which have for so long existed between them; Her Britannic Majesty has named and appointed E. H. Hewett, Esq., her Consul for the Bights of Benin and Biafra, to conclude a treaty for this purpose.

The said E. H. Hewett, Esq., and the said Kings and Chiefs of New Calabar have agreed upon and concluded the following articles:

ART. I. Her Majesty the Queen of Great Britain and Ireland etc., in compliance with the request of the Kings, Chiefs, and people of New

Calabar, hereby undertakes to extend to them, and to the territory under their authority and jurisdiction, her gracious favour and protection.

II. The Kings and Chiefs of New Calabar agree and promise to refrain from entering into any correspondence, Agreement, or Treaty with any foreign nation or Power, except with the knowledge and sanction of Her Britannic Majesty's Government.

III. It is agreed that full and exclusive jurisdiction, civil and criminal, over British subjects and their property in the territory of New Calabar is reserved to Her Britannic Majesty, to be exercised by such Consular or other officers as Her Majesty shall appoint for that purpose.

The same jurisdiction is likewise reserved to Her Majesty in the said territory of New Calabar over foreign subjects enjoying British protection who shall be deemed to be included in the expression 'British subject' throughout this Treaty.

IV. All disputes between the Kings and Chiefs of New Calabar or between them and British or foreign traders, or between the aforesaid Kings and Chiefs and neighbouring tribes, which cannot be settled amicably between the two parties, shall be submitted to the British Consular or other officers appointed by Her Britannic Majesty to exercise jurisdiction in New Calabar territories for arbitration and decision, or for arrangement.

V. The Kings and Chiefs of New Calabar hereby engage to assist the British Consular of other officers in the execution of such duties as may be assigned to them; and, further, to act upon their advice in matters relating to the administration of justice, the development of the resources of the country, the interests of commerce, or in any other matter in relation to peace, order, and good government, and the general progress of civilization.

VI. The subjects and citizens of all countries may freely carry on trade in every part of the territories of the Kings and Chiefs parties thereto, and may have houses and factories therein when, in the estimation of the British Consular or other officers, the state of the country of the Kings and Chiefs will admit of the trade being so extended.

VII. All ministers of the Christian religion shall be permitted to reside and exercise their calling within the territories of the aforesaid Kings and chiefs who hereby guarantee to them full protection.

All forms of religious worship and religious ordinances may be exercised within the territories of the aforesaid Kings and Chiefs, and no hindrances shall be offered thereto.

APPENDIX B

VIII. If any vessel should be wrecked within the New Calabar territories, the Kings and Chiefs will give them all the assistance in their power, will secure them from plunder, and also recover and deliver to the owners or agents all the property which can be saved.

If there are no such owners or agents on the spot, then the said property shall be delivered to the British Consular or other officers.

The Kings and Chiefs further engage to do all in their power to protect the persons and property of the officers, crew, and others on board such wrecked vessels.

All claims for salvage dues in such cases shall, if disputed, be referred to the British Consular or other officer for arbitration and decision.

IX. This Treaty shall come into operation, so far as may be practicable, from the date of its signature.

Done in duplicate on board Her Majesty's ship *Flirt* anchored in New Calabar River, this fourth day of July 1884.

EDWARD HYDE HEWETT.
Their
X KING AMACHRU.
X GEORGE AMACHRU.
Marks

Witness to signatures of King Amachru and George Amachru (signature illegible) Chairman of Court of Equity, New Calabar.

Their
X WILL BRAID
X JOHN BULL
X HORSFALL MANUEL
X BOB MANUEL
marks X YOUNG BRIGGS.

Witness to the above signatures from Will Braid to Young Briggs (signature illegible) Chairman of Court of Equity.

Knight's Beach, New Calabar River, August 16th 1884.

BIBLIOGRAPHY

ADAMS, Capt. John. 1. *Sketches taken during ten voyages to Africa between the years 1786 and 1800.* London, no date.

—— 2. *Remarks on the country extending from Cape Palmas to the river Congo.* London, 1823.

ATKINS, John, Gent. *A voyage to Guinea, Brazil and the West Indies in H.M. ships the Swallow and Weymouth.* London, 1737.

BAIKIE, W. B. *Narrative of an exploring voyage up the rivers Kwora and Binue in 1854.* London, 1856.

BARBOT, James. *An abstract of a voyage to New Calabar river or Rio Real in the year 1699* (in John Barbot's Description)

BARBOT, John. *A description of the coasts of north and south Guinea and of Ethiopia inferior vulgarly Angola.* London, 1746.

BARNES, J. A. *Politics in a changing society.* London, 1954.

BARTH, F. 'Segmentary Opposition and the theory of Games'. *J.R.A.I.* vol. 89, pt. 1, pp. 5–21. 1959.

BLAKE, J. W. *Europeans in West Africa 1450–1560.* Hakluyt Society. London, 1942.

BOLD, Lt. E., R.N. *The Merchant's and Mariner's African Guide.* London, 1822.

BOLER, R. D. and KNIGHT, R. 'Chart of creeks and rivers between Bonny and Brass rivers surveyed by R. D. Boler and R. Knight, September, 1874. *J.R.G.S.* Vol. XLVI. 1876, p. 411.

BOTELER, Capt. Thomas, R.N. *Narrative of a voyage of discovery to Africa and Arabia.* London, 1835.

BURTON, Richard. *Wanderings in West Africa by a F.R.G.S.* London, 1863.

CROW, Capt. Hugh. *Memoirs of the late Capt. Hugh Crow.* Liverpool, 1830.

CROWTHER, Revd. Samuel. *Journal of an expedition up the Niger and Tshadda rivers in 1854.* London, 1855.

DAPPER, O. *Description de l'Afrique.* Traduit du flamand. Amsterdam, 1686.

de CARDI, le Comte C. N. 'A short description of the natives of the Niger Coast Protectorate' (in Mary Kingsley's *West African Studies*). London, 1899.

DIKE, K. O. *Trade and politics in the Niger delta.* London, 1956.

ELLENBERGER, D. F. and MACGREGOR, J. C. *History of the Basuto.* London, 1912.

FORTES, M. and EVANS-PRITCHARD, E. E. *African Political Systems.* London, 1940.

HERTSLET, Lewis. *A complete collection of the Treaties and Conventions between Great Britain and Foreign powers.* London, 1850 onwards.

HOLMAN, James, R.N. *Travels in Madeira, Sierra Leone, Teneriffe, St. Jago, Cape Coast, Fernando Po, Princess Island,* etc. etc. London, 1834.

HUTCHINSON, T. J. 1. *Impressions of Western Africa.* London, 1858.

—— 2. *Ten years wanderings among the Ethiopians.* London, 1861.

JACKSON, R. M. *Journal of a voyage to the Bonny river, 1826.* Letchworth, 1934.

JAMIESON, Robert. 1. *An appeal against the proposed Niger expedition.* London, 1840.

—— 2. *Commerce with Africa.* London, 1859.

JONES, G. I. 1. 'The political organization of Old Calabar', in Forde, D. *Efik Traders of Old Calabar.* London, 1956.

—— 2. Report on the Status on Chiefs. Enugu, 1958.

—— 3. 'Native and trade currencies in Southern Nigeria during the eighteenth and nineteenth centuries.' *Africa,* i, 1958, pp. 43–54.

LAIRD, Macgregor and OLDFIELD, R. A. K. *Journal of an expedition to explore the course and termination of the Niger.* London, 1837.

LANDER, Richard and John. *Journal of an expedition to explore the course and termination of the Niger.* London, 1836.

LEONARD, A. G. *The Lower Niger and its tribes.* London, 1906.

MATHEWS, John. *A voyage to the river Sierra Leone on the coast of Africa.* London, 1788.

NADEL, S. F. *A Black Byzantium.* London, 1942.

OWEN, Capt. W. F. W. *Narrative of voyages to explore the shores of Africa, Arabia and Madagascar.* London, 1833.

PEREIRA, Duarte Pachecho. *Esmeraldo de Situ Orbis.* translated by G. H. T. Kimble. Hakluyt society. London, 1937.

SCHAPERA, I. *Government and politics in tribal societies.* London, 1956.

SMITH, J. *Trade and travels in the gulph of Guinea.* London, 1851.

SMITH, M. G. 'On segmentary lineage systems'. *J.R.A.I.,* Vol. 86, pt. 2, pp. 39–80, 1956.

TALBOT, P. A. *1. Peoples of Southern Nigeria.* 4 Vols. London, 1926.

—— 2. *Tribes of the Niger Delta.* London, 1932.

THOMAS, W. N., R.N. 'On the Oil Rivers of West Africa'. Paper 2. Proceedings of the R.G.S. Section 1872–3, issued as Vol. XVII. July, 1873.

WADDELL, Revd. Hope Masterton. *Twenty years in the West Indies and Central Africa, 1829–1858.* London, 1863.

WALKER, Capt. J. B. 'Notes on the Old Calabar and Cross Rivers'. *Proceedings of the R.G.S.* Vol. XVI. Session 1871–2.

WEST, H. Wenike Brown. *A short genealogical history of Amachree I of Kalabari,* Sankey Press, Yaba, 1956.

R

BRITISH GOVERNMENT RECORDS

TREATIES, CONVENTIONS and AGREEMENTS in Foreign Office files F.O. 93/6/3, 93/6/3 and 97/432, and in Hertslet. Some treaties are absent from the F.O. files and appear in Hertslet only and vice versa.

CORRESPONDENCE and REPORTS consist mainly of Colonial Office correspondence in the series C.O. 82/1–8 for the years 1828 to 1835 and in the Foreign Office correspondence in the series F.O. 2/1–3 and F.O. 2/16 and mainly in the series dealing with the Slave Trade F.O. 84/1–2111. Admiralty records deal mainly with the slave trade and its suppression and have almost nothing to say about the Eastern Delta communities.

Some of this correspondence is published as Parliamentary Papers (referred to as P.P.) again under the general heading 'Slave Trade' apart from special trade reports. The most important of these publications are

P.P. 1842. Vol. XII. which contains Dr. Madden's Report to the Select Committee on the slave trade, on the Western Coast of Africa 1841. (Appendix 3.)

P.P. 1847–8. Vol. XXII, 1849. Vol. XIX, 1850. Vol. IX. which contain the Reports and evidence submitted before the Select Committee on the Slave Trade.

P.P. 1847–8. Vol. LXIV. 5. 'Papers relating to the slave trade, King Pepple and H.M. Naval officers'.

P.P. 1854–5. Vol. LVI. which relates to the deposition of King Pepple. The actual correspondence is in F.O. 84/950.

P.P. 1857. Vol. XVI. which contains Consul Hutchinson's general report on the trade of the Bight of Biafra for the year 1856 (which is also in F.O. 2/16).

P.P. 1865. Vol. LVI. which contains an expurgated version of Consul R. Burton's private letter to Earl Russell. (The complete letter or a copy of it is in F.O. 84/1221.)

P.P. 1873. Vol. LXV. which contains Consul Livingstone's report on the trade and commerce of Old Calabar for the year 1872, and which covers the whole consular district of Biafra and Benin.

NIGERIAN GOVERNMENT RECORDS

Reports, mainly unpublished in the archives of the Government of the Eastern Region.

ADAMS, M. J. Reorganization report on the Bonny clan. 1949.

BEAUMONT, S. P. L. Intelligence report on the Odual clan. 1939.

DEWHURST, J. V. Intelligence report on the Eleme clan. 1936.

DICKINSON, E. N. C. Intelligence report on the Nembe clan. 1933.

ELTON-MILLER, T. Interim report on the Saka clan. 1930.

ENNALS, C. G. T. Intelligence report on the Ndokki clan. 1935.

HARDING, R. W. The Brass and Degema divisions. An enquiry into the possibilities of introducing Local Government into the area. 1955.

HILL, J. N. Assessment report on the Brass district. 1929.

HODGSON, P. C. Intelligence report on the Ogbeyan clan. 1937.

JEFFREYS, M. D. W. Report on the Andoni clan. 1930.

KELSEY, V. C. M. Intelligence report on the Kalabari clan. 1935.

MAYNE, C. J. Report on the Engenni clan. 1929.

NEWINGTON, W. F. H. Further information on the Engenni clan. 1930.

—— Intelligence report on the Ijo clans of the Brass district. 1938.

NEWNS, A. F. F. P. Intelligence report on the Akassa clan. 1935.

—— Intelligence report on the Epie-Atissa group. 1935.

—— Reorganization report on the Kalabari clan. 1947.

—— Report on Comey subsidies in the Eastern Provinces. 1949.

PORTER, J. C. Intelligence report on the Oporoma clan. 1931.

—— Intelligence report on the Okrika clan. 1933.

ROBINSON, G. G. Commissioner. Report of enquiry. Kalabari-Okrika dispute. Published by Govt. Printer. Enugu. 1950.

       should be read in conjunction with:

KALABARI CENTRAL UNION. 'The Kalabari-Okrika dispute. Being the various reports as culled from authentic records'. Privately printed circa. 1950.

WEBBER, H. Intelligence report on the Bonny Tribe. 1931.

Index